NORAD

MCGILL-QUEEN'S/BRIAN MULRONEY INSTITUTE OF GOVERNMENT STUDIES IN LEADERSHIP, PUBLIC POLICY, AND GOVERNANCE

Series editor: Donald E. Abelson

Titles in this series address critical issues facing Canada at home and abroad and the efforts policymakers at all levels of government have made to address a host of complex and multifaceted policy concerns. Books in this series receive financial support from the Brian Mulroney Institute of Government at St Francis Xavier University; in keeping with the institute's mandate, these studies explore how leaders involved in key policy initiatives arrived at their decisions and what lessons can be learned. Combining rigorous academic analysis with thoughtful recommendations, this series compels readers to think more critically about how and why elected officials make certain policy choices, and how, in concert with other stakeholders, they can better navigate an increasingly complicated and crowded marketplace of ideas.

1 Braver Canada
Shaping Our Destiny in a Precarious World
Derek H. Burney and Fen Osler Hampson

2 The Canadian Federal Election of 2019
Edited by Jon H. Pammett and Christopher Dornan

3 Keeping Canada Running
Infrastructure and the Future of Governance in a Pandemic World
G. Bruce Doern, Christopher Stoney, and Robert Hilton

4 The Age of Consequence
The Ordeals of Public Policy in Canada
Charles McMillan

5 Government
Have Presidents and Prime Ministers Misdiagnosed the Patient?
Donald J. Savoie

6 Cyber-Threats to Canadian Democracy
Edited by Holly Ann Garnett and Michael Pal

7 The Canadian Federal Election of 2021
Edited by Jon H. Pammett and Christopher Dornan

8 CETA Implementation and Implications
Unravelling the Puzzle
Edited by Robert G. Finbow

9 Multilateral Sanctions Revisited
Lessons Learned from Margaret Doxey
Edited by Andrea Charron and Clara Portela

10 Booze, Cigarettes, and Constitutional Dust-Ups
Canada's Quest for Interprovincial Free Trade
Ryan Manucha

11 NORAD
In Perpetuity and Beyond
Andrea Charron and James Fergusson

NORAD

In Perpetuity and Beyond

Andrea Charron and James Fergusson

McGill-Queen's University Press
Montreal & Kingston • London • Chicago

ISBN 978-0-2280-1399-0 (cloth)
ISBN 978-0-2280-1400-3 (paper)
ISBN 978-0-2280-1493-5 (ePDF)
ISBN 978-0-2280-1494-2 (ePUB)

Legal deposit fourth quarter 2022
Bibliothèque nationale du Québec

Printed in Canada on acid-free paper that is 100% ancient forest free (100% post-consumer recycled), processed chlorine free

This book has been published with the help of a grant from the Canadian Federation for the Humanities and Social Sciences, through the Awards to Scholarly Publications Program, using funds provided by the Social Sciences and Humanities Research Council of Canada.

Funded by the Government of Canada | Financé par le gouvernement du Canada | Canada | Canada Council for the Arts | Conseil des arts du Canada

We acknowledge the support of the Canada Council for the Arts.

Nous remercions le Conseil des arts du Canada de son soutien.

Library and Archives Canada Cataloguing in Publication

Title: NORAD : in perpetuity and beyond / Andrea Charron and James Fergusson.
Names: Charron, Andrea, author. | Fergusson, James G. (James Gordon), 1954– author.
Series: McGill-Queen's/Brian Mulroney Institute of Government studies in leadership, public policy, and governance ; 11.
Description: Series statement: McGill-Queen's/Brian Mulroney Institute of Government studies in leadership, public policy, and governance ; 11 | Includes bibliographical references and index.
Identifiers: Canadiana (print) 20220259461 | Canadiana (ebook) 20220259666 | ISBN 9780228013990 (cloth) | ISBN 9780228014003 (paper) | ISBN 9780228014935 (ePDF) | ISBN 9780228014942 (ePUB)
Subjects: LCSH: North American Aerospace Defense Command. | LCSH: Command and control systems—Technological innovations—Canada. | LCSH: Command and control systems—Technological innovations—United States. | LCSH: Geopolitics—History—21st century.
Classification: LCC UG735.C3 C43 2022 | DDC 358.4/1450971—dc23

This book was typeset by True to Type in 10.5/13 Sabon

For Eric and Laura

Contents

Figures and Table

FIGURES

TABLE

Foreword

NORAD: *In Perpetuity and Beyond* offers the reader an accurate assessment of current and historical North American continental defense thinking and challenges. The North American Aerospace Defense Command (NORAD) has been a cornerstone of US and Canadian security and a model of military cooperation since its inception. It is a US–Canada binational command, located in Colorado Springs, that provides both nations with aerospace warning, aerospace control, and maritime warning. NORAD has been a remarkable organization for over sixty years. But times are changing, and NORAD in its current form may no longer be a good fit. The authors challenge the reader to understand and consider the policy and military implications of changing North American defence requirements. By linking NORAD's historical rationale and functions to current evolution efforts, the authors help define the problems to be resolved; while many questions remain without answers, the dialogue they are bound to stimulate will contribute to our combined security. This book should be required reading for scholars interested in North American security, policy advisors, and military planners of both the United States and Canadian services.

General (retired) Lori J. Robinson, USAF
Lieutenant-General (retired) Pierre J.J. St-Amand, RCAF

Acknowledgments

This book was several years in the making. It began with three dedicated reports on NORAD, entitled "NORAD in Perpetuity? Challenges and Opportunities for Canada (2014)," "Left of Bang: NORAD's Maritime Warning Mission and North American Domain Awareness" (2015), and "NORAD: Beyond Modernization" (2019), funded by the Canadian Department of Defence's Targeted Engagement Program.[1] As a result of the unprecedented access to successive NORAD command teams, personnel, foreign policy advisors, and government officials on both sides of the border, these reports were the impetus for the authors and the University of Manitoba's Centre for Defence and Security Studies to host Canada's celebration of the sixtieth anniversary of NORAD at the Royal Aviation Museum of Western Canada in Winnipeg on 24 May 2018.[2] A former Chief of the Defence Staff, commanders, deputy commanders, policy advisors, current NORAD personnel, and historians spoke at this incredible event that featured a flyby by 2 CF-18s, not to mention static displays of historical NORAD interceptors (including the VooDoo), the 2018 CF-18 demonstration interceptor, and an amazing cake with a rotating globe that served hundreds. We are very grateful to the support and assistance of Global Affairs Canada, 1 CAD/CANR, 2 CAD and 17 Wing, and the NORAD headquarters.

While immersion into all things NORAD meant that we knew a little more about NORAD, we still had more questions. Building on the incredible scholarship of Joseph Jockel, Joel Sokolsky, and Richard Goette, to whom we are most indebted, we sought to consider the future of NORAD. Along the way, many were instrumental in shaping this book, including many serving and retired NORAD, Canadian and US military and civilian personnel, as well as academics including Troy Bouffard (with special thanks for his polar command plan map), Rob Huebert, Whitney Lackenbauer, Philippe Lagassé, David Perry, Chris Sands, Stephen Saideman, Alan Stephenson, Matthew Trudgen, and many others. All omissions and errors remain solely the fault of the authors.

We owe a particular debt of gratitude to NORAD and USNORTHCOM Command Historian Dr Lance Blyth, whose indefatigable knowledge and patience were instrumental to the success of this and many of our other NORAD projects.

Michael Bechthold provided the wonderful maps, and we thank Richard Goette for permission to use one he commissioned. We thank the North American and Arctic Defence and Security Network and DND's MINDS program as well as the Canadian Defence and Security Network and SSHRC for their financial assistance. We are grateful to Gene Waltz for trying (in vain) to limit the number of acronyms in the book, and librarian Asako Yoshida for finding key documents and helping us to host all of NORAD's unclassified documents on the University of Manitoba's library website.[3] A special thank you to the anonymous reviewers who improved the manuscript, to Maura Blain Brown for indexing, and to Richard Ratzlaff, Lisa Aitken, and Grace Rosalie Seybold at MQUP for their guidance.

Very importantly, we would like to thank the many students who have assisted us with our numerous NORAD projects and helped to inspire us, including: Nicholas Allarie, Christina Aliu, Gift Amadi, Paul Aseltine, Danielle Cherpako, Sam Chiappetta, Laura Conrad, Daniel Chrobak, Marcus Closen, Jay Dion, Roman Ellis, Myles Erickson, Bill Featherstone, Doug Fergusson, Shannon Furness, Nicholas Glesby, Maria Gheorghe, Rory Heaslip, Daniel Kiesman, Daniella Koroma, David Le, Pat McBurnie, Anastasia Narkovich, Victoria Nash, Hannah Payne, Avery Sharpe, Nicholas Suggitt, and Dana Tucker – the next generation of NORAD analysts.

Finally, and especially, a warm thank you to Gen (ret) Lori Robinson and LGen (ret) Pierre St-Amand for their kind foreword and support.

Abbreviations

1 CAD	1st Canadian Air Division
1 WTC	North Tower of the World Trade Center
2 WTC	South Tower of the World Trade Center
9/11	11 September 2001 attacks on the United States using hijacked aircraft
ABM(s)	Anti-Ballistic Missile(s)
ACIA	Arctic Communications Infrastructure Assessment Report in 2011
ACOP	Air Common Operating Picture
ACT	Allied Command Transformation
ADMP	Air Defense Modernization Plan
ADMPOL	Assistant Deputy Minister for Policy
ADSA	All-Domain Situational Awareness
AFB	Air Force Base
AFRICOM	US Africa Command
AI	Artificial Intelligence
AIS	Automatic Identification System
ALCM(s)	Air-Launched Cruise Missile(s)
ANR	Alaskan NORAD Region
AOPS	Arctic and Offshore Patrol Ships (RCN)
AOR	Area of Responsibility
ASW	Anti-Submarine Warfare
AWAC	Airborne Warning and Control
AWACS(s)	Airborne Warning and Control System(s)
BCS-F	Battle Control System-Fixed
BMD	Ballistic Missile Defense
BMDO	US Ballistic Missile Defense Organization
BMEW	Ballistic Missile Early Warning

BMEWS	Ballistic Missile Early Warning System
BNSG	Binational NORAD Steering Group
BPC	Binational Planning Cell
BPG	Binational Planning Group
C^2	Command and Control
C^4ISR	Command, Control, Communications, Computers, Intelligence, Surveillance, and Reconnaissance
CADIZ	Canadian Air Defence Identification Zone
CAF	Canadian Armed Forces
CAFATC	Canadian Armed Forces Arctic Training Centre (in Resolute, Nunavut)
CANR	Canada NORAD Region
CANCOM	Canada Command (precursor to Canadian Joint Operations Command [CJOC])
CANSOFCOM	Canadian Special Operations Forces Command
CANUS	Canada–United States
CAOC	Combined Air Operations Centre
CAP(s)	Combat Air Patrol(s)
CAST	Canadian Air-Sea Transportable Brigade Group
CAUSE	Canadian Arctic Underwater Sentinel Experiment
CBSA	Canada Border Services Agency
CCG	Canadian Coast Guard
CDPD	Continental Defence Policy Division
CDS	Canadian Chief of the Defence Staff
CENTCOM	US Central Command
CFACC	Combined Forces (Canada and US) Air Component Commander
CFMCC	Combined Forces (Canada and US) Maritime Component Command
CFSP	Common Foreign and Security Policy
CHOP	Change of Operational Control
CIA	Central Intelligence Agency
CINC(s)	Commander(s)-in-Chief
CINCNORAD	Commander-in-Chief of NORAD
CIO	Chief Information Officer
CJAMCC	Combined Joint Air and Maritime Component Command
CJCS	Chairman of the Joint Chiefs of Staff

CJFACC	Combined and Joint Forces Air Component Command
CJOC	Canadian Joint Operations Command
CONR	Continental US NORAD Region
COP	Common Operating Picture
COVID-19	Coronavirus Disease 2019 (SARS-CoV-2 is a coronavirus discovered in 2019 and named by the World Health Organization on 11 February 2020)
CSA	Canadian Space Agency
CSDP	Common Security and Defence Policy
CSNI	Consolidated Security Network Infrastructure
CYBERCOM	US Cyber Command
DEFCON	Defence Condition
DEW	Distant Early Warning
DFO	Canadian Department of Fisheries and Oceans
DG	Director-General
DGSPACE	Director-General, Space, Canada
DHS	US Department of Homeland Security
DND	Canadian Department of National Defence
DNSC	Defence NORAD Steering Committee
DoD	US Department of Defense
DoS	US Department of State
DPSA	Defence Production Sharing Agreement
DSCA	Defense Support of Civil Authorities
DSP	Defense Support Program
DSPACED	Directorate of Space Development
EADS	Eastern Air Defense Sector
EAEC	European Atomic Energy Community
ECSC	European Coal and Steel Community
EEC	European Economic Community
EEZ	Exclusive Economic Zone
EU	European Union
EUCOM	US European Command
EvoNAD	Evolution of North American Defence (study)
FAA	Federal Aviation Administration
FBI	Federal Bureau of Investigation
FOBS	Fractional Orbital Bombardment System
FOL(s)	Forward Operating Location(s)

GAC	Global Affairs Canada
GEO	Geosynchronous Orbit
GIDE	Global Information Dominance Exercise
GIUK	Greenland-Iceland-United Kingdom
GLCM(s)	Ground-Launched Cruise Missile(s)
GMD	Ground Based Mid-course Phase Missile Defense
GPALS	Global Protection Against Limited Strikes
HBTSS	Hypersonic and Ballistic Missile Tracking Space Sensor
HCM(s)	Hypersonic Cruise Missile(s)
HGV(s)	Hypersonic Glide Vehicle(s)
IBET(s)	Integrated Border Enforcement Team(s)
ICAO	International Civil Aviation Organization
ICBM(s)	Intercontinental Ballistic Missile(s)
ID	Identification
INDOPACOM	US Indo-Pacific Command
INF	Intermediate Nuclear Forces Treaty
ISR	Intelligence, Surveillance, and Reconnaissance
ITW/AA	Integrated Warning/Attack Assessment
J2	Directorate for Intelligence
J3	Directorate for Operations
JADC2	Joint All-Domain Command and Control
JCS	Joint Chiefs of Staff
JFACC	Joint Forces Air Component Commander
JFCOM	US Joint Forces Command
JLENS	Joint Land Attack Cruise Missile Defense Elevated Netted Sensor System
JTFN	Joint Task Force North
LAX	Los Angeles International Airport
LEO	Low Earth Orbit
LRA	Long-Range Aviation
M/V	Maritime Vessel
MAD	Mutual Assured Destruction
MARV(s)	Manoeuvrable Re-entry Vehicle(s)
MCC	Military Cooperation Committee
MDA	US Missile Defense Agency
MERP	Canadian Maritime Emergency Response Protocol
MIRV(s)	Multiple Independently Targeted Re-entry Vehicle(s)
MND	Canadian Minister of National Defence
MOTR	US Maritime Operational Threat Response

MOU	Memorandum of Understanding
MSOC(s)	Marine Security Operations Centre(s)
MW	Maritime Warning
N2C2	NORAD/USNORTHCOM Command Center
NAADM	North American Air Defence Modernization
NATO	North Atlantic Treaty Organization
NAVCanada	Canada's Air Navigation Service Provider
NAVNORTH	US Navy North
NAWS	North American Warning System
NCA	National Command Authorities
NDS	National Defense Strategy
NEADS	US Northeast Air Defense Sector
NMCC	National Military Command Center
NMD	National Missile Defense *or* National Missile Detection
NMIO	National Maritime Intelligence Integration Office
NORAD	North American Air (later Aerospace) Defence Command
NORTHCOM	US Northern Command
NTOG	Naval Tactical Operations Group
NWP	Northwest Passage
NWS	North Warning System
NWTDP	Northern Watch Technology Demonstration Project
ONE	Operation NOBLE EAGLE
OST	Outer Space Treaty
PACAF	US Pacific Air Force
PACOM	US Pacific Command
PEOC	Presidential Emergency Operations Center (a.k.a. White House Bunker)
PJBD	Permanent Joint Board on Defense
PO	Polar Orbit
POTUS	President Of The United States
PRC	People's Republic of China
RADARSAT	Ground Earth Observation Radar Satellite
RCAF	Royal Canadian Air Force
RCMP	Royal Canadian Mounted Police
RCN	Royal Canadian Navy
R&D	Research and Development
RFP	Request for Proposal
RN	UK Royal Navy

RPAS	Remotely Piloted Aircraft Systems (drones)
SAC	US Strategic Air Command
SACEUR	Supreme Allied Commander Europe
SACLANT	Supreme Allied Commander Atlantic
SAM(s)	Surface-to-Air Missile(s)
SAR	Search And Rescue *or* Synthetic Aperture Radar
SARS	Severe Acute Respiratory Syndrome
SCEAND	Standing Committee on External Affairs and National Defence (House of Commons)
SDI	US Strategic Defense Initiative ("Star Wars")
SEA	Single European Act
SecDef	US Secretary of Defence
SIPR	Secret Internet Protocol Router network
SLBM(s)	Submarine-Launched Ballistic Missile(s) *or* Sea-Launched Ballistic Missile(s)
SLOC	Sea Lines Of Communication
SNMG	Standing NATO Maritime Groups
SOCOM	US Special Operations Command
SOSUS	Deep-water Sound Surveillance System
SPACECOM	US Space Command
SPP	Security and Prosperity Partnership of North America
SRR	Search and Rescue Region
SSBN(s)	Strategic Ballistic Missile Submarine(s) (nuclear-powered)
SSE	*Strong, Secure and Engaged* (Canadian Defence White Paper, 2017)
SSN	US Space Surveillance Network
START I	Strategic Arms Reduction Treaty
STRATCOM	US Strategic Command
THAAD	Theatre High-Altitude Area Defense
TOR	Terms Of Reference
TRANSCOM	US Transportation Command
UCP	US Unified [Combatant] Command Plan
UNDRIP	UN Declaration on the Rights of Indigenous Peoples
USA	United States Army
USAF	United States Air Force
USAFRICOM	United States African Command
USAFSPC	US Air Force Space Command
USCENTCOM	US Central Command

USCG	United States Coast Guard
USCYBERCOM	US Cyber Command
USEUCOM	US European Command
USFFC	US Fleet Forces Command
USINDOPACOM	US Indo-Pacific Command
USN	United States Navy
USNORTHCOM	US Northern Command
USPACOM	US Pacific Command (1947–2018)
USSOUTHCOM	US Southern Command
USSPACECOM	US Space Command
USSTRATCOM	US Strategic Command
VCDS	Vice Chief of the Defence Staff (Canada)
WADS	Western Air Defense Sector
WMD	Weapons of Mass Destruction
Y2K	Year 2000 (refers to events related to the formatting and storage of calendar data or dates just prior to and after the year 2000)

NORAD

Introduction

The North American Aerospace Defence Command (NORAD) is the only binational military command in the world. Rather than working in parallel through two separate chains of command each focused on national defence, NORAD integrates assigned (mainly air force) personnel from Canada and the United States to achieve a unity of effort. NORAD is reflexively pointed to whenever Canada–United States relations look shaky in other issue areas. NORAD's commander can reach out to the president of the United States (POTUS) and the Canadian prime minister separately or simultaneously, to warn of air and maritime threats and confirm guidance to defend North America. No other countries enjoy this level of integration and trust in the other, and yet the command is still rarely studied in depth or understood. With emerging peer competitors in Russia and China, advancing technologies (including hypersonic weapons), and new ways of waging war, North America is as vulnerable now, if not more, than it was during the Cold War. This book traces the response of NORAD to geopolitical and technological changes, especially since 9/11, and pays particular attention to the decisions made by the military leadership and the continental defence technocratic experts.

NORAD was created because the United States and Canadian Air Forces foresaw the advantages of treating the airspace above North America as indivisible. If the Soviet Union did not distinguish between Canadian and American targets, why should either country organize itself as if it did? The decision to share capabilities and defend the air approaches of North America jointly was the result of functional logic; the Air Forces drew upon technological and organizational solutions to deal with a common problem, the air threat posed by the Soviet Union. We use this functional logic as a lens to trace the evolution of changes to NORAD more recently, and argue that the shared and joint defence of North America continues to be important and ideally, at least according to functional logic, should extend to other domains (including the joint defence of the maritime and cyber domains). Political barriers, especially Canadian fears around sovereignty, however, remain a brake on such action; indeed, even thinking about an all-domain North American Defence Command is rejected by politicians out of hand.

Too few people study NORAD and understand both its complexities and its possibilities. This book is intended to be part of a triptych[1] building from two of the very best of the few academic studies of NORAD. Richard Goette's *Sovereignty and Command in Canada-US Continental Air Defence: 1940–1957*[2] outlines how NORAD came to be, and Joseph Jockel's *Canada in NORAD 1957–2007: A History*[3] details the changes to NORAD since its operational start in 1957. The biggest changes to NORAD, however, have happened since 2006, when it was given a new mission and the NORAD Agreement was signed in perpetuity. This third book builds on the excellent scholarship of Goette and Jockel to trace NORAD's recent history, one that is marked by technological and command and control innovations, and now by unprecedented threats. Two constant threads run through the books. The first is a deep curiosity about the command and the decisions taken in the face of inevitable geopolitical and technological changes, and the second is the functional lens that all three books employ.

In many ways, NORAD represents the ideal case for the utility of functionalist/neo-functionalist theory, which investigates "needs" identified by experts and the resulting cross-national efforts to meet those needs.[4] In other words, integration between Canada and the United States to achieve continental defence has been guaranteed by shifting focus from the value-laden and highly controversial grounds of high politics to the technical aspects of a problem (e.g., the need for aerospace defence) via solutions encouraged by a variety of functionally based, cross-national ties.[5] NORAD represents the "endpoint" of integration driven by the need to defend North America. While Canadians have always been wary of being too close to US military strategy, especially as it relates to ballistic missile defence, concerns about the erosion of Canadian national sovereignty should there be expanded defence integration (for example an expanded NORAD mission suite beyond the air/missile domain) are misplaced. The conjunction of the new emerging political-strategic environment and new military technologies is creating the conditions for NORAD to be, in theory, connected in more domains. In practice, however, both political and military service concerns mitigate against opening the NORAD Agreement; after all, one never knows what one may lose when agreements are negotiated. Rather, changes are expected in processes, command and control, and the use of new technology that will stretch terms of reference as far as they can. Nonetheless, there is a deterministic element to this future process, and it begins with the repercussions of 11 September 2001 (9/11).

Though the 9/11 attacks against the continental United States were a failure of its number one mission (to prevent an air attack on North America), NORAD's continuation was never questioned. 9/11 was a watershed in the history of the evolution of CANUS North American defence cooperation and integration. On the surface, the changes appear to be modest, including new feeds of information to the internal air picture and new US Federal Aviation Administration (FAA) personnel in the NORAD Headquarters in Colorado Springs. The creation of a new American combatant command on 1 October 2002 with an area of responsibility that includes the continental United States, Alaska, Mexico, Canada, parts of the Caribbean, and the maritime approaches needed to be absorbed by technocrats and politicians.[6] United States Northern Command (USNORTHCOM) created acute, immediate problems for Canada, but once it became clear that NORAD's aerospace warning and control missions were not subordinated to the new USNORTHCOM, a steady rhythm was re-established.

In reality, however, everything had changed. NORAD had evolved into a "new" organization taking on a homeland counter-terrorism role as a function of the new focus on internal airspace. The US-driven response to 9/11 cemented the recognition, on both sides of the border, that the defence and security of North America was indivisible. Whether the political side of the equation recognized this reality is beside the point. The functional side drove the response.

At the heart of a future defence solution for North America lie three important considerations. First, as the air and maritime domain threat environments merge into a single, integrated domain as a result of technology (for example, a long-range cruise missile launched from a maritime platform transforms into an air threat), existing service and command seams will need to be overcome and similar to the indivisibility of the airspace, logic suggests a truly combined (including both nations) and joint (including all military services) approach to the defence of North America is a possibility.

Second, USNORTHCOM is likely to become the primary driver of future command arrangements because of its existing maritime control mission and its responsibility in other domains as well. Since its inception, it has struggled for recognition as a combat command no different from the other regional commands established in the US Unified [Combatant] Command Plan (UCP). Recent NORAD and USNORTHCOM commanders – General Eberhart (2000–04), Admiral Keating (2004–07), General Renuart (2007–10), Admiral Winnefeld (2010–11), General Jacoby (2011–14), Admiral Gortney (2014–16), General Robinson (2016–18), General O'Shaugnessy (2018–20), and General VanHerck (2020–present) – have all sought to remove USNORTHCOM's image as a command simply undertaking defense support of civil authorities (DSCA) missions (support to civilian agencies dealing with areas affected by floods, fires, etc.), and to eliminate the pejorative perception of it being "sleepycom" – not involved in serious defence issues as are the Indo-Pacific or European commands. Indeed, with the rise in great power competition, attention is returned to the importance of homeland defence and both NORAD's and USNORTHCOM's mandates.

Finally, the NORAD aerospace command and control (C^2) structure is readily adaptable to the maritime world and could be to other domains as well if desired. Air tasking orders emanate from NORAD Command but execution of the air defence battle falls to the regional NORAD commands. Each regional command, in turn, has a commander from one nation and a deputy from the other on a regional basis. Thus, the Alaskan NORAD Region (ANR) and Continental NORAD Region (CONR) have an American commander and Canadian deputy, and the Canadian NORAD Region (CANR) has a Canadian commander and American deputy. As such, although embedded within a binational structure, each has a national flavour.

Of course, functional theory is not political and military service reality. There is deep reluctance, on both sides of the border, to integrate more domains into the NORAD mission suite politically, and a preference by military services other than the Air Forces to continue to operate bilaterally.

While an all-domain, binational North American defence command is unlikely, all of the conditions that led to the creation of NORAD seem present in the maritime world and in other areas. As a result of exceptional economic, social, cyber, and industrial integration between Canada and the United States, an attack on one country in any domain is bound to affect the other country. Defence requirements can no longer be considered in isolation from multiple, civilian authorities and local communities. The functional process will be neither easy nor straightforward. Nonetheless, the vision of the US Department of Defense (DoD) for joint all-domain command and control (JADC2)[7] opens the door for a reimagination of the formerly stovepiped organization of commands and commanders in domain-specific silos. While on paper it makes sense to connect sensors from all of the military services, including allied data and information, practically speaking, it is incredibly complicated. Not only are there intricate technological requirements, but it also assumes no service rivalries, egos, or resource fights. In times of great power competition and a changing threat environment, patience is not a virtue. Bold changes are needed, and with those changes will come either a new, modernized NORAD or a marginalized one.

This book is arranged into seven chapters. Chapter 1 begins with a brief reminder of the reasons for the creation of NORAD, its numerous Agreement renewals, and its evolution until the 1990s. It also outlines the functional theory – the main lens of analysis. Chapter 2 recounts the stunning events of 9/11 with particular attention to the Canadian perspective. While the official *9/11 Commission Report* captured many details about NORAD's role on that day, the Canadian side was not covered therein.[8] While 9/11 represents a failure for NORAD, given its aerospace defence mission, it survived and adapted. Not only was the NORAD Agreement then signed in perpetuity, but an additional maritime warning mission was added to its suite of responsibilities. Chapter 3, therefore, delves into the maritime warning mission in earnest. From its rocky beginnings to its first maritime warning in 2010, four years after NORAD was assigned the task, this mission remains underrated and understudied. And yet, given new technology and the merger of domains, it could well be one of the most important missions for NORAD in the future.

Chapter 4 shifts to the perennially and proverbially difficult Arctic region and its many challenges, especially the renewal of the North Warning System (NWS) within the wider concept of NORAD "modernization" or the need for NORAD to prepare for future threats and literally "modernize." This, of course, is not NORAD's first attempt at modernizing, but it is likely to be the most ambitious, given the US Department of Defense's push to achieve JADC2.

Undergirding the functional decisions made to warn and respond in times of crisis, in the maritime and aerospace domains, is NORAD's command and control (C^2) architecture. Chapter 5 deconstructs the multiple roles ("hats") of the commanders, discusses the roles of force employers and generators, and adds the complicated US UCP. While NORAD is recognized within the UCP as the "twin" to USNORTHCOM and is fundamental to the defence of the homeland, and literally hovers above the problematic area of responsibility (AOR) seams created by the various other commands, NORAD is often forgotten and is rarely referenced in US strategies.

Chapter 6 reinvestigates the blurring of the air and space domains made possible by new weapons, especially hypersonic weapons, which do not follow a ballistic missile trajectory but can travel at very high speeds in sub-orbital space, and which are manoeuvrable, thus defying existing defence systems. The other issue is the future of continental ballistic missile defence, to which NORAD provides the warning, but USNORTHCOM executes the kill mission, leaving Canada out of the decision-making loop.

Chapter 7 concludes with future domains of interest for NORAD, including the cyber and land domains, and returns to the functional theory that suggests a multi-domain North American command is the logical next step, given the current and future threat environments. Of course, one can never divorce such decisions from politics – the important brake on, and needed oversight of, potentially limitless technocratic ambitions.

NORAD has had a long and storied history. It ensured the protection of North America through the Cold War and withstood both political hypersensitivity and inanition. Even when the main US adversary, the Soviet Union, ceased to exist, NORAD adapted and changed, turning its attention to supporting drug interdiction efforts in the late 1980s.

9/11 could have meant the end of NORAD, as it failed to prevent airborne threats in the form of civilian aircraft from destroying the Twin Towers in New York, hitting the Pentagon, crash-landing in Pennsylvania, and killing thousands. Instead, NORAD became the twin to USNORTHCOM, dedicated to continental defence. Indeed, confidence in NORAD was renewed and resulted in it acquiring a new mission, maritime warning, and the Agreement was signed in perpetuity.

These days, North America has never been more vulnerable, given new geopolitical competition in the form of not one but two near and peer competitors (Russia and China, respectively) with access to new technology in the form of hypersonic weapons; rogue states such as North Korea and Iran with nuclear weapons; and violent extremists – and all resorting to grey zone tactics. In response, Canada and the United States are investigating ways and means not only to modernize NORAD, in its infrastructure, processes, and command and control architecture, but to fundamentally rethink the importance of homeland defence and what it means to defend North America.

While it is always dangerous to predict, the arguments for NORAD, in its existing or expanded form, are compelling. That being said, failing to appreciate its importance can create the conditions for its marginalization. With sixty-plus years under its belt, brief spurts of political attention, and a very small but dedicated epistemic community advocating for more resources and NORAD's continued success, will NORAD be replaced, remain status quo, or continue to take on more of the defence of North America? Time will tell.

1

NORAD's Origins: It's All Functional

The binational North American Aerospace Defence Command (NORAD) remains a unique defence relationship in the world of international politics. At the same time, it is a relationship that is little studied in the academic world, reflected by the existence of only a few major monographs that are either government-issued or Canada-centric.[1] Moreover, neither the American nor Canadian governments have paid much attention to NORAD, with both placing their defence emphasis on missions abroad. Nor are many Americans or Canadians aware of its mandate, other than in the broadest of terms (e.g., to "track Santa" at Christmastime); NORAD's primary role in the collective defence of North America is far from the minds of most.

Even though NORAD is largely out of sight and out of mind, both the American and Canadian governments periodically pay attention to the relationship within the broader context of Canada–United States (CANUS) defence relations. Until 2006, this piquing of interest coincided with the renewal process of the binational agreement outlining the missions and intentions of the command.[2] In 2006, NORAD was renewed indefinitely.[3] This renewal in perpetuity only served to push NORAD further "underground" politically and publicly. Now, NORAD only emerges from the political shadows on occasions when capabilities need modernizing, largely due to the significant associated costs, which cause momentary media angst in Canada. NORAD's emergence into the public eye, however, is short-lived. NORAD also appears on relatively rare occasions around the process and publication of Canadian Defence White Papers.[4] Even then, NORAD receives little attention other than confirmation of its importance. For example, in the Canadian Defence White Paper (2017) *Strong, Secure and*

Engaged (*SSE*), references to NORAD are relatively general and vague. It points out the importance of NORAD modernization, tied directly to the aged NWS, and hints at the possibility of modernizing NORAD's mission suite. But no details are provided, and no dollars are ascribed to NORAD specifically. The bulk of *SSE* (as with past defence policies) is directed to overseas missions, to the acquisition of new military equipment, and to the well-being of people, arguably all very important issues as well. Despite NORAD modernization and NWS renewal being billed as priorities, the follow-up 2018 Defence Investment Plan had no budget for these priorities,[5] and only a relatively small amount of "new" money targeted for NORAD appeared in the 2021 Canadian Federal Budget.[6] That NORAD needs modernizing and the NWS, renewal, but that little funding and/or political attention was raised, is largely status quo.

Of course, there is a coterie of civilian and military officials within both the Canadian Department of National Defence (DND) and the US Department of Defense (DoD) who are tasked with managing the NORAD file within the broader context of CANUS defence relations.[7] A smaller number of officials within Global Affairs Canada (GAC) and the US Department of State (DoS) are also tasked to this file. The relevant Canadian Parliamentary Committees and US Congressional Committees also, on occasion, take up NORAD as a topic, but though in the case of Congress, as twin to USNORTHCOM issues by virtue of their dual-hatted commander. Finally, formal, direct political engagement is largely limited to the co-chairs of the CANUS Permanent Joint Board on Defense (PJBD), both of whom are political, civilian appointments. The PJBD, however, has normally met only twice a year, and of late, it has met only annually.[8] All appointments, both governmental and political, to the PJBD are brief, with the participants entering the NORAD world for a couple of years before moving on. On both sides of the border, PJBD and NORAD assignments may advance careers but are rarely a springboard to the top positions in either military.[9]

This leaves the NORAD file to NORAD, and the mainly military personnel assigned to it to consider its future. Just prior to 9/11, NORAD was the near-exclusive domain of the Royal Canadian Air Force (RCAF) and the United States Air Force (USAF).[10] Although NORAD remains air force–dominant, since 9/11, personnel from the other military services and other government departments/agencies have joined it. In the Canadian case, this has primarily entailed the assignment of Royal Canadian Navy (RCN) personnel to NORAD, largely as a function of NORAD's acquisition of a maritime warning (MW) mission in 2006.[11]

In the American case, this includes members of the United States Navy (USN), the United States Army (USA), and the United States Coast Guard (USCG), and civilian personnel from a variety of American governmental agencies, largely as a function of two factors: linking NORAD to the internal North American air picture after 9/11, which brought in FAA personnel,[12] and solidified the marriage of USNORTHCOM to NORAD, evident in the position of commander of USNORTHCOM being dual-hatted as commander of NORAD. Reflective of this new reality, since 9/11, the roll of commanders of NORAD and USNORTHCOM has included three USN admirals (Keating, Winnifeld, and Gortney – all Navy pilots) and one US Army general (Jacoby, Airborne). On the Canadian side, every NORAD deputy commander and Canadian NORAD regional commander and deputy regional commander has been an RCAF pilot; not even another trade within the RCAF has been considered.[13]

Despite this expansion of different personnel and other government departments, especially on the US side, NORAD remains the exclusive purview of the military, notwithstanding the presence of US non-DoD officials, and a political advisor from GAC and from DoS. In the broader context, considering the lack of political attention paid on both sides of the border, this means that NORAD is, in many ways, the primary expert on and driver of North American defence cooperation. On the rare occasions when North American defence comes under political and, to a lesser degree, public scrutiny, NORAD emerges as the expert interlocutor. This is evident, for example, in the futurist Evolution of North American Defence (EvoNAD) study, a broad-reaching study of how North America can prepare to defend against threats in all domains (air, maritime, cyber, aerospace, space, and land), originated by NORAD and subsequently mandated to NORAD by the PJBD.[14]

Leaving NORAD decisions and policy direction largely to the military, of course, raises question about the state of civil-military relations on both sides of the border. But, as discussed in greater detail in the following chapters, NORAD's role as the driver of deeper and broader North American defence cooperation and integration is conditioned by a clear recognition of what the political traffic will bear. The key point, however, which is vital to understanding NORAD and CANUS defence cooperation and future North America defence integration, is NORAD's role as the driver of all three. In this regard, NORAD is a bureaucratic entity, no different from any other bureaucratic entity, and exists to serve a functional purpose; in NORAD's case this is, for now, primarily the air defence of North America. The functional logic that led to the creation of NORAD is, now and in the future, creating the conditions for further CANUS defence integration, which could lead to the creation of a multi-domain (air, land, sea, cyber, and space) integrated North American Defence Command. This future is the product of the various strategic and political factors that brought about the creation of NORAD in the first place.

NORAD'S FOUNDATION

Even though only a small number of academics within the defence community in Canada and the United States pay attention to North American defence cooperation or to NORAD, there exists a general consensus on the foundation of NORAD, which, arguably, extends to GAC and DND on the Canadian side, and to DoD and DoS on the American side. The source of this consensus resides initially in President Roosevelt's 1938 unilateral guarantee that the United States would not stand idly by if a third party attacked Canada. World War II, after all, was looming. Prime Minister Mackenzie King was in the audience at the Queen's University (Kingston, Ontario) graduation address given by President Roosevelt. The prime minister, however, was not expecting such a pledge during Roosevelt's acceptance speech for his honorary degree. The prime minister clapped politely, but took two days to respond to the pledge, stating:

> we, too, have our obligations as a good and friendly neighbour, and one of them is to see that, at our own instance, our country is made as immune from attack or possible invasion as we can reasonably be expected to make it, and that should the occasion ever arise, enemy forces should not be able to pursue their way, either by land, sea or air to the United States across Canadian territory.[15]

In other words, Canada would not allow itself to be used by a third party to threaten or attack the United States. On this basis and in the context of war in Europe, Canada and the United States (really William Lyon Mackenzie King and Roosevelt) negotiated the one-page press release now known as the Ogdensburg Agreement (1940), which tied the national defence of Canada and the US together, and established the PJBD to provide study and recommendations to the governments of both Canada and the United States for the defence of "the north half of the Western hemisphere."[16] A year later, Canada and the United States issued the Hyde Park Declaration on defence industrial cooperation.[17] With the entrance of the United States into the war in December 1941, CANUS defence cooperation deepened, especially in the area of RCN-USN cooperation and coordination in the protection of allied convoys across the Atlantic and defence production.

Following the end of the war, North American defence cooperation continued and deepened as a function of the emergence of the Cold War.[18] Even though the Soviet Union lacked the capability to threaten North America with long-range aviation (LRA) or bombers in the initial years of the Cold War, defence planners on both sides of the border recognized that it would only be a matter of time until the Soviet Union acquired this capability, which would be married to nuclear gravity bombs following the Soviet Union's first detonation of an atomic device in 1949. In some ways, the legacy of the allied strategic bombing of Nazi Germany and Imperial Japan was simply transferred into projections of future Soviet strategic capabilities. As a result, Canada and the United States, under the PJBD, established the Military Cooperation Committee (MCC) in 1946 to provide advice on dealing with this eventuality. The net result was the coordination of the air defence of North America, which, in turn, led to the creation of three early-warning radar lines: the Distant Early Warning (DEW) line across the Canadian far north, the Mid-Canada line roughly located at the northernmost point beyond which trees cannot grow, and the Pinetree line just north of Canadian population centres (figure 1.1). In addition, reflecting Canada's disparity in size and resources, the governments agreed to fund the creation of these lines under a division that saw the United States paying the lion's share.[19]

At the same time, both governments also agreed that the interception of incoming Soviet bombers should be coordinated and undertaken as far north from North American population centres as possible. Subsequent coordination established the foundation for integration of operational control of Canadian and United States air defences in the continental United States, Canada, and Alaska under an integrated command responsible to the Chiefs of Staff of both countries. This allowed for authoritative control of all air defence weapons that could be employed against an attacker. The idea was

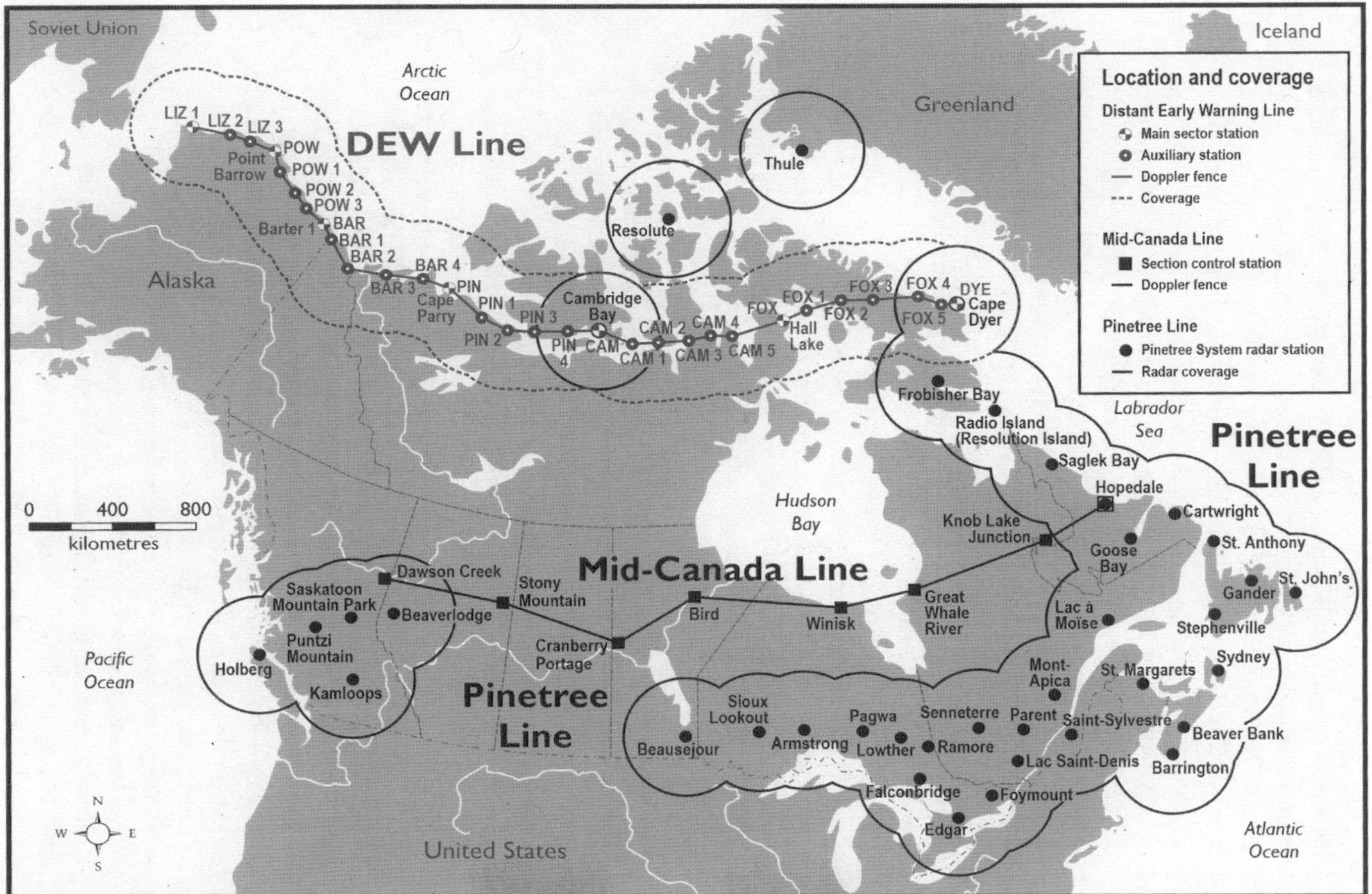

1.1 Pinetree, Mid-Canada, and Distant Early Warning (DEW) radar lines, 1958

not new; indeed, the principle of an integrated headquarters exercising operational control over assigned forces was de rigueur for the North Atlantic Treaty Organization (NATO) and was noted in the preambular note penned by then-Ambassador to the United States for Canada N.A. Robertson addressed to the Acting Secretary of State Christian Herter.[20]

These two factors, air early warning and coordinated air defence, created the functional logic leading to the establishment of an integrated binational North American Air Defence Command. The command became operational in September of 1957, with the political confirmation of its existence taking place in the form of a signed binational agreement on 12 May 1958.[21] The parties agreed that the commander-in-chief of NORAD (CINCNORAD) and deputy commander would not be from the same nation. With the agreed location of the Command first at Ent Airforce base in Colorado Springs (home of US Continental Air Defense Command) (1957–66), later in Cheyenne Mountain (1966–2006), and then at Peterson Air Force Base (2006–present; renamed Peterson Space Force Base in 2021), the commander of NORAD has always been an American, and the deputy commander a Canadian. The staff are integrated joint personnel of both countries.

The regional sub-commands, in turn, reflect the binational nature of the overall NORAD command structure. Binational means that Canada and the United States jointly defend North America, rather than Canada defending Canada and the United States defending the United States in parallel (which would be a bilateral arrangement). The regional commands, consisting of ANR, located in Anchorage, Alaska, CANR in Winnipeg, Manitoba, and CONR in Panama City, Florida, mirror this arrangement. ANR and CONR have a three-star US commander (lieutenant general) with a one-maple-leaf Canadian deputy (brigadier-general). CANR has a two-maple-leaf Canadian commander (major-general) and a one-star US deputy (brigadier general).

Legally, the collective defence of North America, and thus NORAD, resides under the 1949 North Atlantic Treaty (or Washington Treaty), which established NATO. Via the Treaty's Article 5, signatories are committed to the collective defence of each other under Article 51 of the United Nations Charter (the right of self or collective defence), if one of the members is attacked by an adversary not a member to the Treaty.[22] At the same time, however, NORAD was never a NATO component command; none of the European allies, for example, participated in PJBD deliberations, and none were present in NORAD.[23] NORAD was and remains, at least for the time being, an exclusive Canada–US club, in part reflecting the American and Canadian bias in seeing NATO as a European collective defence arrangement, consistent with their prioritization of the "away" game.[24]

NORAD's and thus the commander's authority over the defence of North America initially entailed two primary missions: warning of an air attack and defence against an air attack on a north-south vector through the Arctic. The former involves the assessment of an air attack, and the latter concerns the employment of air- and land-based point defences to detect, deter, and defeat such an attack.[25] In terms of the air defence component, this entailed the authority to task Canadian and American interceptors (initially CF-101 Voodoos and F-102s, now CF-18s and primarily F-16s) to undertake the air defence of North America, based upon the annual national commitment of RCAF and USAF resources to the NORAD command. Air tasking orders, based upon these resources, were transferred to the regional commands to conduct the air defence battle.

Thus, the process of North American air defence entails a centralized command authority, and a decentralized execution authority. The NORAD commander (or, in their absence, the deputy commander) allocates force levels in accordance with pre-approved plans for the regions. The NORAD commander sets the force level, given threat levels, which prescribes regions with particular assets for the execution of operations. The execution of the air defence battle falls to the regional commands. In effect, the execution of the air defence of Canada per se becomes the responsibility of the Canadian commander of CANR, whereas the air defence of Alaska or the continental US would fall to the American commanders of ANR and CONR respectively. In their absence, CANR would come under the American deputy commander, and ANR and CONR under the Canadian deputies.

This is the heart of the unique *binational* command structure. Both countries remain in command of their national air defence, yet both countries might find that their national air defence, or air control as defined in the NORAD agreement, is under the authority of the other nation. A Canadian might have to command and defend American air space and an American might have to command and defend Canadian air space. In effect, North America is an integrated air defence world with a seamless air control and defence arrangement, and with it, an embedded North American mindset. NORAD personnel, regardless of nationality (American or Canadian), become North Americans. As Jockel so aptly put it, there was and is "No Boundary Upstairs"[26] (borrowed from a comment made by General Charles Foulkes, Canada's first chairman of the Chiefs of Staff Committee), and so American and Canadian air defence interceptor assets may move across the border unhindered.[27] This was extended during the Cold War to permit US strategic bombers to fly over Canadian territory even though these bombers remained under the exclusive authority of US Strategic Air Command (SAC).

In the evolution of CANUS air defence cooperation and the initial years of NORAD, the central concern was the requirement to defend North America from a Soviet LRA attack launched across the Arctic, ostensibly envisioned as part of a Soviet land offensive in Europe – a repeat of World War II, but this time with nuclear weapons. By the 1960s, however, the key function of NORAD was not the air defence of North America exclusively, but the protection of American strategic nuclear retaliatory capabilities from a pre-emptive, disarming first strike. In other words, NORAD evolved into a key component of the Western/American strategic nuclear deterrence posture to prevent a third World War.

The shift from air warning/air control (or defence) to a deterrence function for NORAD in the 1960s was largely driven by the emergence of long-range intercontinental ballistic missiles (ICBMs) and submarine-launched ballistic missiles (SLBMs) married to nuclear warheads. With their emergence, the concept of defence became fully supplanted by the concept of deterrence as the cornerstone of Western security. Necessarily, NORAD's mission evolved to provide early warning of an ICBM/SLBM attack in order to protect the SAC's nuclear retaliatory capabilities, in terms of its land-based ICBM stockpile, and its long-range bomber fleet, located across the northwestern US.[28]

NORAD, therefore, acquired the ballistic missile warning mission in the mid-1960s. The first renewal of the Agreement in 1968 left NORAD missions as they were, but Canada acquired an "anti–ballistic missile" clause to reinforce the fact that NORAD was not involved in active ballistic missile defence and therefore precluded such a mission in future renewals.[29] NORAD's mission was to provide an assessment of whether North America was under ballistic missile attack, labelled an integrated tactical warning/attack assessment (ITW/AA). Similar to its original air warning mission, NORAD did not "own" the warning assets. The radar lines (especially the DEW line) and the US Ballistic Missile Early Warning System (BMEWS)[30] are national assets, not binational ones, notwithstanding the joint funding arrangements and the replacement of the DEW line in the 1980s by the NWS.[31] As such, NORAD had (and has) always been a supported command as a function of national air and ballistic missile warning assets. At the same time, NORAD, through its ITW/AA function, supported US SAC and the Canadian and US National Command Authorities (NCA). In the ballistic missile case, NORAD's function was to provide sufficient time for the US NCA to release its land-based ICBMs and strategic bombers to undertake a retaliatory strike before Soviet ICBMs hit these targets.[32] This early warning reduced the Soviet incentive to launch a first strike during a potential crisis, ensuring the "stability" provided under the condition of Mutual Assured Destruction (MAD).[33] Canada and the United States agreed to renew NORAD in 1973, but the term was abridged to only two years on the request of Canada, whose government wanted time to consult with the public on continued participation within NORAD, given the US MAD doctrine.[34]

The 1975 renewal of NORAD recognized that ballistic missiles were a growing problem. While Canada would assist with aerospace warning, NORAD would not participate in missile defence, as enshrined in the 1968 ABM exclusion clause in the renewed agreement. The changing threat meant that NORAD command would: a) assist each country to safeguard the sovereignty of its airspace; b) contribute to the deterrence of attack on North America by providing capabilities for warning of attack and for defence against air attack; and c) ensure an appropriate response against an attack, should deterrence fail, by providing for the effective use of the forces of the two countries available for air defence.[35]

By the late 1970s, American and Canadian defence planners recognized that the air-breathing threat to North America (a missile or aircraft with an engine requiring intake of air for combustion of fuel) had further changed. With the development of air-launched cruise missiles (ALCMs), no longer would Soviet LRA need to penetrate deep into North American airspace to release their nuclear gravity bombs. Now, Soviet LRA only needed to reach ALCM launch points in the high Arctic of North America. Moreover, ALCMs, because of their small diameter and ground-hugging flight characteristics, obviated the requirement for three radar lines. Particularly, the Mid-Canada and Pinetree lines were obsolete, and the crewed DEW line required significant upgrading. As a result, the former lines were dismantled, and the DEW line upgraded into a series of short- and long-range radars designed to track Soviet LRA over the Arctic approaches to North America and vector NORAD interceptors to these targets prior to their reaching their ALCM launch points. Forward operating locations (FOLs) were created across the Canadian north to launch NORAD interceptors in a crisis.

The 1981 renewal of NORAD was essential to keep pace with Soviet activity. First, it changed the "A" in NORAD from "air" to "aerospace." Second, it removed Canada's thirteen-year caveat preventing it from participating in missile defence, made possible because the United States and Soviet Union signed the ABM Treaty.[36] The new CF-18 Hornet fighters were delivered to the Canadian Forces by 1988 (as were the CP-140 Aurora maritime patrol aircraft, to replace the ageing Argus in airborne anti-submarine warfare [ASW] operations), representing significant Canadian contributions. The NORAD objective was to destroy the Soviet bombers (the "archers" in NORAD parlance) before they could release their ALCMs (the "arrows"), thereby securing US SAC retaliatory forces and protecting CANUS population centres. Against the backdrop of many US modernization projects, including the ambitious Strategic Defense Initiative (SDI) and the 1985 North American Air Defence Modernization (NAADM) Agreement, the 1986 renewal of the NORAD Agreement, negotiated at a time when the Cold War seemed to be heating up, required Canada to be extra sensitive to the US's homeland defence concerns.[37]

It was not at all certain from the Canadian perspective, however, that Canada would agree to the renewal. Throughout 1985, the Standing Committee on External Affairs and National Defence (SCEAND) debated the pros and cons of renewing or rejecting the NORAD Agreement. President Reagan's SDI was cited as a chief reason not to renew, as SDI was presumed to change Canada's role to defending US targets from *retaliatory* strikes by the Soviets that the US provoked.[38] Renewal was ultimately chosen, mainly because NORAD officials convinced the Canadian government that NORAD was necessary despite the new CF-18s, which were insufficient to defend Canada unilaterally. Canada needed NORAD's protection and the RCAF and USAF were jointly considering how to prepare for a Soviet assault. Plans were hinted at in the 1987 White Paper *Challenge and Commitment: A Defence Policy for Canada*, which stated that the USAF would forward-deploy US Airborne Warning and Control System (AWACS) aircraft to Canadian air bases and that USAF interceptors would be deployed to Canada during a crisis.[39] NORAD seemed more needed than ever before.

Almost everyone was caught off guard when the Berlin Wall fell, requiring a rethink of CANUS military priorities generally and NORAD specifically. Consequently, in 1992, the command completed a "NORAD Strategy Review" study, which documented the wide-ranging changes in the security environment since the end of the Cold War.[40] This new geopolitical era required NORAD to evolve again. With its original rationale to defend North America from an air attack obsolete, and its subsequent rationale to provide sufficient warning time for a decision to launch SAC retaliatory forces and thus ensure the creditability of the US strategic deterrent in the context of MAD no longer applicable either, NORAD had to find a new raison d'être. Using its warning assets, NORAD turned its attention to the American war on drugs, in addition to continued surveillance of pariah states (or states of concern) and, to a lesser extent, non-state actors.[41] Despite the new roles, NORAD officials throughout the 1990s were deeply concerned about the future of the institution in the absence of either an air-breathing threat to North America or a threat to US strategic retaliatory capabilities. Fortuitously, the lack of political attention paid to NORAD, because of the end of the Cold War and a significant degree of bureaucratic inertia, meant that NORAD's future was never really in doubt from a strategic perspective, but it might have been from a fiscal perspective. The end of the Cold War meant considerable threat reductions and financial savings. Dealing with a recession, Canada especially looked poised to pull back dramatically from NATO and NORAD. Not surprisingly, the 1994 Defence White Paper noted that Canada's contribution to aerospace surveillance, missile warning, and air defence would be reduced significantly, owing to a more peaceable world and deficit dilemmas. Canada remained within NORAD, however, as it was still the most cost-effective command to protect North America and kept Canada's foot in the US door.[42] As argued by Joel Sokolsky, Canada would do less and with less,[43] but abandoning NORAD was not an option. NORAD was thus renewed in 1991, 1996, and 2000 (coming into effect March 2001).

The survival of NORAD in the 1990s in the absence of its primary rationale for existence speaks directly to the place of NORAD within the political calculations of Canada and of the US. With neither the American nor Canadian governments paying particularly close attention to NORAD except as it related to wedge issues at the time of renewals, it never reached the level of political focus that called for direct and deep scrutiny and examination. Nor did NORAD entail significant investment costs for either government; the modernization of the NWS had been completed by 1988, and DND and DoD were able to reduce their annual resource commitments to NORAD to the point where Canada, for example, only committed two fighter interceptors to NORAD in the 1990s, and the United States transferred its NORAD resource commitments to the Air National Guard.[44] NORAD, as the institutional symbol of CANUS defence cooperation, however, could not be dissolved lest that be interpreted as a comment on the special relationship as a whole. The functional logic underpinning the institution and the relationship remained in place, even if it was absent from political calculations. In other words, NORAD's flexibility to adapt to new missions, an unpredictable future, and NORAD's place as the institutional heart of North American defence cooperation generated no incentives for either government to direct their attention towards NORAD specifically, nor to dissolve the command.

EXPLAINING NORAD WITH FUNCTIONALISM

To understand NORAD, one needs to consider the Soviet perspective and the functional logic that made NORAD inevitable. The consensus explanation for NORAD's existence begins with the Roosevelt and Mackenzie King declarations that tied Canadian and American defence together. This was reinforced by defence cooperation during World War II, which set in place a "habit" for both countries to perceive the defence of North America as inextricably linked, fundamentally as a function of geography and the reality that the only direct military threat was initially an air-breathing one, followed by a ballistic missile one. While American and Canadian attention remained focused throughout the Cold War upon the central front in Europe, the Soviet Union's air-breathing/ballistic missile threat to North America could not be separated on an American/Canadian basis. Simply, American population and industrial centres are too close to Canadian ones. Relative to the flight times of Soviet LRA, ballistic missiles, and subsequently ALCMs, neither Canada nor the United States would be able to distinguish their specific, intended targets. As a result, North America was, in effect, a single target, dictating a common and coordinated response. In other words, the defence of Canada and the United States, and thus North America, was indivisible. Defending North America dictated a North American response, rather than two national ones.

This geostrategic reality, in turn, was reinforced by the historical experience of CANUS defence cooperation in World War II, and by a common heritage, language, and shared values. Moreover, once the Washington Treaty creating NATO was signed in 1949, any prospect that the Soviet Union might differentiate between Canada and the United States simply evaporated. In addition, with the 1941 Hyde Park Declaration, general economic integration, and the 1957 Defence Production Sharing Agreement (DPSA),[45] North America emerged as a single defence industrial base for all intents and purposes. As a result of all of these factors, the defence of Canada and the United States became inextricably linked, and thus, for the Soviet Union, a single North American target set.

These factors strongly suggest that North American defence cooperation and thus NORAD were inevitable and deterministic, although the literature shies away from this conclusion. In the 1970s, an alternative explanation emerged, which arguably came to dominate Canadian defence theory: Nils Ørvik's "defence against help" theory.[46] Ørvik's 1973 thesis encapsulates, in short, a presumed fundamental fear of successive Canadian governments: if Canada doesn't provide at least minimum levels of defence against external threats so as not to leave the United States vulnerable, the United States will undertake unilateral actions without consultation and threaten, if not violate, Canada's sovereignty. In effect, "defence against help" is supposed to explain Canadian motives in the evolution of the North American defence relationship and predict that Canada will do more, rather than less, to guard against that "help." While the theory, on the surface, appears attractive to explain North American defence cooperation and NORAD, it is deeply problematic. Ørvik's empirical cases concern neutral or non-aligned small powers, rather than a small power such as Canada initially aligned with the United States prior to World War II, and subsequently allied with the United States through the 1949 North Atlantic Treaty.[47] Regardless, neither the deterministic inevitability argument nor the "defence against help" thesis can adequately explain NORAD's existence. Both may explain the recognition by Canada and the United States of the need to cooperate in the air defence of North America, but neither can explain why a binational approach was the result, especially when all other aspects of North American defence cooperation, at least for now, remain bilateral. The answer to why binational and not bilateral for air defence lies with a body of theory rarely, if ever, applied to the defence sector: functionalism and its post–World War II successor neo-functionalism.

Functionalist/neo-functionalist theory has exclusively resided in the intersection of two dilemmas. Both found their origins in the Interwar Period (1919–39). The first dilemma concerns the emergence of new technologies from World War I with implications that could not be managed solely on a national basis.[48] For example, the development of the airplane, which enabled the movement of people and goods across national borders, could only be managed by cooperation among states to establish common rules and procedures.[49] This cooperation, in turn, required the engagement of technical, rather than political, actors. Simply, the problem was a technical, apolitical one, as all states had a common interest in ensuring air safety.

The second dilemma was directly related to the disaster that was World War I, which was viewed within the emerging functionalist literature as hopefully the last in a long series of European civil wars. Recognizing the transnational implications of the new technologies on display during World War I, functionalists/neo-functionalists, led by David Mitrany, posited that their implications provided the means to promote a peaceful, integrated European polity – the underlying normative component of the theory. The empirical case, which emerged after World War II, was initially the European Coal and Steel Community (ECSC), designed to transnationalize two foundational elements of national war-making capabilities at the time. The net result was an almost exclusive concentration on European integration, beginning with the ECSC, followed by the European Atomic Energy Community (EAEC), the European Economic Community (EEC), and now the European Union (EU). Politics and technology merged as the means to ensure perpetual peace in Europe, driven by the apolitical reality of new technologies. Apolitical, technologically driven cooperation among states, initially based on self-interest, created the stepping stones for further cooperation as governments came to recognize its benefits. As a result, cooperation spilled over into a wide range of areas, slowly engaging political issues, and in the process, eroding nationalism and leading to integration.

Arguably, embedded within functionalist/neo-functionalist integration theory resides the argument that defence is the final step to complete integration and the creation of a supranational political entity. As the "habit" and benefits of initial functional integration expand into new issue areas, nationalist predilections and identity will slowly succumb to a supranational identity. In other words, from initial technical cooperation/integration follows deeper economic integration, leading to foreign policy and ultimately defence integration. Along this path, new supranational political institutions emerge to manage cooperation.

This linear, deterministic path is evident in the evolution of the ECSC over time into the EU. Coal and steel and atomic energy cooperation/integration set the foundation for the Treaty of Rome, which in turn led to the Single European Act (SEA), and then to a Common Foreign and Security Policy (CFSP), and now to the establishment of a Common Security and Defence Policy (CSDP). Along the way, supranational institutions emerged, such as the Court of Justice of the European Union, a European Parliament, a European political process, and a European bureaucracy – all of the elements of an emerging federalist political entity. Of course, this path has not been smooth, and it remains to be seen whether the rhetoric of a CFSP and CSDP will be truly and fully translated into reality. For now, significant foreign policy differences remain among the European states, especially the major European powers within the EU, and despite some degree of defence cooperation, centred primarily on the Franco-German axis, the prospects for an integrated, operational European army remain bleak. Politically, some members of the EU remain neutral, and others, especially the Eastern Europeans, continue to see NATO as the backbone of their defence and security; a view reinforced by the re-emergence of Russia as the primary threat. Finally, the UK's formal withdrawal from the EU (via Brexit) represents a major blow to the linear integration process, and its future implications for the EU remain to be seen, as does the devastation of the COVID-19 pandemic to budgets and common foreign and defence policies.

In contrast to functionalist/neo-functionalist integration theory almost entirely dominated by the European experience and process, and its normative underpinnings, North America followed a different path, one that began within the defence world, and largely remained there. This different path, in turn, significantly explains why functionalist/neo-functionalist integration has not been applied in either the case of North America or the defence world as a whole.

New military technologies created the requirement and conditions for defence integration, of which NORAD is the prime example. These new technologies, specifically (in terms of airpower) ballistic missiles and nuclear weapons, served to shrink time and space. In the context of the East/West Cold War rivalry, dominated by the United States and the Soviet Union, the time for a decision to strike shrank from days to hours and then to minutes, and the problem of space/distance disappeared as both superpowers obtained the capability to strike quickly and globally. In effect, nuclear weapons married to advanced long-range delivery systems could completely destroy a nation in minutes. A war could be over in thirty minutes, thereby giving no time for nations to enter into cooperative defence relationships.[50] Alliances required permanency, not least because of the need to develop and coordinate defence/war plans, which, in turn, dictates that alliance members commit forces to a central command and control (C^2) structure and process. In other words, national defence forces within an alliance structure had to be integrated, and this integration has been driven by functional demands. Thus, functionalism/neo-functionalist theory provides the explanation for NORAD's longevity, not the "defence against help" theory.

In the case of NORAD, coordinating the air and then aerospace defence of North America in the Cold War strategic environment was a technical problem that could only be resolved by the technical experts: air force planners and operators. Once the political sides of the equation agreed that the air/aerospace defence of North America, in this environment, was indivisible, the foundation was set to turn the solution over to the technical experts. These experts, on both sides of the border, were part of the "community of airpower," speaking a common language and part of a common culture. Of course, this did not mean that the political world simply disappeared from the process. As the negotiations unfolded and evolved, political decisions had to be made, not least in terms of budget allocations and the implications of a major American military presence in Canada.[51] This was, in part, the function of the PJBD: to provide political advice on the foreign and defence policies of Canada and the United States. Even so, once matters were handed over to the technical experts, technocrats provided the options and recommendations in a bottom-up process, through two channels – the PJBD and the nations' respective defence departments – with the ultimate decision made by the civilian political leadership, which may be understood as a blessing. This process, in turn, provided the means for the technical experts to understand what would be politically possible. At the same time, the civilian political leadership had limited grounds to question the final recommendations.

Of course, there was nothing inevitable in the process that began in the wake of World War II and ended with the unique NORAD binational command structure. The air force technical experts did not start the process with NORAD in mind as the final outcome. Instead, over time, and in response to the strategic environment, each recommendation/decision on air defence cooperation in some ways led to the next, driven by logic, efficiency, and operational and cost effectiveness. It is in this sense that NORAD emerged as simply the next logical, efficient, and effective step in cooperation, to be replicated when the next new technological development occurred: long-range ballistic missiles. It is this very functionalist/neo-functionalist process which again came into play on 9/11. NORAD had to respond to a new strategic political environment and new, emerging military techniques, if not technologies.

CONCLUSION

In many ways, NORAD represents the ideal case for the utility of functionalist/neo-functionalist theory. NORAD represents the end state of integration, beginning with a functional response to the technological problem of needing to defend North America. Functionalism in a defence environment resides in the theory's first dilemma – dealing with technology – more than the second – an integrated North American polity. New threats are likely to require more and more integration of other domains in the defence world to deal with technological advancements. While Canadians have always been wary of being too close to US military strategy, especially as it relates to ballistic missile defence, their concerns about the erosion of national sovereignty, should there be expanded defence integration (for example, an expanded NORAD mission suite beyond the air/missile domain), are misplaced. The conjunction of the new emerging political-strategic environment and new military technologies are creating the conditions for a further evolution of NORAD and perhaps even its mission suite. The temporal/political process, especially in Canada, will be neither smooth nor linear. Nonetheless, there is a deterministic element to this future process, and it begins with the repercussions of 9/11.

2

The 9/11 Tragedy and the "New" NORAD

From its origins in post–World War II air defence cooperation, NORAD has adapted to the changing technology-driven defence environment. From an air warning/air control (defence) mission, NORAD acquired a ballistic missile warning mission with the advent of intercontinental/submarine-launched ballistic missiles (ICBMs/SLBMs) and then revised its air missions with the advent of air-launched cruise missiles (ALCMs). NORAD then moved to support the US War on Drugs just before the end of the Cold War in 1988. Despite some expectations that NORAD would fade away with the demise of the Soviet Union, its continued existence speaks to a resilience underpinned by past success, and an embedded culture within DND and DoD and their respective air forces that perceives North American defence as indivisible relative to the threats of the day.

The 2000 renewal of NORAD by exchange of diplomatic notes (effective 21 May 2001) was remarkable only for its timeliness. Canada was keen to avoid an entanglement with US elections and US discussions of their National Missile Detection (NMD) program.[1] The NORAD Agreement was unaltered – it continued to assume that the world was as it was, and that the United States was the unipolar power with no peer competitors. NORAD's missions remained to track aerospace threats from outside of North America. The control mission was planned for and exercised, but not expected to be needed. Indeed, NORAD was often referenced pejoratively as "SNORAD" post–Cold War. It was harder and harder to convince politicians that funding for upgrades to NORAD was necessary and/or warranted.

The shock of 9/11 was another event to which NORAD would have to adapt. Neither nation looked to solely national responses to the terrorist attack. Indeed, hijacking an aircraft is a criminal act, and law enforcement (FBI or RCMP) have the lead in dealing with a hijacked aircraft. However, given 9/11's circumstances, NORAD was the obvious, immediate solution, and the NORAD C^2 architecture and weapons platforms provided the logical means to react; the commander of NORAD was simultaneously the commander of USSPACECOM and answered directly to the Secretary of Defense as well as to the Canadian Chief of the Defence Staff for NORAD. On the other hand, 9/11 was not like any event NORAD or the CANUS security and defence community could have imagined.

On 11 September 2001, NORAD did respond, even though its surveillance architecture was unprepared for the speed and scale of the connected events that made up 9/11. NORAD's priority was to warn of and react to external threats against North America. With the advent of missiles in the 1960s, the need for internal domestic air space visibility declined. Although there were various attempts by NORAD to raise the issue of the need to consider the air space inside North America, the investments required were simply not made available. On 11 September 2001, therefore, NORAD was looking outside of North America for inbound threats; it was not anticipating any from "inside."

As per its deter, detect, and defend motto of 2001, NORAD's steps after detecting a threat were to assess the nature of the attack, deploy the national resources dedicated to the command, and execute the air defence of North America on a regional basis. 9/11, however, was very different, involving an internal threat to North America. Indeed, a flight originating in North America was, by definition, deemed "friendly." Since NORAD needed to react quickly and since information was coming from mainly civilian sources, the immediate NORAD response was from a regional air defence sector rather than from the NORAD Command Center in Cheyenne Mountain. The US Northeast Air Defense Sector (NEADS) under CONR was the first to be notified of a rogue plane. Nevertheless, NORAD battle staff were immediately in the operational loop.

On 9/11, the NORAD battle staff were already stood up in all air defence sectors and regions and at the Cheyenne Mountain Operations Center. NORAD was participating in a global strategic exercise (VIGILANT GUARDIAN), conducting a real-world scenario of a counter-air operation against Russian bombers operating primarily in ANR and CANR. All NORAD alert aircraft were armed as a result of this counter-air operation exercise. The Russians also had an exercise scheduled on 11 September and had long-range bombers in their high north. The NORAD night shift was preparing to hand over to the day shift when the initial request for assistance with a "possible" hijacked aircraft was received.

At that time, the protocol for a hijacking in the United States was as follows. If the FAA, via a controller, suspected a hijacking over the continental United States, then after trying to contact the plane in question or the parent company of the aircraft and other planes in the vicinity to set the aircraft back on course, the FAA would seek unarmed fighter(s) from NORAD. But, in order to do so, multiple levels of notification and approval "at the highest levels" of government were required. As outlined in the *9/11 Commission Report*, the FAA's hijack coordinator – the director of the FAA Office for Civil Aviation Security, headquartered in Washington, DC – would contact the Pentagon's National Military Command Center (NMCC), which would contact the office of the Secretary of Defense for approval to take action, which would then be transmitted down the NORAD chain of command.[2] This process was under way when the first aircraft struck the North Tower of the World Trade Center (1WTC).

On 9/11, because of the confusion and misinformation and because the hijackings were coordinated suicide attacks, the official protocol was overtaken by events. In parallel with existing procedures (which were not fast enough to cope with the multiple events), the FAA's Boston Center, which was tracking American Airlines Flight 11 (en route from Logan Airport in Boston to Los Angeles International Airport [LAX]), reached out to NEADS directly at 8:37:52 am ET to report a suspected hijacking.[3] NEADS's battle commander Colonel Robert Marr (USAF) called to battle stations two F-15 alert aircraft at Otis Air Force Base in Falmouth, Massachusetts, and then ensured that the CONR commander, Major General Larry Arnold (USAF), and NORAD battle staff in Cheyenne Mountain were informed. The F-15s took off at 8:46, at the same time that Flight 11 hit 1WTC in New York, approximately nine minutes after NEADS received notice that there was a hijacking. Much is made of the nine minutes, but this response time was the minimum required to launch after a NORAD scramble call. Crews must run to aircraft, strap in, and initiate start sequences. Indeed, it was the most notice NORAD would have about any of the planes.[4] The pilots had very little information as to the direction in which to head or about the events transpiring, and were directed toward military-controlled airspace off of Long Island to avoid New York–area air traffic.

At the NORAD Operations Center in Cheyenne Mountain, MGen Eric Findley (RCAF), director of Combat Operations, issued a NORAD-wide call to battle stations. This meant all alert aircraft in every air defence sector and region were made ready for immediate air defence operations. By now, the day shift had arrived, and the battle staff doubled in size in Cheyenne Mountain.

At 9:03:02 am ET, United Airlines Flight 175 (also en route from Boston to LAX) flew into the South Tower of the World Trade Center (2WTC) at about the same time as NEADS received a phone warning of another hijacking. NEADS directed the F-15s already in the air to Manhattan, where they established a combat air patrol over the city at 9:25, but now they were low on fuel. This was a routine peacetime procedure to de-conflict air traffic. FAA controllers expected a period of time for negotiations, as in past hijackings. This explains the apparent lack of urgency to intercept immediately. (And of course, no one was entirely sure which plane to intercept and where.) NEADS placed fighters from Langley Airforce Base in Virginia on battle stations, given the low fuel of the airborne interceptors and evolving events.

MGen Findley directed the establishment of an air threat conference to ensure better situational awareness between all NORAD regions and air defence sectors, as well as with other participants. Many other agencies (Canadian and American) were added to this operational conference call.

Meanwhile, American Airlines Flight 77 (a Boeing 757 en route from Washington Dulles to LAX), which had been reported missing by the FAA and was assumed crashed, was re-acquired by Dulles and Reagan National controllers. Reagan National controllers vectored a nearby unarmed National Guard C130H cargo aircraft to identify and follow the aircraft. The National Guard aircraft reported that the Boeing 757 had hit the Pentagon at 9:337:46 am ET.[5] By chance, NEADS was informed of this third aircraft while chasing down reports that American Airlines Flight 11 might still be airborne. It made sense to clear the skies, and NORAD and the FAA discussed doing so. The FAA Command Center's national operations manager, Ben Sliney, ordered all FAA facilities to instruct all aircraft in US airspace to land at the nearest airport, and to ground/stop all flight operations. It was his very first day on the job. The *9/11 Commission Report* notes 4,500 commercial and general aviation flights landed without incident.[6]

At 9:36, the FAA's Boston Center called NEADS to report an aircraft closing in on Washington, DC. Airspace for the Langley fighters was cleared by NEADS but the fighters were heading east, not north, and for a number of reasons connected to the fog of information and misinformation, and following normal procedures to de-conflict with other air traffic, those fighters were not in a position to respond to Flight 77. NEADS did not have the full radar picture and the FAA lost the hijacked aircraft once its transponder was turned off. Only when the hijacked aircraft approached close enough to a radar near the airport did the FAA re-acquire it. By this time, it was clearly too late for NEADS to intercept the aircraft. Adding to the confusion were several false reports of additional aircraft to track.

NORAD was blind. Its radars were on the periphery of the United States and Canada (looking out), and the battle control system was designed to prioritize tracks coming at North America from abroad. Each new track, which had to be manually entered, would cause another existing track to be deleted, without the operator knowing. The years of financial neglect and old technology were coming home to roost.

Meanwhile, Russia cancelled its bomber activity and assured everyone that it had no part in what was taking place. VIGILANT GUARDIAN was terminated, and the counter-air operation was cancelled. Clearly, the situation was increasing tensions, and the question of how extensive the attacks would become forced the United States to declare Defense Condition 3 (DEFCON 3 is a higher state of force readiness) for its forces globally.[7] It was the fastest way to increase military preparedness and implement high force protection and cyber security conditions.

The last hijacked plane, United Airlines Flight 93 (en route from Newark International Airport to San Francisco International Airport), was tracked by the FAA's Cleveland Command Center, which requested military assistance from the FAA's Command Center. As the FAA was still fixated on the Pentagon strike, Flight 93 crashed in Pennsylvania at 10:03:11 am ET before any action could be taken by the military. No one from the FAA had requested military assistance per the protocol, nor was information about Flight 93 passed along to NEADS, which was tracking the flight after a call from the military liaison at FAA's Cleveland Center approximately four minutes after Flight 93 crashed.[8] The FAA had, however, notified the Secret Service, which notified the White House, which informed the National Military Command Center (NMCC). The Secret Service ordered jets to be scrambled "weapons free" for the Air National Guard at Andrews Air Force Base in Maryland by order of Vice-President Dick Cheney, as President G.W. Bush was sequestered on Air Force One to ensure his safety since the status of the attacks was unclear, and communication was difficult. The vice-president, Navy Commander Anthony Barnes, National Security Advisor Condoleezza Rice, White House Communications Director Karen Hughes, Secretary of Transportation Norman Mineta, and others, per protocol, evacuated to the "White House bunker," officially known as the Presidential Emergency Operations Center (PEOC). Defense Secretary Rumsfeld instead rushed to the Pentagon to assess the damage.[9]

"Weapons free" means that the decision to shoot rests with those in the cockpit. In the background, the White House was seeking confirmation from the president on a shoot-down confirmation for Flight 93 to be communicated to NORAD for the NEADS fighter jets. A modified Security Control of Air Traffic was coordinated between NORAD and the FAA. In effect, the FAA retained control of airspace, but all aircraft, except those engaged in air defence and military operations or first response (medical and law enforcement aircraft), were grounded immediately. At 10:24 am ET, the FAA announced the diversion of all US-bound trans-Atlantic and trans-Pacific flights to Canada. Every 90 seconds, a pilot requested to enter Canadian airspace.[10] Deputy Minister of Transport Canada Margaret Bloodworth authorized, by phone, the entry of these flights into Canada. The Canadian Forces took "executive control" of Canadian airspace by 11:30 am ET, and by 12:16 pm ET, US airspace was cleared. Operation YELLOW RIBBON[11] was launched at 12:28 pm ET by Canadian Minister of Transport David Collenette as hundreds of stranded international passengers were taken in by communities across Canada. Two hundred and thirty-nine planes, with more than 30,000 people on board, were hosted by Canadians.

While the whereabouts of key US decision-makers has been reviewed in documentaries, the whereabouts of Canadian decision-makers has been studied less. That morning, Minister Collenette (Transportation) was delivering a keynote speech to 2,000+ North American airport executives at the Palais de Congrès in Montreal. The audience was extremely restless as news of the attacks on the Twin Towers spread among the delegates. Canada's Foreign Affairs minister, John Manley, was flying on Air Canada from Frankfurt to Toronto, due to arrive later in the afternoon, and the US ambassador to

Canada, Paul Cellucci, was now stranded at Calgary International Airport because, at 10:43 am ET, NAVCanada notified all pilots in Canada that flights were cancelled.[12] In addition, Canada's key military leaders happened to be in Europe along with the other NATO Chiefs of Defence.

General Ray Henault, Canada's Chief of Defence Staff, arrived in Hungary from Italy aboard a NATO chartered aircraft around 3:00 pm local time (9:00 am ET) on 9/11, and was attending his first military committee tour with fellow NATO Chiefs of Defence. A Military Tour was traditionally hosted each year by one of the Chiefs of Defence. In this case, Italy and Hungary collaborated to conduct a combined military committee tour, and Hungary was receiving the Military Committee for the very first time as a new member of the Alliance, having joined NATO in 1998 at the same time as Poland and the Czech Republic. The Canadian minister of National Defence, Art Eggleton, was in Bulgaria visiting his counterpart for discussions regarding NATO training.

General Henault spoke to Prime Minister Chrétien from Hungary by phone about the events connected to 9/11 and assured him of his intent to return to Canada as soon as possible, and confirmed that the Acting Chief of Defence (the Vice Chief of the Defence Staff [VCDS], LGen George Macdonald) was the general's representative in Canada. Minister Eggleton was also in touch with the prime minister by phone and relayed his intention to return home ASAP as well.

Knowing that air traffic had been curtailed broadly, and anxious to return home, General Henault contacted Minister Eggleton in Bulgaria, who agreed (at the general's request) to reroute the Challenger aircraft the minister was flying on to Budapest to pick up the general later that evening on 9/11 and to stage through Brussels for the return to Canada as soon as possible.

Minister Eggleton and General Henault arrived in Brussels around 3:00 am on 12 September (local time) and attended the meeting of NATO Ambassadors at NATO HQ held the next morning to discuss the terrorist attacks. The meeting was chaired by Canadian Ambassador David Wright, then the dean of NATO ambassadors. The discussion was sobering to say the least, but no decision was made regarding the source of the attack against the United States.

During the flight to Brussels, the Challenger crew advised Henault and Eggleton that they would require a twenty-four-hour crew rest period before returning to Canada. That was significant, since it meant that the minister and the general would be unable to return to Ottawa until 13 September at the earliest. During the night, staff located a Canadian Forces A-310 Airbus that was overnighting in Madrid, Spain on a round-the-world trainer. The crew was directed to relocate to Brussels and to plan to fly to Ottawa from Brussels as soon as crew flying time regulations permitted.

The crew relocated to Brussels on 12 September 2001 during the day, and a notice was sent out to all military and parliamentary members who were on trips to Europe, and to diplomatic and public servants also potentially stranded on the European continent, that the Airbus would be leaving for Ottawa at 5:00 pm local time on 12 September. The aircraft had a significant number of people aboard when it left Brussels.[13] The passengers arrived in Ottawa at around 5:30 pm ET on 12 September 2001. Meetings with the prime minister, his Cabinet, General Henault, RCMP Commissioner Giuliano Zaccardelli, National Revenue Minister Martin Cauchon (who was also responsible for borders and customs), and Michael Kergin, Canada's ambassador in Washington, took place. Chrétien also spoke to Canadian Alliance Leader Stockwell Day and Bloc Québécois Leader Gilles Duceppe, but he could not reach President Bush. Canada was putting in place the emergency measures needed and bracing for the next steps.

NORAD HEADQUARTERS

On 9/11, the commander of NORAD, General Eberhart (USAF), was at NORAD Headquarters at Peterson Air Force Base, Colorado Springs, and took the immediate calls from the Pentagon during and after the attacks. He later travelled to Cheyenne Mountain Operations Center in the morning and continued communication with the Pentagon and key authorities. The Canadian deputy commander, Lieutenant-General Pennie (RCAF), was in Washington, DC attending meetings. On 10 September 2001, he had had meetings at the Pentagon in the section destroyed on 9/11. NORAD sent a plane to bring LGen Pennie back to the NORAD Headquarters in Colorado Springs. Flying past the smoldering Pentagon was emotionally painful. The third in command, Canadian Director of Combat Operations MGen Eric Findley, was in charge of the NORAD battle staff in Cheyenne Mountain. MGen Findley had long had several things on his mind: how to manage an emerging divergence between NORAD and the FAA on the operational necessity of the existing joint surveillance radars, how to expedite the allocation of resources for operations, and how to move forward on a new battle control system. A long night was drawing to a close (and VIGILANT GUARDIAN was well underway) when the request for NORAD assistance with a "possible" hijacking took place. As that process was being executed, the initial reports of a spectacular airplane crash into one of the World Trade Center towers were received. NEADS was already taking tactical action in the Northeast, but the situational awareness was not overly clear. With an additional, though fuzzy, indication of another hijacked aircraft, it was time to declare NORAD-wide battle stations, and to begin a more earnest discussion with the FAA. The situational awareness improved after the establishment of an operational conference loop. However, there were several reports of additional hijacked aircraft that added to the uncertainty. Americans and Canadians began the hard work of coordinating a more expansive response, as units with fighters, air refuelling tankers, and AWACS aircraft started sending in "we are ready, where do you want us to deploy?" calls. Liaison with the US Pacific Air Force (PACAF) took place to ensure that the air defence of Hawaii (not a NORAD responsibility) was in lockstep with NORAD responses. At Cheyenne Mountain, the two three-foot-thick, 23-ton blast doors were closed – one of the very few times the doors have ever been shut outside of exercises.

CANR was commanded by MGen Steve Lucas (RCAF), but he was at Canadian Forces Base Bagotville on 11 September. BGen Angus Watt (RCAF), the CANR Director of Operations, was quick to declare that every available fighter was operationally ready for employment. As diverted commercial aircraft began to appear in Canadian airspace, NORAD tracked all arriving aircraft. One aircraft flying over the Pacific and scheduled to land in Anchorage, Alaska, for fuel was apparently directed by the FAA to "squawk" the hijack code – for what reason is not clear. That craft, Korean Airlines Flight 85, did change its transponder to code 7500, the hijack code. ANR (commanded by Lt Gen Norton Shwartz [USAF]) directed the intercept of KAL 85 with F-15s and, in coordination with CANR and air traffic control authorities in both Canada and the United States, had the flight escorted to Whitehorse, Yukon. The aircraft landed in Whitehorse with a large surprise – another of the company's 747 cargo aircraft (KAL Flight 281) had landed at Whitehorse as well. It was an anxious time for NORAD; an aircraft indicating that it was hijacked in Canadian airspace, escorted by fighters from ANR with shoot-down authority from the prime minister if needed, was bound to raise heart rates. Restraint was the watchword.

The *9/11 Commission Report* focused mainly on CONR, based in Florida, as it oversaw NEADS, which was physically closest to the crises. What is referenced in the *Report*, although not entirely clear, is that the shoot-down order for NEADS's F-15s seems to have been passed to the NORAD chain of command, including the CONR commander, via an air threat conference call. The CONR commander messaged his personnel about the order, but confusion and concern about the instructions persisted and NEADS's fighters from Otis Air Force Base (Cape Cod, Massachusetts) and Langley Air Force Base (Virginia) were told to ID, type, and tail the aircraft, not to shoot.[14] After all, there was much confusion at the time, and so the intent was to hold fire until the last possible moment out of an abundance of caution. Meanwhile, the jets from Andrews Air Force Base (the District of Colombia's Air National Guard) circling Washington, DC had shoot-down orders. The White House officials thought the shoot-down message had been received by all of the pilots, but there is no evidence, according to the *9/11 Report*, that NORAD knew about the other jets.[15]

More and more aircraft joined NORAD's air defence response and two US carrier battle groups on each coast were added for additional surveillance and armed response. As evening fell, there were hundreds of fighters engaged in combat air patrols (CAPs) over vital areas of the United States, organized by the NORAD battle staff under the direction of MGen Eric Findley. They were later coined OPERATION NOBLE EAGLE or ONE. It was immediately acknowledged that this new mission would have to be sustained for a long time and that it was going to be a "marathon" rather than a sprint. ONE was a North American operation, but Canada did not direct CAPs over all of its cities as was required for US cities. The United States continued with the ONE patrols for months owing to the vulnerability felt by the US government, but also because the US Air Force was large enough to accommodate the increased tasking orders. Initially, there were several CAPs in Canada, but they were managed primarily by CANR in Winnipeg and they required additional forward operating locations to handle the patrols, which could not be sustained in perpetuity.

With the combat air patrols established in the early evening of 11 September, MGen Findley had his first chance to look at the very tired battle staff. His "night" shift had now been on duty for well over twenty-four hours and it was time to establish a revised operational routine. The "night" shift was to go home, rest, and return as the day shift. The original day shift carried on for their "twenty-four-hour watch," and a new battle rhythm was underway.

The Canadian and US governments' responses to the events on 9/11 remain a case study in all that was wrong with North America's approach to homeland security – not just NORAD, but the entire defence and security architecture and way of thinking. It was clear that drastic changes in the United States and Canada were required.

The immediate response of both governments was to integrate the internal North American air picture into the previously exclusively external picture NORAD had for the air domain. NATO AWACS aircraft were deployed from Germany to the continental United States (Oklahoma) to augment domestic AWACS radar coverage. As Jockel notes, this was the first time NATO assets were sent to protect the US homeland.[16] The lack of radar feeds to provide the internal air picture, however, was a major problem that needed to be fixed more systematically and structurally. NORAD had been underfunded for decades. The tracking systems were out of date and could not handle more feeds. NORAD did have unfunded plans, but it still took over six months to increase the capacity of the computer systems; that increase was massively more than the capability available at the time of 9/11. The FAA radars also needed upgrading, as they had been too heavily dependent on secondary transponders from cooperative aircraft. FAA radars had not been "tuned" to get raw data for years, so they were only effective with cooperative targets using transponders (which amplify the radar return signal). The 9/11 hijackers had turned off their transponders to avoid detection, so the FAA lost the aircraft and had a hard time finding them again. The planes could only be seen once they were much closer to a given radar.

Eventually, the FAA, Transport Canada, and NAVCanada began providing internal radar feeds into NORAD Headquarters to complement NORAD's NWS radar feeds. This required the FAA to dispatch personnel to the NORAD Headquarters in Colorado Springs to monitor their feeds and provide assistance. Additional military staff were brought in as well to cobble together a more complete internal radar picture and begin work on a new battle control system.

Canada did not send NAVCanada and/or Transport Canada personnel to Colorado Springs principally because of Canada's considerably lower air traffic numbers. Nonetheless, NORAD evolved to acquire an integrated internal and external air picture of North America, thanks to funding from Washington for the necessary upgrades.

Despite the technological and other challenges at the time, the NORAD solution was the only viable response to the 9/11 attacks. A hijacked aircraft in the United States could fly north to strike Canadian population centres and vital national infrastructure, and vice versa, especially as major North American cities are located relatively close together. At the same time, the centralized control, decentralized execution nature of NORAD provided the solution for possible national exceptions in approaches to the question of intercepting and destroying hijacked aircraft. In the United States, this authority was vested in the Secretary of Defense, whereas in Canada, this authority remained with the prime minister as the NCA. Regardless, NORAD's structure provided the solution for potentially different political perspectives and responses to attacks originating from within the United States or Canada. Regular exercises practising the execution of this authority were and are conducted, but whether or not processes in either nation remain fast enough to respond to an actual event(s) is an open question.

Operation NOBLE EAGLE (ONE), launched in the evening of 9/11, became a permanent functional solution to a deterrence gap within North America. As the patrols continued for days and months afterward, the US Air National Guard took on more of the burden from NORAD-assigned forces. Canada had to increase the number of CF-18s assigned to NORAD duty from four to twelve – a small contribution in comparison to the three-hundred-plus on duty for at least the initial months following 9/11.[17] US interceptors concentrated on New York, Washington, DC, and wherever the president happened to be. Canada focused on large southern Canadian population centres. ONE decreased in frequency and numbers over time, but is now a permanent mission to protect the skies above key city centres and major national events, beginning with the 2002 Winter Olympics in Salt Lake City, Utah. In all cases, time from identification to interception of a possible air attack is highly dependent on the event's proximity to the closest intercept base or air patrol. For example, Canada's only two fighter bases, where dedicated NORAD assets were deployed (and still are), are located at Cold Lake, Alberta and Bagotville, Quebec, notwithstanding the temporary relocation of some CF-18s to Trenton, Ontario, Comox, British Columbia, and Greenwood, Nova Scotia immediately after 9/11.

9/11 could have meant the end of NORAD, given that its mission to protect North America from air attacks had essentially failed. At the time, however, NORAD was seen as the hero – it was widely acknowledged that the circumstances were unprecedented and that NORAD had been indispensable in terms of the immediate, follow-on response to 9/11, especially in the form of ONE. Disappearing NORAD was never a viable option from either a Canadian or an American perspective. Changes to the UCP, however, did contemplate a subordinate NORAD briefly before the final plan was published in 2002. A review of the UCP had been scheduled prior to 9/11. Chairman of the Joint Chiefs of Staff (CJCS) General Richard B. Myers, USAF (former NORAD commander from 14 Aug 1998 to 18 Feb 2000), however, suggested it was the appropriate time to consider a new UCP configuration, given 9/11.[18] This was followed up with a twenty-four-star letter (representing six four-star generals) to the Secretary of Defense Rumsfeld advocating for a UCP review.

The UCP has undergone many changes since its first iteration in 1946[19] and therefore the creation of a new combatant command, USNORTHCOM, was in some ways not surprising. One of the most significant changes to the UCP occurred in 1986 to fix inter-service rivalries, which were viewed as being partially responsible for the failures in Vietnam, the Iran hostage crisis, and the US intervention in Grenada. The Goldwater-Nichols Act[20] required combatant commanders (then known as commanders-in-chief or CINCs) to report directly to the Secretary of Defense, rather than through the CJCS and along strict service lines, to promote jointness – army, navy, marine, and air force working together.[21] The CJCS was out of the operational chain of command.

Prior to 9/11, the world, according to the US command plan, was divided among five CINCs and NORAD: US Joint Forces Command (JFCOM), with responsibility for land and maritime defense of the US continental states and provision of military assistance to civil authorities; NORAD for aerospace defence; and US Pacific Command (PACOM),[22] US Southern Command (SOUTHCOM), US Central Command (CENTCOM), and US European Command (EUCOM) for their geographic areas of responsibility. Combatant commands were expected to manage strategic relations with countries within their AOR. There were also four functional commands headed by combatant commanders (four-star generals) assigned worldwide functional responsibilities not bounded by geography: US Space Command (for which the NORAD

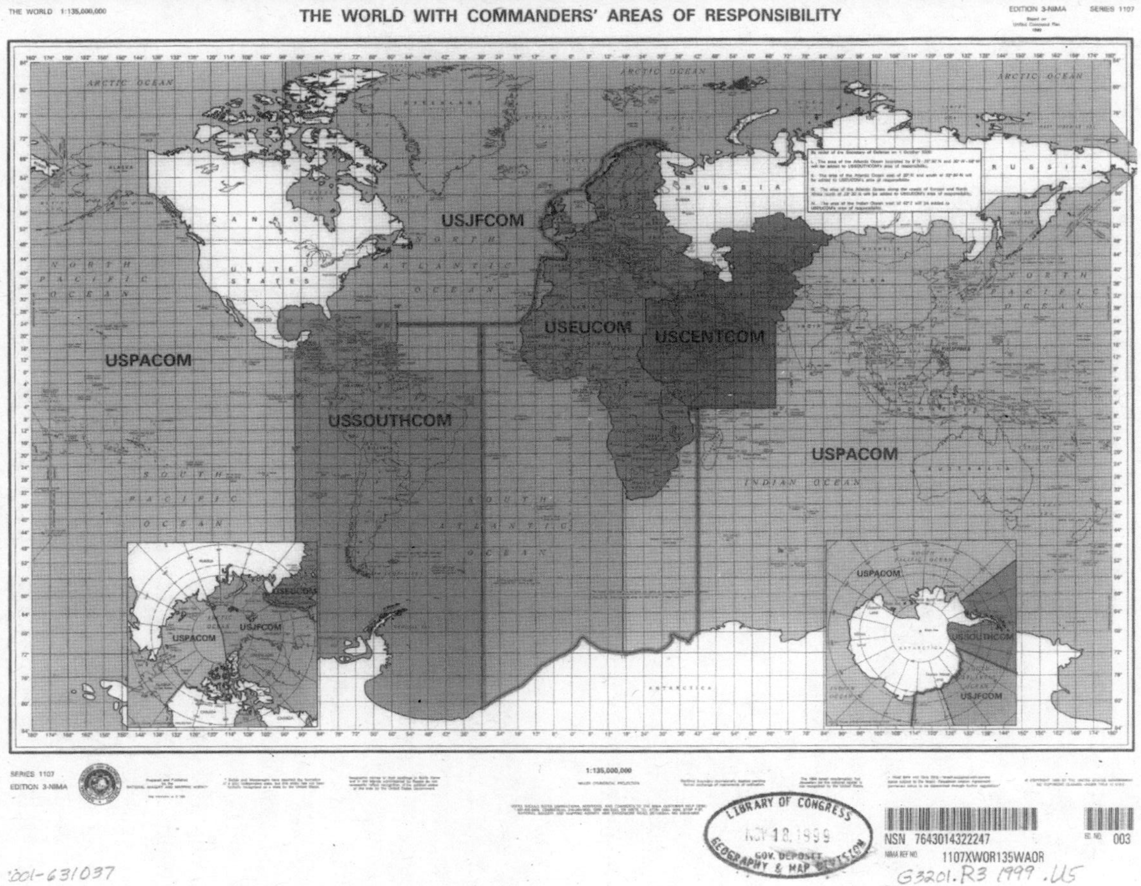

2.1 UCP just prior to 9/11

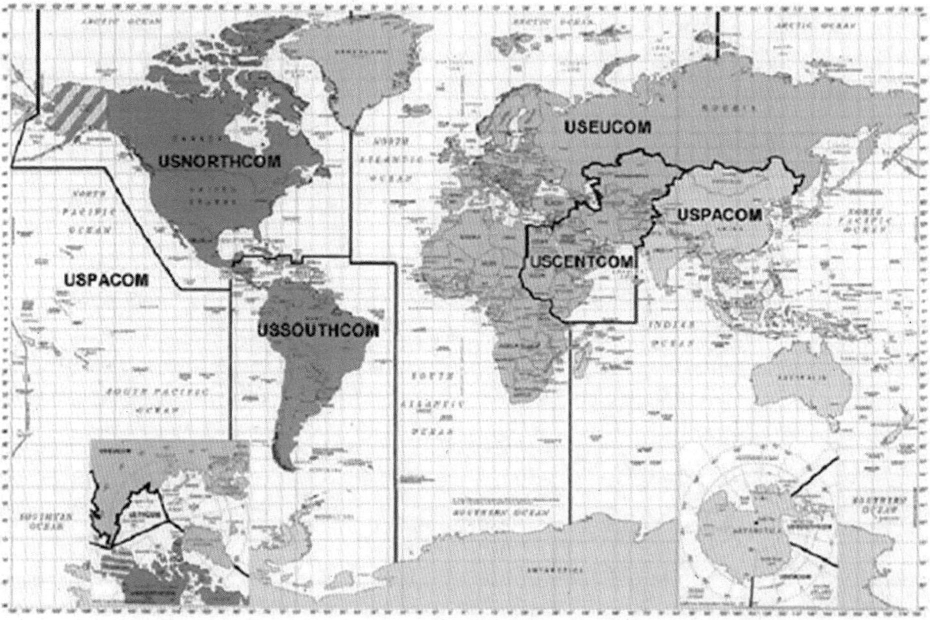

2.2 UCP as of 17 April 2002

commander was dual-hatted), US Special Operations Command, US Strategic Command, and US Transportation Command.[23] There was no CINC with regional responsibility for the lower forty-eight states, Canada, or Mexico, which seems unthinkable today; NORAD provided aerospace warning and air control and JFCOM provided maritime and land assets to the continental United States only. The NORAD commander reported to the US SecDef and to the Canadian CDS.

On 17 April 2002, Secretary of Defense Donald H. Rumsfeld and Chairman of the Joint Chiefs of Staff Gen Richard B. Myers announced changes to the UCP. A new combatant command, USNORTHCOM, was created and assigned the mission to defend the United States and support the full range of military assistance to civil authorities. US Joint Forces Command shifted to focus on transforming military forces and USEUCOM (which also covered Africa)[24] took over more of the European side of the Atlantic and extended into the Arctic. Finally, the term "CINC" was dropped in favour of "combatant commanders." The president was to be the only commander-in-chief.

USNORTHCOM was now a "home" command with air, land, maritime, and cyber assets. The question became, what to do with NORAD?

Canada was consulted and many options were analyzed, including a "larger and expanded" NORAD with a USNORTHCOM element. In other versions, NORAD would become a subcommand under the new USNORTHCOM. (This was never really possible, as a binational command could not legally fall under a national command.) It was also recommended that USSOUTHCOM and STRATCOM be downgraded to sub-unified commands, which was possible given that they would fall solely under national command. The Canadian part of NORAD, therefore, was not the reason for the potential subordination of NORAD, although Canada's rebuff of more mission suites for NORAD (including maritime and land operations), as was initially floated, is noted as one of the reasons for the flirtation with NORAD's potential downgrade.[25] Above all, NORAD's evolution as *the* air defence arm of North America had become ingrained in Canadian and US thinking, and little evidence suggests that scrapping NORAD in favour of strictly national responses was considered seriously.

NORAD's acquisition of an *internal* air defence function in response to 9/11 (as exemplified by ONE) was not a significant departure from its traditional two primary missions: aerospace warning and control. The changes involved integrating more information and personnel. Specifically, more civil radar feeds needed to be integrated into NORAD processes and civilian FAA personnel into the NORAD headquarters on the watch floor. 9/11 had shown that military cooperation and connections with air traffic control authorities were not sufficient; rather, a full air traffic picture was needed. NORAD needed also to have reach-back to Transport Canada and NAVCanada for information on the Canadian flight picture, although personnel from there were not relocated to Colorado Springs. In addition, there were two important political ramifications that required many long conversations with legal experts. The first was what the protocols would be should NORAD interceptors be required to shoot down a plane (and potentially a civilian, commercial plane instead of an enemy combatant) within North American territory. The other was how NORAD would interact/integrate with the new USNORTHCOM.

NORAD AND USNORTHCOM

Prior to 9/11, no formal national command for US continental defence existed, only NORAD, a binational command, operating strictly in the air domain. 9/11 created the impetus for homeland defence, and with it, a Department of Homeland Security (DHS) for the United States. While Canada did not conduct a 9/11 Commission–like investigation, it was evident that changes in Canada would be needed as well, although they were prompted more by the considerable slowing of commercial road traffic with the United States than by the failed air response. When the House of Commons resumed sitting on 17 September 2001, an emergency debate was held, beginning with speeches from the five party leaders: Stockwell Day (leader of the Canadian Alliance and of the Official Opposition), Gilles Duceppe (leader of the Bloc Québécois), Alexa McDonough (leader of the New Democratic Party), Joe Clark (leader of the Progressive Conservative Party), and Jean Chrétien (leader of the Government and of the Liberal Party).[26] In the speeches, NORAD was mentioned directly only three times and in the most perfunctory of ways.[27] Canada responded to subsequent US UCP changes and to the creation of the DHS by striving to remain interoperable and similar in command architecture. The creation of USNORTHCOM prompted the creation of Canada Command (CANCOM) in 2005, and the creation of the DHS was matched, but not replicated, by the establishment of Public Safety and Emergency Preparedness Canada in 2003, although legislation for Public Safety had begun in February 2001, many months before 9/11, prompted by Y2K, ice storms, and other disasters.

The thinking and process leading to USNORTHCOM is not easy to discern. The memoirs of Donald Rumsfeld, at the time US SecDef in the George W. Bush administration, make no mention of the thinking or process, or the place of Canada relative to the decision.[28] Nor is there any public material from Canadian government officials on Canadian thinking during the process leading to USNORTHCOM, which is not surprising, as USNORTHCOM was dedicated solely to US defence, in which Canada had no say. As noted by then–LGen George Macdonald, Vice Chief of the Defence Staff, to a Senate Committee at the time: "NORTHCOM is a US unified command and it would be quite extraordinary for [Canada] to participate in that."[29] Academic accounts are also limited, referencing confidential sources.[30]

In the United States, 9/11 precipitated the political requirements for a joint homeland defence command to encompass North America. This automatically raised questions about the place of NORAD within a new US joint command. Rumsfeld apparently raised the option of combining USNORTHCOM and USSOUTHCOM into a single command for Western Hemisphere defence and security: i.e., an

Americas' Command. As for NORAD, it would simply slide under that new US Americas' Command as the air component for the defence of Canada and the United States. The Americas' Command was subsequently rejected; it would have involved sliding NORAD under USNORTHCOM, which, for Canada, was a political non-starter. Such an arrangement would make NORAD subordinate to a US command, contrary to the NORAD agreement of a balanced command of equals. Canada would, in effect, become the junior partner in the defence of North America, likely unleashing a domestic political backlash around the loss of Canadian sovereignty.[31]

In addition, closely following 9/11, Rumsfeld apparently tasked NORAD to examine deeper and broader CANUS North American defence cooperation, which would lead to the establishment of a binational planning group in NORAD. Sometime during the year-long process from 9/11 to the formal creation of USNORTHCOM, Rumsfeld apparently approached Minister of National Defence Art Eggleton with a proposal to expand NORAD from an air-only binational command to an all-domain combined and joint binational command – a North American Defence Command.

One logic behind such a command was the recognition that potential terrorist threats to North America could include maritime and/or land components. Cargo ships containing large quantities of explosives, or possibly a nuclear weapon, could be employed by terrorists to strike at North American ports, and their cargoes could be transported through the North American rail network to strike at inland targets. As NORAD had provided the functional solution to the air defence issue in the wake of 9/11, so it was also the obvious functional response to threats emanating from the maritime and land domains. In addition, longstanding maritime cooperation between the RCN and the USN, as well as longstanding bilateral protocols on land cooperation in response to natural disasters, reinforced the viability of a North American Defence Command – even the acronym "NORAD" could remain unchanged.

For Canada, however, a multi-domain binational command was simply premature and a "bridge too far." The United States saw 9/11 in Pearl Harbor terms – a direct attack on the homeland that demanded bold, fast solutions. Canada, in contrast, required time to reflect and negotiate. Eggelton's response was to open the door to further and perhaps deeper defence cooperation, but not to all-domain integration. Canada was caught on the horns of a dilemma, as Eggleton's response reveals. To turn the United States down, out of hand, without any due diligence or consideration, raised the spectre of Canada being a defence and security liability for the United States, likely driving it to unilateralism in North American defence, and, in a worst-case scenario, leading it to eliminate NORAD. To agree to the proposal raised the fears of a divisive, internal debate on the loss of Canadian sovereignty, especially in terms of land forces, and an internal ideological struggle within the ruling Liberal Party, which had to guard against accusations of abandoning Europe in favour of the United States on the right side of the political spectrum and losing sovereignty to the United States on the left.[32]

Thus, the Canadian response was not an outright no, but a willingness to discuss possible greater defence cooperation. The United States, however, had already decided to create a new command. In the fall of 2002, formal discussions began with US Defense and State Department officials on the full range of possible future North American defence cooperation, with one exception: ballistic missile defence. NORAD could continue to warn of an incoming missile attack, but Canada (and therefore NORAD) would not respond to it. USNORTHCOM, which was formally stood up on 1 October 2002, subsequently assumed that mission. USNORTHCOM's mandate was "to provide command and control of Department of Defense (DoD) homeland defense efforts and to coordinate defense support of civil authorities (DSCA)."[33] USNORTHCOM was to deter, detect, and defeat threats to the United States, conduct security cooperation activities with allies and partners, and support civil authorities. Its area of responsibility was to include air, land, and sea approaches and encompassed the continental United States, Alaska, Canada, Mexico, and the surrounding water out to approximately 500 nautical miles. NORAD, in contrast, had no area of responsibility but a global area of operations as it related to aerospace warning and a North America–wide scope as it related to aerospace control. Canada agreed to marry NORAD to the new USNORTHCOM because NORAD was a twinned rather than a subordinate command, operating within the functional air domain – separate, yet inseparable.[34]

The NORAD-USNORTHCOM marriage entailed three major components. The commander of NORAD was now double-hatted as the commander of NORAD/USNORTHCOM. (Future commanders, especially General Robinson (2016–18), insisted that the "/" should be an "and" to distinguish the very different mandates of these commands.) USSPACECOM (the other command of the NORAD commander prior to 9/11) was now part of the new USSTRATCOM, completely separate from USNORTHCOM and NORAD, but also housed within Cheyenne Mountain. Beneath the dual-hatted US commander resided a Canadian NORAD deputy commander and an American USNORTHCOM deputy commander. The command centre/operations centre was eventually co-located at Peterson Air Force Base in Colorado Springs in 2012, and the Cheyenne Mountain complex was designated the alternate location. The command centre, subsequently labelled the NORAD/USNORTHCOM Command Center (N2C2), was fully integrated, with Canadian (NORAD) personnel working alongside American (NORAD and USNORTHCOM) personnel.[35] The only exception was the Joint Operations (J3) section, given the different mandates of the commands. As NORAD and USNORTHCOM had different mission sets, there had to be a J3 for NORAD (N/J3) and a separate J3 for USNORTHCOM (NC/J3).[36] Finally, the marriage of equals became evident with the creation of the tri-command structure for the management of North American defence cooperation, subsequently consisting of the Canadian Joint Operations Command (CJOC),[37] NORAD, and USNORTHCOM.

As has long been the pattern in CANUS defence relations, the United States was the initiator and Canada the responder to the changes wrought by 9/11 and the establishment of USNORTHCOM. This is not unique to the CANUS relationship; all nations, allied or not, face little choice but to react and respond to initiatives launched by the leading military power. Arguably, it is more pronounced in the case of Canada as a function of sharing the continent with the United States; North American defence is indivisible and the economies are closely intertwined. Even so, this has never meant that Canada simply "buckles under" to American unilateral decisions, such as with the creation of USNORTHCOM. On the contrary, Canada has always been able to ensure that Canadian national interests are taken into account in the process from decision to implementation, and the United States has always been sensitive to Canadian interests in a relationship of sovereign equals (albeit occasionally after being reminded). Canada has put a brake on unilateral US decisions, such as in 1993 when the US Joint Chiefs proposed downgrading NORAD's command status given the lack of a Soviet threat.[38] In the case of ballistic missile defence (BMD), the United States proceeded unilaterally to develop such capabilities, and the Martin government's 2005 decision not to participate (reflecting the mood of 60 per cent of Canadians in one poll who opposed participation in ballistic missile defence) had little appreciable impact on the relationship.[39] US and Canadian officials approved amendments to the NORAD Agreement authorizing NORAD to make missile warning information available to US commands involved in ballistic missile defense.

In terms of the US unilateral decision to establish USNORTHCOM after Canada rebuffed an expanded NORAD, the Canadian government could do nothing to stop it. Indeed, attempting to do so would simply have been counter-productive and politically dangerous for the relationship, given the priority attached to US homeland defence and security in the wake of 9/11. Instead, the Canadian government could only limit the potential damage that might result from a USNORTHCOM generating an image of Canadian subordination. In this, the United States was a willing partner, being sensitive to potential Canadian domestic political fallout. Reflecting this sensitivity, Rumsfeld, following 9/11, approached NORAD for options, clearly indicating that the defence of the United States could not be separated from the defence of Canada. Rumsfeld, however, was inclined to action, not study.[40]

Soliciting advice from NORAD, which led to the creation of the binational planning cell and its successor the Binational Planning Group (BPG), reflects two important factors. First, it indicated that Rumsfeld's preferred solution was a North American one, rather than a unilateral one. In other words, consciously or not, North American defence was indivisible and NORAD was the functional institutional solution. Second, Canadian agreement to do so provided the solution to the Canadian dilemma of saying no or caving in to the United States. The net result of the BPG's deliberations lead to two significant developments, which speak directly to the significance of NORAD and lay the foundation for future binational North American defence integration: the indefinite renewal of NORAD and its acquisition of a new non-aerospace defence mission, maritime warning, effective 12 May 2006.

THE "NEW" NORAD

On 8 November 2002, NORAD received the Joint Meritorious Unit Award for exceptional service and achievement in defending North America from 11 September 2001 to 10 September 2002.

There was still much to be done, however, including General Eberhart's testimony to the 9/11 Commission on the role played by NORAD. At the change-of-command ceremony on 5 November 2004 from General Eberhart to the first ever non–Air Force commander, Admiral Tom Keating (USN), Eberhart was awarded two honours: the US Defense Distinguished Service Medal (with second oak leaf cluster) and Canada's Meritorious Service Cross (military division). The Canadian citation lauded Eberhart's "strong vision and tenacious pursuit of bi-national support for the common defense of North America," which "contributed significantly to the advancement and defense programs critical to Canada."[41] Cheyenne Mountain was crucial to that defence, but it was also becoming more crowded. USNORTHCOM moved into the mountain with NORAD. Hundreds of millions of dollars of upgrades were made, but within less than a year, Admiral Keating (2004–07) called for a relocation, stating that the amount of vehicle traffic wending its way to and from the mountain every day could be a liability during a crisis.[42] The decision was made to move both commands and the command operations' centre to Peterson Air Force Base. The move was completed by 2008, and in 2012, the NORAD and USNORTHCOM headquarters building at Peterson Air Force Base was renamed the Eberhart-Findley Building in honour of US Air Force General (ret) Ralph E. Eberhart and Royal Canadian Air Force Lieutenant-General (ret) Eric A. Findley for their efforts on 9/11. Cheyenne Mountain remains the alternate command centre and is occupied by the Global Strategic Warning/Space Surveillance Systems Center.

In 2006, Canada and the United States agreed to the indefinite renewal of NORAD and the assignment of a maritime warning mission to the command. On the surface, these two actions do not appear to be linked. The former was a political decision, and the latter a functional one. Yet, in removing the political debates in Canada that generally accompanied NORAD renewals, and taking a small step forward in binational defence integration, they are inherently linked nonetheless. Both have set the stage for future integration outside of the public and political limelight.

During its relatively brief lifespan, the BPG issued an interim report in 2004 and a final report in 2006 on options for the defence of North America.[43] Both reports examined the full scope of possible CANUS/North American defence and security cooperation frameworks. Ten recommendations were made by the BPG. It examined a number of national policies (e.g., the 2002 *US National Security Strategy Report* and Canada's 2004 *Securing an Open Society: Canada's National Security Policy*) that covered the unilateral, national defence of the United States and Canada and identified gaps (capabilities) and seams (geography and command-and-control considerations) between these policies. The BPG found that, from national perspectives, both Canada and the United States had already articulated the need for enhanced security cooperation in their national documents, as well as in the Security and Prosperity Partnership signed by Canada, the United States, and Mexico.[44] NORAD seemed the optimal organization to address the gaps in national policies because it was an extant agreement that did not require creating yet another new organization or require new funding sources. It had the crucial continental mandate and had proven itself a flexible organization.

However, the BPG recognized that NORAD was focused only on the aerospace domain. The proposed maritime warning mission for NORAD would, in theory, address a gap between the aerospace and maritime domains, but would leave surveillance and control to national commands. Including land as another part of NORAD's expanded mission suite was rejected due to political and legal restrictions, cost, and the existence of Memoranda of Understanding (MOUs) that already allowed for bilateral assistance. The reports covered the range of possibilities, including multi-domain (air, land, and maritime) defence integration. Most importantly, the BPG introduced guiding concepts that would subsequently inform future discussions for North American defence cooperation: i.e., the need to consider gaps and seams.

Gaps refer to the capability side of the defence equation, relative to the "new" threat environment, which subsequently coincided with the resumption of Russian LRA flights across the Arctic Ocean and down the East and West Coasts of North America in 2007. Of particular concern were emerging new technologies, which provided higher speed and longer range for Russian and potentially Chinese ALCMs. The age and utility of the NWS and the placement of CANUS forward operating locations for the disbursement of NORAD interceptors during a crisis also came to the fore. Specifically, no longer was the issue of the NWS simply about replacing one-for-one the existing radars, which would be required by 2025 at the end of their serviceable lifespans. Rather, the system needed "renewal" and upgrades to deal with the "new" ALCM threat. Similarly, the utility of the existing FOLs in Inuvik, Yellowknife (used more by the Canadian Army and Rangers), Goose Bay, Rankin (which was not used), and Iqaluit became problematic because of the limited range of the Canadian NORAD interceptors and the greater distance provided by long-range ALCMs. The preferred NORAD counter-capability had been to neutralize the bombers prior to reaching their ALCM launch points, but this would mean stopping bombers near, if not in, Russian territory.

Seams, in contrast, had a geographical and C^2 component. Geographically, in the context of the terrorist threat, this entailed the possibility that terrorists could exploit the border between Canada and the United States in the absence of agreed-upon C^2 protocols on defence responsibilities. Directly related were other C^2 seams as a function of the US UCP. Specifically, a C^2 seam existed between NORAD/USNORTHCOM and USEUCOM in the North Atlantic and USPACOM (later USINDOPACOM) in the Northern Pacific. And in the Arctic, there were four seams: USEUCOM, USNORTHCOM, USPACOM, and NORAD. A further C^2 seam later emerged between NORAD (which had been twinned with USSPACECOM) and USSTRATCOM in relation to the air and space domains.[45]

The final C^2 seam, directly related to the terrorist threat, concerned defence and civil national security authorities. Potential terrorist threats in the maritime and land domain came under the jurisdiction of the DHS and the Canadian Department of Public Safety, as well as other civilian agencies in both countries. The terrorist threat was a "police" problem, and in neither country does the military police the public or possess constabulary authority.[46]

The logic behind this C^2 seam can be primarily linked to 9/11. In the wake of the attack, a US Congressional committee was established to investigate what was, for all intents and purposes, an intelligence failure. The results indicated that all the information about and warning of an attack were present, but divided among different agencies, similar in many ways to the Pearl Harbor intelligence failure in 1941. In other words, all of the pieces of the puzzle were there, but there was no overarching organization or agency to assemble them. As the intelligence failures of Pearl Harbor informed the 1947 National Security Act,[47] so too did 9/11 demand the restructuring of American internal national security architecture to include a dedicated DHS to eliminate the internal seam.

While the creation of DHS arguably resolved the internal intelligence/security issue, it was insufficient to deal with the transnational nature of the terrorist threat.[48] There still existed a border seam with Canada, which required some form of deeper cooperation and coordination in two respects. Canada faced the same problem as the United States, with multiple departments and agencies potentially possessing pieces of the terrorist threat puzzle. Lacking any overarching department to put the pieces together, Canada created Emergency Preparedness Canada (renamed Public Safety Canada), which had a coordinating function, not an operational one, as did DHS.

Second, given their level of economic integration and the fact that terrorists could exploit this by cross-border movement, both countries needed to cooperate and integrate their intelligence pictures to create a seamless North American picture. The next obvious step was to coordinate and, in effect, functionally integrate their responses to an identified North American threat – hence the underlying logic of establishing an integrated multi-domain defence command with air, maritime, land, and cyber responsibilities. The role of the armed forces is not to be the lead responders during a disaster, but rather to be second responders in support of civil authorities, especially if there are high numbers of casualties and/or widespread and critical infrastructure damage. This support role was not new but was traditionally tied to natural disasters such as hurricanes and floods, or to crisis management after a nuclear attack. Furthermore, depending upon the location of a natural or human-made disaster and of national military bases, a centralized North American command structure could enable quicker and more effective responses. The civilian population directly affected by a disaster would likely not care if Canadian or American military members responded, only how quickly relief was provided.

Of course, this was yet another political "bridge too far," reinforced by a military mindset that privileges its overseas combat functions (which, to be fair, are very challenging and do consume a lot of attention) over requests for assistance to civil authorities. As such, the response to the CANUS seam was threefold. The first was to tighten the CANUS border, which, in turn, forced the Canadian government to negotiate arrangements to reduce the potential economic effects of a thicker border on the free flow of goods and people across it. The second was the expansion of integrated border enforcement teams (IBETs) of Canadian and American police forces.[49] This solved the "border" issue on land and water because combined CANUS teams would simply ensure that Americans issued arrest warrants on US soil/water and Canadians on Canadian soil/water. The third was to establish a system in which the US and Canadian intelligence pictures, including the maritime pictures, were integrated into a North American situational awareness picture both nations could access.

Of course, on the surface, this appears unrelated to NORAD. In reality, these steps were foundational to the "new" NORAD that emerged after 9/11. Furthermore, they served as the linkage between indefinite renewal and NORAD's new maritime warning mission in 2006. If maritime platforms could launch air threats (cruise missiles, for example), then a maritime warning mission would partially address the border seam problem related to the US UCP command structure. Now that NORAD was married to USNORTHCOM, the latter having representation from dozens and dozens of civilian security agencies and, importantly, US naval and Coast Guard personnel, NORAD's maritime warning mission was not as foreign as many first believed. The indefinite renewal of the binational agreement ensured that apprehensions connected to NORAD's expanded mission suite would not be raised regularly at the political level, as was the custom with past NORAD renewal processes, which required considerable bureaucratic resources to complete.

CONCLUSION

9/11 was a watershed in the history of the evolution of CANUS North American defence cooperation and integration. On the surface, the changes appear to be modest, including new feeds of information on the internal air picture and new FAA personnel and liaisons with Transport Canada. USNORTHCOM created more acute problems for Canada, but once it became clear that NORAD's aerospace warning and control mission were not subordinated to the new command, a steady rhythm was re-established.

In reality, everything had changed. NORAD had evolved into a "new" organization, taking on a homeland counter-terrorism role as a function of the new focus on internal airspace. The US-driven response to 9/11 cemented the recognition on both sides of the border that the defence and security of North America were indivisible. Whether the political side of the equation recognized this reality is beside the point. The functional side drove the response. And, while the rest of the Canadian and US militaries and politicians were focused upon the "away game" in Afghanistan and Iraq, NORAD and its twin USNORTHCOM were left to concentrate on North America.

3

The Maritime Domain and NORAD's Warning Mission

In 2006, NORAD, an exclusively aerospace-domain command, acquired a new mission in a new domain: maritime warning. The new mission had little if anything to do with traditional military threats to North America. With the Cold War long over, a globally dominant United States, and the absence of any existential military threat to North America, the new mission was simply part of the fall-out from 9/11, and one response to the American-led "war on terror."

Roughly a decade later, however, the transformed geopolitical and geostrategic environment placed traditional military threats back on the defence agenda. This did not mean that the terrorist threat to North America had simply disappeared. On the contrary, the two combined in some ways to merge homeland defence and security, especially within the maritime domain. The nexus of this merger of threat environments was largely the function of a common technology, which cut across the traditional state and non-state divide; for example, an otherwise peaceful merchant ship becomes a platform from which to carry or launch conventional weapons or weapons of mass destruction (WMD). In keeping with new thinking about homeland defence, focus turned from the "arrows" (the weapons) to the "archers" (the launch platforms).

While non-state terrorist organizations did not and do not possess the advanced, long-range sea-launched cruise missile capabilities of Russia and China, cruise missile technology had diffused, and the likelihood that terrorists might employ a cruise missile from a merchant ship could not be ignored. Indeed, this likelihood had been one of the rationales for NORAD's maritime warning mission, even though the defend and defeat side of the equation (at least from a maritime perspective) was not part of NORAD's mission. Operationally, defeating a threat fell into the hands of national naval and constabulary forces; NORAD's warning mission ensured that intelligence from the sources that had it was shared with the people who needed it.

New, long-range SLCM capabilities, Russia's in particular, raised doubts that naval forces could intercept the archers before they reached their launch points. In other words, the maritime threat environment could morph into an aerospace one if missiles, drones, or other air-breathing threats were launched from a ship or submarine. The problem is that while NORAD may warn of a maritime threat, it cannot defeat it if it is not an air-breathing threat. The same functional logic that called for NORAD to have an aerospace warning *and* air defence role should also apply in the maritime domain. This, in turn, suggests that a binational solution in a different or "new" maritime threat environment is required, one that goes beyond the longstanding bilateral nature of naval cooperation between Canada and the United States.

In order to understand this new maritime environment and NORAD's potential future role, it is useful to examine the origins and evolution of NORAD's maritime warning mission. This examination then exposes the obstacles faced by NORAD in engaging the existing North American maritime organizations. This naturally leads to a review of the defence challenges confronting North America and CANUS defence cooperation.

MARITIME WARNING

NORAD's maritime warning (MW) mission was a function of 9/11 in two ways. First, analysts recognized that one of the potential avenues for a future terrorist attack was from the maritime domain. For example, waterborne imports by foreign container trade to US ports in 2000 measured 81,075,637 metric tons. In 2017, it was 167,200,155 metric tons, representing a 106 per cent increase.[1] The concern is that terrorists might obtain a merchant ship and use it as a weapons platform to attack coastal cities in one of three ways: loading the ship with explosives for detonation on arrival, dropping mines, or using the ship to launch some simple or crude type of cruise missile. In addition, a freighter could carry a container full of explosives and offload it in port for transportation to high-value targets along the integrated North American rail and road transportation network. In the worst-case scenario, terrorists might be able to use weapons of mass destruction against North America. As a result, full and complete maritime domain awareness was a pressing requirement, especially for the United States.

Second, it quickly became apparent that the 9/11 attacks succeeded due to structural intelligence failures. All of the information related to the attacks had been present in pieces within the multi-actor American domestic intelligence world, but the pieces had not been fully shared, and there was no overarching agency present to put them together. To resolve this, the United States responded by placing the various agencies under the new centralized Federal Department of Homeland Security. Canada established a new department, Public Safety and Emergency Preparedness Canada (now Public Safety Canada),[2] as well as a new continental command, Canada Command (now Canadian Joint Operations Command), to match the scope and size of USNORTHCOM with its multiple service components.[3] USNORTHCOM is charged with deterring, detecting, and defeating threats to the United States, conducting security cooperation activities with allies and partners, and supporting civil authorities – the last of these duties becoming more onerous with climate change.

Even so, the maritime sector largely replicated the pre-9/11 intelligence structure, with no central agency on either side of the border positioned to collate and assess the wide range of maritime intelligence information gathered by many civilian and military maritime agencies on both sides of the border for different purposes.[4] While each nation might generate an integrated national solution, the nature of maritime traffic begged for some form of a cross-border solution. With ships approaching North America transiting through one state's maritime zone to the other's, ships moving between Canadian and American ports, and cargo offloaded in a Canadian port destined for the United States and vice versa, at a minimum, intelligence information needed to be shared across the border. As noted in the BPG's two reports, there existed a maritime "seam" between Canada and the United States that might be exploited by terrorists or adversarial states.[5]

Of course, cross-border cooperation and information sharing had long existed. But it was "stovepiped" because of differing mandates, jurisdictions, and authorities among multiple government departments and agencies. Thus, for example, the RCN[6] and USN continued to work closely together as they had beginning in World War II, throughout the Cold War, and beyond, but their defence mandates focused upon traditional state-level naval threats, not potential security threats posed by merchant ships. Similarly, the Canadian Coast Guard (CCG) and United States Coast Guard (USCG) also worked closely together, but concentrated upon safety and regulatory maritime issues.[7] The same was true for other functional areas, such as policing, border control, and immigration.

On both sides of the border, and in terms of cross-border relationships, there existed multiple maritime domain and intelligence "pictures," but no integrated single North American maritime Common Operating Picture (COP) to provide complete domain awareness, which would entail an understanding of the Atlantic and Pacific approaches, as well as the Arctic (the latter becoming increasingly important as a function of climate change). As well, there was no overarching North American agency assessing the maritime COP in its entirety. Both a complete, common picture and a central agency were needed.

Beyond these two factors, a third political consideration was also arguably at play. In the immediate wake of 9/11, Canada had turned down the Rumsfeld proposal to establish a multi-domain North American Defense Command.[8] Canadian officials were concerned that a "no" to any changes to NORAD might have significant consequences for the future of defence cooperation. There was also the matter of how to navigate the US decision to establish a new combatant command (USNORTHCOM). This new command could potentially step into NORAD's shoes, bringing command consistency to the relationship across all domains on a bilateral basis, thereby eliminating the valuable Canadian influence opportunities that came from the NORAD *binational* relationship, and increasing the prospects of US unilateralism and the marginalization of Canada in the North American defence relationship. In other words, Canada had to do something to ensure NORAD was not marginalized, given USNORTHCOM's size and North American area of responsibility,[9] and the easiest and least politically problematic option was to accept maritime warning as NORAD's third mission.

The Canadian government communicated a willingness to examine possible binational options or solutions to the new post-9/11 threat environment. Bilateral discussions began in the fall of 2002, with one Canadian caveat: ballistic missile defence was to remain "off the table." These discussions subsequently led to the establishment in

NORAD of a Binational Planning Cell (BPC), subsequently superseded by the BPG, with a broad, multi-domain analytical mandate to identify options for future defence cooperation. In its recommendations in its Interim and Final Reports, maritime warning was the "low-hanging fruit," with few political ramifications, unlike "bi-nationalizing" the other areas, especially the land domain.

NORAD, of course, had a long, established record in early warning. NORAD's core aerospace early warning mission was, in effect, an assessment mission through its integrated warning/attack assessment function for inbound aerospace threats. In this context, NORAD was supported by national surveillance assets. NORAD was a "supported" command: it did not own any of the assets on which it depended. The new maritime warning mission would be similar to this core mission. NORAD provided an assessment from nationally collected information and intelligence. NORAD would not duplicate existing maritime procedures and arrangements, but would simply consider the information, applying a North American lens.[10] Moreover, like its ballistic missile warning/assessment mission relative to US strategic nuclear forces, a maritime warning generated by NORAD would be transmitted to the respective national maritime command authorities for action.[11] There would be no dedicated NORAD maritime intercept assets, nor command authority as in the case of the air control component of NORAD's mission suite.[12] In military parlance, NORAD would operate only "left of bang," meaning warning before a threat became active.

Beyond its experience in the aerospace domain, NORAD's maritime warning mission was based upon significant developments that occurred at both the national and bilateral levels quickly after 9/11.[13] The first pressing requirement was to encourage intelligence-sharing to counter the "stovepiped," multiple-actor maritime world. Both countries took steps to promote intelligence-sharing across their respective maritime communities. For example, Canada established Marine Security Operations Centres (MSOCs) in 2004, with representation from the primary maritime actors. At the national level, Canada established the Inter-departmental Maritime Security Working Group.[14] The United States created the National Maritime Intelligence Integration Office (NMIO) to facilitate and coordinate maritime intelligence-sharing, but not until January 2009.[15]

NORAD, however, is not formally engaged with these actors in their processes. Instead, NORAD resides at the end of the maritime intelligence "food chain." In particular, the navies are responsible for generating a national maritime COP, which includes intelligence from the military and civil sectors. The integrated North American maritime COP is generated by US Naval Forces Northern Command (USNAVNORTH commander to USNORTHCOM),[16] located in Norfolk, Virginia, which receives the Canadian maritime COP from the RCN's operational support and intelligence centre (TRINITY) in Halifax[17] in addition to information from allied partners. The subsequent North American maritime COP is transmitted in various forms, after filters have been applied to scrub out nationally sensitive information.

NORAD became one of the recipients of this maritime COP. NORAD's and USNORTHCOM'S operation centre's maritime desk receives the maritime COP, but provides no input into the process, and has no direct involvement in its creation.[18] If necessary, the maritime desk can reach out directly to CANUS security and defence offices for clarification, but NORAD's main function is as an intelligence fuser. At the end of the chain, NORAD sees much of what others have seen and assessed. NORAD provides a final set of eyes on the maritime COP and may choose to issue a maritime advisory (of an emerging threat) or warning (of a confirmed threat), through formal mechanisms, to the respective maritime communities and actors and, if necessary, to the respective NCAs.

Not surprisingly, NORAD's entrance into the maritime defence and security domain was not an easy one, and the maritime community was not welcoming of NORAD's perceived usurpation of a navy-only activity. While some, such as US Admiral Vern Clark, the Chief of Naval Operations in 2002, recognized the need to track inbound vessels, the preference was to have a separate "maritime NORAD" rather than for NORAD to have a maritime role.[19] Besides the fact that the decision to assign a MW mission to NORAD was top-down, with apparently little if any input from the maritime security community, what role was there for an aerospace-dominant NORAD? The lack of a strategic communication plan to the multifaceted maritime community, and especially the respective navies, was also not helpful. The aerospace and maritime domains were also distinctly different. For example, speed is vital in the process from threat identification to response in the aerospace domain, but it is not in the maritime domain, simply because ships move slowly, or so went the common refrain amongst critics of the new role for NORAD. NORAD J-32 assessors, critics continued, would simply see what others in the community had also seen and assessed, and thus NORAD appeared as not only redundant, but also as a veiled critique of or attack on the analytical work of the maritime community. Finally, NORAD's entrance into the maritime world raised fears that a new maritime warning mission was the first step to NORAD assuming maritime control from the navies, highlighting environmental jealousies.

These critiques and fears, however, were misplaced. First of all, the NORAD of the past had significantly transformed. It was no longer an exclusively aerospace military organization, reflecting the blending of the heretofore separate defence and security domains. Post-9/11 developments brought US civilian FAA personnel into the command, and the establishment of the BPC and BPG brought naval personnel and USCG personnel into the fold. Second, the creation of USNORTHCOM was instrumental in bringing military and civilian personnel in many domains into contact with each other and, by extension, with NORAD personnel. USNORTHCOM's co-location with NORAD headquarters, a dual-hatted common commander, an integrated NORAD USNORTHCOM Command Center (N2C2) and its maritime control mandate that extended over the coastline and out approximately 500 nautical miles in the Atlantic, all helped to transform the NORAD environment and mindset.[20] USNORTHCOM, with its responsibility in the maritime and land domains, brought USN, USCG, and other civilian security personnel into the headquarters. Personnel from roughly sixty other US government departments (OGDs) were represented in USNORTHCOM, and thus accessible to NORAD.[21]

NORAD's twinning to USNORTHCOM gave it a unique place within the maritime domain awareness community and structure. Although both Canada and the United States recognized the importance of intelligence-sharing nationally and bilaterally, both imposed filters relative to their respective national maritime COPs. TRINITY, for example, did not provide the full maritime COP to relevant Canadian OGDs, but only information relevant to their mandates and authority. Highly classified defence information is removed. Similarly, elements of the Canadian maritime COP also contain information for Canadian "eyes only" and are thus not part of the maritime COP communicated to US Fleet Forces Command/NAVNORTH. Similarly, the US maritime COP contains information for American "eyes only." For example, the USN does not provide information on submarine activity, especially concerning nuclear-powered strategic ballistic missile submarines.

NORAD, by its placement at the end of the assessment line, possessed a unique capability in this regard. While the maritime warning mission resided in the N/J-32's Maritime Division, maritime personnel were transferred to the N2C2 as part of a 2019 transformation. The N/J-32 is now responsible for domain awareness. Regardless, maritime assessors at the N2C2 have the capacity to reach back to the classified Consolidated Security Network Infrastructure (CSNI) system to obtain the unfiltered Canadian maritime COP. They also have access to intelligence information from USINDOPACOM and USSOUTHCOM via access to the Secret Internet Protocol Router network (SIPR). Assessors may also connect to NORAD and USNORTHCOM's J-2 (N-NC/J2) intelligence division for additional information to support their assessment process and can access USNORTHCOM intelligence assets in place, which include non-defence security actors in general and the USCG in particular. They can also reach back to any and all of the maritime domain awareness (MDA) and warning actors for additional information and clarification relative to NORAD's MW mission. No other actor in the maritime security world possesses these capabilities, and thus NORAD is uniquely placed partially because it is "outside" of the formal processes.

In addition, NORAD's MW value-added role "left of bang" (i.e., before a critical incident) is the product of other important considerations. NORAD's commander has direct access to each nation's NCA. The commander, if necessary, possesses the ability to elevate an advisory or warning[22] quickly and directly to the NCA, especially if the slow-moving maritime threat suddenly transforms into a rapid-moving air threat or is noticed late; for example, a merchant ship hijacked off the coast, or one that is suddenly not reporting at traffic buoys, might be detected with a fresh set of NORAD eyes. The commander can also identify and examine problems that might emerge in the MDA/MW process and bring them to the direct attention of the NCAs.

NORAD is also the only actor that possesses a truly North American perspective. The other MDA/MW actors are constrained by their respective national and departmental/agency mandates, jurisdictions, responsibilities, and cultures. In the absence of NORAD, there would be no formal integrated structure in place to provide a truly North American assessment, which reflects the problem of national and/or departmental/agency seams as raised by the BPG. NORAD sees and thinks North America.

While there is no evidence of a maritime warning failure which was detected only by NORAD, its MW function is not simply redundant in a negative sense. Its place at the end of the process, its unique cross-border access points, and its North American perspective all provide a measure of assurance that a potential threat is not missed as a function of national and bureaucratic factors. No one wants another 9/11-like event in any domain.

The first test for NORAD's maritime warning role, however, didn't come until three years after the mission was acquired. The M/V *Ocean Lady*, a derelict freighter that had left from Pangkal Pinang, a port city on Indonesia's east coast, popped up off the coast of British Columbia in June 2009. This voyage exposed the lack of intelligence/information-sharing among the organizations involved (among other issues), creating lessons learned for future, improved cooperation.[23] The 2010 M/V *Sun Sea*, carrying 492 Sri Lankans to British Columbia in August 2010, demonstrated improved information-sharing and NORAD's value-added, such that all of the relevant security and defence actors were aware of the ship's approach. Most importantly, NORAD issued its first maritime warning with the *Sun Sea*. Issuing a warning, however, did not quite fit the circumstance, and so NORAD created a new category of "advisories."

But while NORAD was now issuing these notices, there was no feedback loop to NORAD as to what national actions had been taken vis-à-vis the notices.[24] This meant that it was difficult for NORAD to gauge the relevancy, timeliness, and usefulness of its products. This lack of feedback, however, was somewhat hidden, given that national representatives within NORAD could access this information informally and "everyone knew everyone" in the maritime community, especially on the Canadian side. This informality was widely accepted, but it did mean that the few key naval personnel within NORAD became vital as the go-to sources for information. On the one hand, this made for quick answers when needed because the key source phoned his/her key source for the relevant information. On the other hand, it meant that there was no redundancy in the system and single points of failure were created when *the* go-to person changed positions.

Even after NORAD issued its first warning in 2010, few in the security world connected NORAD to this function, as it was still perceived as a uniquely aerospace organization. NORAD had to communicate with and educate the maritime security community about its role and

Table 3.1
Maritime advisories and warning since first issued in 2010

Year	*# Issued*	*Year*	*# Issued*
2010	1*	2016	11
2011	0	2017	6
2012	4	2018	5
2013	9	2019	14
2014	14	2020	7
2015	3	2021	7

* This situation occasioned the only "warning," but gave rise to the new "advisory" category, which was deemed more appropriate for similar circumstances in future.

value to the maritime community. NORAD, therefore, introduced a series of formal table-top exercises to the maritime security community. These exercises, in turn, worked to break down existing cultural intelligence barriers among the disparate number of actors. NORAD and USNORTHCOM also played a significant role in the creation of a Canadian/US Maritime Stakeholders' Conference beginning in 2010, which met annually until 2019 and included Canadian and US officials from most of the maritime security actors. In addition, NORAD also facilitated the breaking down of interdepartmental and national barriers in the move to establish an agreed-upon MDA lexicon.[25] So as not to prejudice future court cases or interfere with law enforcement activity, the entire community needed to be able to reference a vessel and the issue of concern without revealing sensitive information. For example, NORAD could track vessels that might be a vector of contamination (such as COVID-19) to North America. And yet, the maritime warning role for NORAD has been mostly constrained to pure defence threats. Despite, for example, repeated concerns about North Korea's sanctions-busting activity at sea[26] and NORAD's global area for warning purposes, there is reluctance to expand NORAD's warning mission to wider homeland security issues. This is not surprising given that NORAD is low in the US's national security hierarchy.

Alongside the functional value of MW, NORAD, intentionally or not, became a catalyst for enhancing interdepartmental and bilateral maritime defence and security cooperation. In this regard, ironically, the "outsider" spurred greater cooperation out of the fear that failure might lead to NORAD taking over the full spectrum of the maritime defence and security domain. If the maritime security actors failed to cooperate and fully share intelligence, and this failure led to a disaster that could have been averted à la 9/11, an expanded NORAD maritime mission loomed as a potential option.

Of course, even after more than a decade, NORAD continues to face organizational obstacles as a maritime "outsider," and suspicions of a bigger NORAD maritime agenda have not disappeared. NORAD has had to continue to work hard within the community to communicate and demonstrate its value-added contribution and defeat lingering perceptions of being an alien aerospace organization in a maritime world. This extends not only to interactions with this community, but also to interactions with other areas within the command itself. Repeatedly, the MW mission has been overlooked in favour of other priorities, and the maritime warning cell within NORAD is still under-resourced and has bounced from operations to intelligence back to operations again. Ensuring that new commanders recognize the importance of the MW mission, and thus dedicate the necessary resources, remains a perennial concern. Failure in this regard, whether relative to the maritime community or to NORAD's senior command, might create calls to go back to the pre-2006 status quo, and leave North America without an overarching organization to provide an integrated, North American perspective on maritime defence and security.

PERHAPS MARITIME CONTROL?

Notwithstanding suspicions within the maritime defence and security world, there is no evidence of a "hidden" NORAD agenda. The process leading to the decision to give NORAD a MW mission through to its implementation fails to highlight such duplicity. Certainly, by virtue of the initial Rumsfeld proposal and the mandate of the BPC/BPG, consideration was given to a NORAD binational maritime control mission. Even so, once Canada had said "no" to a multi-domain North American Defence Command, political and organizational barriers made a NORAD maritime control mission a non-starter. Nor is there any evidence at the senior levels of NORAD, nor at the level of the national commands, that significant attention was paid to the possibility. Indeed, one of the problems for the maritime warning mission has been the general lack of attention to it. What is more, the naval personnel attached to NORAD to execute the MW mission had their hands full in this regard, and had not, entirely, shed their national naval identities. In addition, for the United States, the problem of North American maritime control had been somewhat solved by the creation of USNORTHCOM, and the respective navies were fully satisfied with a long tradition of close and deep bilateral cooperation.

Certainly, thinking about maritime control relative to NORAD did not entirely disappear, but considerations in this regard were embedded in studies of future decades. In particular, both the internal NORAD Next study, initiated by NORAD Commander (Army) General Jacoby (2011–14), and its successor, the Evolution of North American Defence (EvoNAD) study, blessed by the PJBD in 2017 and begun under General Lori Robinson (2016–18), contain maritime components. Even so, looking far into the future does not make for a hidden agenda.

Regardless, maritime *control* is on the North American defence agenda, even if it is not directly on the NORAD agenda. The rediscovered maritime threat environment of long-range SLCMs, both existing and under development, raises significant issues for the existing bilateral maritime command and control structure and process. This evolving environment has direct similarities to the "new" air threat environment of the early Cold War, initially addressed through bilateral cooperation, which, over time, created the functional logic for a binational solution via NORAD. It may be only a matter of time until both navies and/or senior commands go down the same path. There are, of course, numerous organizational, structural, and cultural impediments to moving towards a binational solution.

Bilateral naval cooperation between Canada and the United States dates back at least to World War II and has continued to this day.[27] This cooperation, of course, stems from overarching common political, strategic, economic, and cultural interests, embedded beneath the relationship formally established by Roosevelt and King in 1940, and cemented as allies in World War II and subsequently within NATO. This cooperation has also been supported by a common naval heritage and culture, similar, in some ways, to the relationship between the RCAF and USAF. The USN was culturally influenced by the Royal Navy (RN), as was the RCN.[28] Even more deeply embedded in their naval culture was a fierce independence from the other services, largely a function of naval vessels at sea being unable to communicate with NCAs (roughly until the development of wireless radio), creating a situation where the captain of the ship was "god." As a result of this history and tradition, navies arguably remain the most independent of all the military services, always watching for interlopers.[29] Of course, this has softened over time, and certainly the USN and USCG work hand in glove as well as with the US Marine Corps. As Canada's Coast Guard (a specialized agency within Fisheries and Oceans Canada) has a safety mandate, it is limited in its capacity requiring support from the RCN, especially beyond the Exclusive Economic Zone (EEZ) (i.e., beyond 200 nautical miles offshore).

There are also other factors beyond culture to consider. The USN is the global "blue-water" naval power, whereas the RCN lacks the capability to undertake such a role in a sustained fashion, especially with the loss of Canada's destroyers. The RCN can only truly operate on a global scale within a larger naval coalition, ideally one led by the USN. This is reflected in the ability of RCN vessels to integrate into a USN Carrier Task Force under US command. Whereas the USN possesses naval capabilities across all naval dimensions, the RCN is limited, with a small fleet that shrank dramatically after World War II, given changing geopolitical realities. Frigates, with anti-submarine warning capabilities and helicopters, were seen as the future need.

USN strategic thought, which embraces nineteenth-century US strategist Alfred Thayer Mahan's counsel to control the seas,[30] has never really considered North America as integral to its projection of sea power. Instead, the USN nurtures an offensive mindset and culture evident in the development of the Forward Maritime Strategy in the 1980s.[31] While it is difficult to discern whether or not the RCN quietly yearns to be a disciple of Mahan, it is largely resigned to a defensive role. Thus, during the Cold War, the RCN was primarily focused upon anti-submarine warfare to protect the sea lines of communication (SLOC). A Canadian frigate today within a USN Carrier Task Force primarily serves as a defensive picket. Of course, politically, Canadian governments have remained comfortable with a defensive, reactive maritime role, similar in many ways to NORAD's defensive posture.

There are certain areas that pose a challenge for a binational maritime solution. Specifically, these relate to the strategic submarine world, especially in the Arctic. The Arctic Ocean is the location where Russian SSBNs are bastioned, as the Soviet ones were. It is also the place where USN SSNs transit, including, according to some accounts, through the Northwest Passage (NWP).[32] Canada has no existing capacity to operate underneath the ice, and the USN has no interest in sharing intelligence about under-ice activities with Canada or anyone else. Nor is the Canadian government truly interested in "knowing" officially because of potential political ramifications, given Canada's classification of the NWP as historic internal waters.

Until recently, there was no pressing requirement, similar to the aerospace domain, to shift to a binational solution. The aerospace domain, because of the speed of the threat, created an environment in which agreed-on intercept plans are well-established and practised, which is part of the functional logic underlying the binational solution. The maritime domain is a slow-moving one, allowing for a bilateral solution. Also, during the early stages of the Cold War, the primary maritime threat was to the SLOC, not directly to the North American continent per se, notwithstanding forward-deployed Soviet SSBNs. Today, however, SLOC protection is no longer a pressing requirement, and new technologies and strategies have dramatically altered the maritime environment.

The successful nature of World War II anti-submarine RCN/USN cooperation could simply be extended into the Cold War era, whereas air defence cooperation was a distinct and new requirement demanding a new approach. In this regard, the new approach, which led to NORAD, was driven by the two air forces in a "bottom-up" process. In addition, the RCAF dedicated a significant number of air defence assets in a more equal relationship. With the "new" maritime threat today, Canada's naval contribution is dwarfed by USN capabilities, not to mention its very small number of quick-reaction alert fighters.

Procedures have long been in place and undertaken, on rare occasions in the past, for naval assets to be placed under NORAD command. For example, on 9/11, a USN aircraft carrier's air assets, located off the coast of New York, were "CHOPed" (change of operational control) over to NORAD command. More recently, the USN and RCN have engaged more directly in the annual NORAD VIGILANT SHIELD exercises, and, of course, USNORTHCOM has a North American maritime control mission to which the RCN contributes on a bilateral basis.

All of these factors explain not only why close bilateral naval cooperation did not evolve into a binational solution, but also why the RCN, and especially the USN, are likely to be reluctant supporters of a future binational solution. In the absence of their willing support, neither government is likely to impose a binational solution. Nonetheless, neither the RCAF nor the USAF thought that the ultimate end state of their initial bilateral air defence cooperation would be a binational solution. In this regard, the transformation of the maritime threat environment, and the resulting merger of the air and maritime domains, creates similar functional conditions that will likely drive the two naval commands to the same conclusion.

The new maritime threat environment is markedly different from the past. During the Cold War, the maritime threat was primarily to the sea lines of communication between North America and (NATO's) Europe. Even though the expectation was that a war in Europe would rapidly escalate to a nuclear exchange, there was also the possibility that such a war might be contained and require the movement of significant military resources to Europe in a repeat of World War II. Indeed, Canada, as part of NATO, agreed to provide a rapid deployment force by air and sea to support Norway.[33] Today, however, North American adversaries possess very long-range surface and sub-surface SLCMs that can directly threaten North America. This is especially true for the North Atlantic, but also for the Pacific as Chinese capabilities evolve.

In the wake of the end of the Cold War, the North Atlantic was removed from the defence agenda. The Russian Fleet largely disappeared from the North Atlantic. NATO's Supreme Allied Commander Atlantic (SACLANT) was disbanded and replaced by Allied Command Transformation (ACT). The USN's 2nd Fleet (Atlantic), formed in 1950, was eliminated in 2011, although re-established in August 2018 with a two-maple-leaf Canadian naval officer (Rear Admiral Steve Waddell) named as vice-commander in 2019. In the interim between 2011 and 2018, Allied naval cooperation and operations shifted to support UN and NATO operations – for example, in the Persian Gulf and off the Horn of Africa. Anti-submarine exercises and training became a very low priority, and the requirement to reinforce NATO's northern flank (Norway) disappeared.

With the transformation of the political environment occasioned by conflict in Crimea, Ukraine, and Syria, the initial allied naval response concentrated on the Baltic and Black Seas and the Mediterranean, directly related to the two Standing NATO Maritime Groups (SNMG) under Allied Maritime Command, located at Northwood, United Kingdom.[34] Subsequently, with the return of Russian naval activity in the North Atlantic, NATO re-established a new Atlantic Command – Allied Joint Force Command Norfolk, commanded by the new dual-hatted 2nd Fleet commander. In 2018, NATO undertook its first major Arctic and North Atlantic exercise since the end of the Cold War, called TRIDENT JUNCTURE.[35]

In many ways, the allied response was simply the Cold War past made present in three distinct ways. First, the new Joint Force Command Norfolk, at least from the continental NATO European perspective, appears as a return to an emphasis on SLOC between North America and Europe. Second, in terms of the US UCP, the region beyond USNORTHCOM's 500-nautical-mile AOR is in USEUCOM's area of responsibility. Third, reflecting the USN's forward maritime strategy of the 1980s, and evident in the 2018 NATO TRIDENT JUNCTURE exercise, the strategy is to move naval strike forces in the case of a crisis quickly north of the Greenland-Iceland-United Kingdom (GIUK) Norway gap to threaten Russian naval forces before they can filter out into the North Atlantic.[36]

In contrast to the Cold War, the prospect that a modern crisis or war in the far eastern reaches of NATO would require a massive mobilization of national resources and the movement of large numbers of forces and supplies from North America to Europe is modest for now, but increased attention is turning to the capabilities and intentions of Russia and China. Nuclear weapons and the fear of escalation act to limit the objectives sought by an adversary. Modern warfare, evident in high-tech, long-range precision strike forces, places large conventional forces at significant risk, and the concentration of forces is a military liability in this environment. In other words, a war is likely to be over long before North American resources could be mobilized and shipped by sea.

Moreover, no nation possesses the capability to mobilize national resources as they did in World War II. War of today and in the future is "come as you are." Few other than China possess plans for mobilization and the rapid transformation of civilian production to military production. Modern management and production processes are not amenable to rapid transformation. There are few if any well-trained inactive conscript forces at the ready, and training civilians to employ high-tech military equipment cannot be done overnight. As far as the submarine threat goes, existing Russian and Chinese capabilities are concerning.[37] Russia, however, is incapable of suddenly ramping up submarine production. Expansion at Chinese submarine production yards suggests they can produce more and do so relatively quickly.

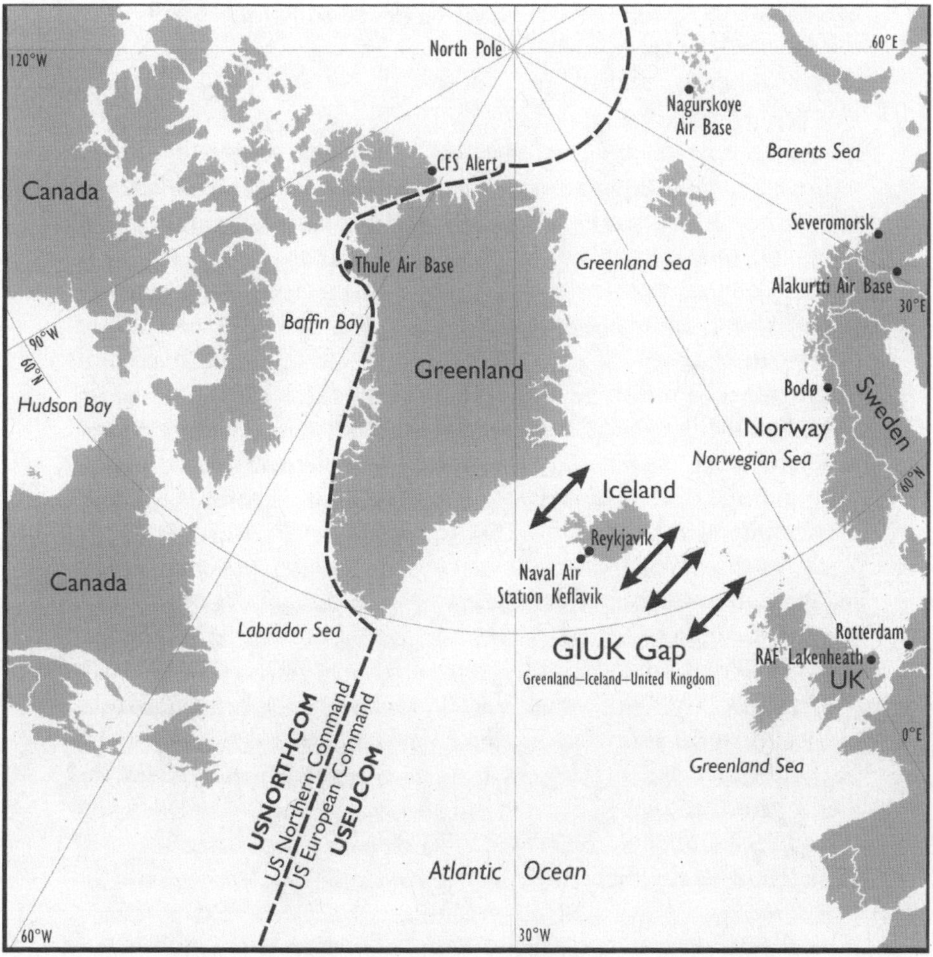

3.1 Map of the Greenland-Iceland-United Kingdom (GIUK) Norway Gap

Of course, this does not negate the strategic logic of allied naval forces moving north to strike at Russian naval assets before they filter out into the Atlantic south of the GIUK Norway gap. Indeed, in a crisis in Eastern Europe, allied naval forces are likely to move north of the GIUK Norway gap to threaten Russian surface and subsurface capabilities in their adjacent waters. Such movement could potentially serve valuable deterrence purposes. Of course, how the Russian navy will respond is unpredictable. Regardless, the anti-submarine campaign is likely to take place in the upper regions of the North Atlantic.

This campaign, and the deterrence utility attached to it, does not ensure that submarines will not be able to filter south of the GIUK Norway gap. Even a small number of cruise missile submarines would pose a significant threat to North America, a threat that would transform into an air-breathing one upon SLCM launch. Moreover, the long-range distance of a modern SLCM places the threat far beyond the intercept range of air assets, and of existing North American surveillance and reconnaissance capabilities. As a result, the defence of North America requires the integration of naval air defence assets into NORAD capabilities, similar to air national defence assets committed annually to NORAD command. Certainly, naval assets are used in Operation NOBLE EAGLE. This integration suggests that a NORAD maritime control mission could overcome the C^2 seam that exists between naval strategy and the air defence of North America.

The RCN's national AOR extends only to the edge of Canada's EEZ (to 200 nautical miles, which is approximately 230 miles or 370 kilometres). In the case of USNORTHCOM, its AOR extends 500 nautical miles into the North Atlantic, well short of the range of Russian SLCMs. USEUCOM's AOR extends across the rest of the North Atlantic, but its attention and whatever forces are assigned to it in a crisis are likely to be moved far north of the GIUK Norway gap. As a result, the area south of the GIUK Norway gap and east of USNORTHCOM's AOR is neglected and could be exploited by Russia in particular. This suggests that the existing command-and-control seam in the Atlantic is a liability.

At the same time, the maritime threat environment is effectively merging with the air threat environment. Producing a separate maritime COP and Air Common Operating Picture (ACOP) appears problematic. Ideally, what is needed is all-domain awareness. This, in turn, raises issues concerning the integration of air and maritime command and control potentially into a single command, instead of two distinct command-and-control structures, a binational air and a bilateral maritime structure.

The outlines of this evolution are already in place. Both the RCN and USN recognize that greater cooperation is needed, especially at the operational and strategic levels. Until recently, cooperation has largely been exercised at the tactical level, as in the case of the Naval

Tactical Operations Group (NTOG), hosted by the USN's 5th Fleet, in the summer of 2019.[38] Requirements for greater cooperation are now on the table, which of course raise issues of the respective roles and functions of the two navies. In the near term *the relationship* is likely to remain a bilateral one in which the USN has the lead, but *the procedures* that emerge will likely mirror the binational solution in all but formal agreement à la NORAD. The functional logic of a binational solution will, or perhaps should, merge over time, as it did in the 1950s leading to NORAD.

CONCLUSION

At the heart of a future binational solution lie three important considerations. First, as the air and maritime domain threat environments merge into a single, integrated domain, existing service and command seams will need to be overcome to reflect a truly combined and joint approach to the defence of North America.

Second, USNORTHCOM is likely to become the primary driver of future command arrangements as a function of its existing maritime control mission. Since inception, it has struggled for recognition as a combat command no different from the other regional commands established in the US UCP. Recent NORAD commanders, from Admiral Gortney (2014–16) to General Robinson (2016–18) to General O'Shaugnessy (2018–20) to General VanHerck (2020–present), have sought to remove its image as a command simply undertaking DSCA missions (aid during floods, fires, etc.). Indeed, with the rise in great power competition, attention is returned to the importance of homeland defence and both NORAD's and USNORTHCOM's mandates.

Finally, the NORAD aerospace C^2 structure is readily adaptable to the maritime world. Air tasking orders emanate from NORAD but execution of the air defence battle falls to the regional NORAD commands. Each regional command, in turn, has a commander from one nation and a deputy from the other on a regional basis. Thus, ANR and CONR have American commanders and Canadian deputies, and CANR has a Canadian commander and an American deputy. Although embedded within a binational structure, each has a national flavour.

Similarly, the existing maritime C^2 structure would entail regional operational commands on the East and West Coasts, mirroring the existing national structures. Each of these commands, in turn, relative to regional location, would have a Canadian or American commander and an American or Canadian deputy respectively. Air and naval tasking orders would emanate from a Combined Joint Air and Maritime Component Command (CJAMCC) and above would be a NORAD strategic headquarters.

Of course, there will be significant obstacles, among which the nations' respective navies, and the USN in particular, stand out. Moreover, this evolutionary path may well be an uneven one. Given the greater level of cooperation over time on the East Coast of North America, the primacy of the Russian maritime threat for the time being, and the peculiar place of the Pacific in USN culture, one may see initially greater integration on the Atlantic, before the Pacific.

NORAD's expansion into the maritime domain will also naturally face political barriers surrounding sovereignty. Even so, the binational solution would not undermine Canadian or American authority in their respective waters and out into their EEZs. As in the case of the air domain, both Canada and the United States can apply national air support for missions short of defence. Similarly, both would be able to task naval forces to support OGDs and non-defence missions as well.

Even though a binational outcome is not inevitable, all of the pressures that led to the creation of NORAD appear present in the maritime world. The process will not be easy or straightforward. Nonetheless, the merging of the air and maritime defence domains requires a new command structure and C^2 process to ensure the credibility of the North American deterrent posture through an effective and efficient defence. And nowhere are deterrence and all-domain awareness more pressing than in the Arctic.

4

The Perennial and Proverbial Arctic Conundrum

In 2007, Russia resumed its long-range aviation (LRA) (bomber flights) over the Arctic Ocean and down the East and West Coasts of North America. There was nothing particularly ominous about this resumption at the time from a geostrategic perspective. Nor was there anything politically nefarious about these flights. One could easily conclude they were training flights, of little or no consequence. The United States was still focused on its war on terrorism and climate-related events were making headlines, especially the now-infamous NASA map of the shrinking Arctic ice.[1] Russia was a key member of the Arctic Council and had just chaired the Council successfully from 2004 to 2006.[2]

Several months after Russia reportedly undertook a cyber-attack on Estonia (a NATO member since 2004) in April and May 2007,[3] Russia went to war with Georgia.[4] Admittedly, both sides deserved part of the blame for the war, but many observers perceived Russia's military actions as a response to Georgia's expressed desire to join NATO and the decision of the NATO alliance to "keep the door open" to future Georgian membership and to that of other former Soviet Republics, including Ukraine. Still, none of these events, individually or collectively, suggested that Western relations with Russia were necessarily on an adversarial path reminiscent of the Cold War. Indeed, during this period, Russia and the United States negotiated and signed the New START agreement, which then-President Obama sold as a restart of positive relations with Moscow.[5] Meanwhile, NORAD had been renewed in perpetuity in 2006 and had a new maritime warning mission.[6] NORAD had conducted thousands of ONE sorties since the evening of 9/11 and had made the decision to relocate the NORAD headquarters from Cheyenne Mountain to a dual-purpose NORAD and USNORTHCOM Command Center (N2C2) at Peterson AFB, which opened in time to celebrate NORAD's fiftieth anniversary in 2008. In Canada, 22 Wing in North Bay (Canada's Air Defence Sector base)[7] received an upgrade to its air surveillance and control system from an old AN/FYQ-93 to a new Battle Control System–Fixed (BCS-F), but the auditor general noted all sorts of cost overruns and unilateral decisions made by DND.[8] It would seem that internal modifications and budget overruns were top-of-mind for NORAD, as opposed to thoughts about Russia.

In 2011, the Putin government announced an ambitious military modernization program.[9] While some saw the program as a direct challenge to American military superiority and thus politically directed against NATO and the United States, the program could also be interpreted as the simple need for Russia to modernize its ageing and outdated nuclear and conventional forces. The recovery of the Russian economy, largely thanks to its oil and gas resources, had finally provided surplus capital for investment in modernization. In other words, there was nothing particularly ominous about this ambitious program. NORAD provided air security assistance to the Government of Canada for the 2010 Vancouver Winter Olympics and reaffirmed its historical mission, adopting the combined NORAD and USNORTHCOM vision: "With our trusted partners, we will defend North America by outpacing all threats, maintaining faith with our people and supporting them in their times of greatest need. 'WE HAVE THE WATCH.'"[10]

In 2013, China, Italy, Japan, India, Korea, and Singapore were accepted as Observers to the Arctic Council to join the United Kingdom, France, Germany, the Netherlands, Poland, and Spain. The eight Arctic states (Russia, Canada, the United States, Norway, Denmark, Finland, Sweden, and Iceland) had agreed to a few Arctic-related agreements, including an important Search and Rescue Agreement.[11] The Arctic was referenced as "high North, low tension."

A year later, however, Russia's actions were interpreted collectively as part of a pattern to confront the West and the United States and to restore Russia to Great Power status by re-establishing the former Soviet sphere of influence, identified in Russian foreign policy as the "near abroad." Underpinning this "new" interpretation was the

Putin government's decision to annex Crimea in response to internal developments in Ukraine, which Putin described as a "coup." Following the annexation of Crimea, Moscow instigated and supported an armed insurrection that seized control of major portions of the Donbas region and began an armed conflict that continues. At the same time, Russia also escalated its support to the Assad regime in the Syrian Civil War, subsequently tipping the military balance in the regime's favour.

Russia is seen as a revisionist power, seeking to undo the results of the end of the Cold War and the collapse of the Soviet Union, and directly threatening NATO in Europe and the United States and Canada in North America. The events since 2007 now tend to be perceived as a clear, conscious political and strategic pattern confirmed by the unprovoked attack on Ukraine in February 2022. In many circles, particularly within NORAD, Russia is the persistent and proximate threat to North America, and its chief and likely avenue of attack is via the North American Arctic, though, according to the US UCP, EUCOM is chiefly responsible for Russia.[12]

Beyond Russia, however, the United States and the West now face the additional challenge of the People's Republic of China (PRC) – the most anticipated peer and pacing competitor to the United States. Dramatic Chinese economic growth instituted by Deng Xiaoping's 1979 modernization program provided the surplus capital over time for the relatively rapid modernization of China's military forces. Modernization, in turn, was reinforced by the shock of the American-led, nearly cost-free expulsion of Iraqi forces from Kuwait in 1991. China watched and learned. The Malacca Strait remains a choke point for its exporting ambitions and China seeks to expand its influence and reach in the world to ensure its security and resources. Rapid technological gains and science breakthroughs (often copied)[13] mean that China is now a space power, seeks to dominate the Asia Pacific region, and is determined to ensure it has a say and influence in the international regimes of the world from which it believes it was systematically excluded.[14] The Obama administration responded with a policy pivot toward the Asia-Pacific region, requiring a significant number of the United States' naval assets to be redeployed to the renamed Indo-Pacific theatre.[15]

Chinese economic growth has continued, with expectations that its economy will surpass the United States in terms of gross domestic product, barring unforeseen events (such as the fallout from the

COVID-19 pandemic, continued internal strife, and an uncounted domestic debt burden). China's ambitious "One Belt, One Road" initiative, with its land and maritime components stretching westward and its penetration into Africa and beyond, presents a challenge to the United States. China's new strategic doctrine, supported by new, advanced military technologies, is designed to gain control of the Pacific maritime approaches and deny the ability of the United States, or more specifically the USN, to intervene in the region.[16] At the same time, China has undertaken numerous aggressive steps to reinforce its claimed territorial waters in the South and East China Seas, and to reject and ignore the Permanent Court of Arbitration's ruling on China's South China Sea claims vis-à-vis the Philippines.[17]

China and Russia are now considered peer competitors to the United States, but whereas Russia is the main concern from an Arctic perspective, China is the main adversary worldwide. In contrast to the United States, Canada is more circumspect about naming specific states, preferring to refer to the return of Great Power politics[18] or to refer to China as problematic in a South China Sea context and Russia in an Eastern European context in official documents. The term "adversary" appears only three times in Canada's 2017 defence policy. The post–Cold War era of American dominance and hegemony has come to an end. In its place, a Great Power triangle has emerged which is likely to dominate international politics for the foreseeable future, notwithstanding the possibility that India will also shortly join the club. As a result of the emergence of these powers, deterrence and defence have re-emerged as pressing issues for the United States and its allies across the globe, and especially for NORAD's ability to respond to this new geostrategic environment as the (air/aerospace) defender of North America.

Although deterrence cuts across the traditional air, land, and sea domains and includes outer space and the cyber world, most pressing for NORAD are the new challenges faced from advanced military technologies in the air domain; NORAD's traditional mission suite of aerospace warning and aerospace control (air defence) cannot keep up with the new air- and space-based weapons. These technologies have rendered the ability of NORAD to detect air-breathing threats with the existing NWS obsolete.[19] Thus, NWS renewal, if not outright reimagining, is at the top of NORAD's latest modernization agenda. NWS renewal presents numerous challenges, especially in the context of existing technology, costs, and the impact of climate change in the Arctic. There is also the complicated political and economic environment confronting both Canada and the United States, not to mention the importance of buy-in by Indigenous communities across the Arctic. Both states must give due consideration to the obligations outlined in Article 30 of the UN Declaration on the Rights of Indigenous Peoples (UNDRIP).[20]

THE NEW CAPABILITY THREAT ENVIRONMENT

Long before Russia re-emerged politically as an adversary to the West, primarily occasioned by its annexation of Crimea, NORAD military intelligence had begun to issue warnings of a new generation of technologically advanced Russian military capabilities. At the strategic nuclear level, these included a new generation of ICBMs and sea-launched ballistic missiles (SLBMs). In the air-breathing domain, there was a new generation of ALCMs and SLCMs. In addition, intelligence picked up the development of hypersonic weapons, which can potentially be launched from a ballistic missile, aircraft, or sea-based platform, fly at very high speeds at the lower reaches of outer space, and are manoeuvrable during flight.[21] Taken together, this meant that the resumption of Russia LRA flights was perceived in much more ominous terms.

For NORAD, the particular and most pressing concern was the implication of the new generation of cruise missiles relative to its traditional, primary missions of aerospace warning and control. The replacement of the original DEW line in the 1980s with the NWS, along with the dismantling of the Mid-Canada and Pinetree lines and the development of FOLs across the Canadian far north, had been in direct response to the first generation of Soviet ALCMs.

The objective for NORAD was to detect and intercept Soviet/Russian LRA, the "archers" in NORAD parlance, before they reached their launch points in the high north, because of the difficulties in tracking cruise missiles (the "arrows") in flight due to their small radar cross-sections and ground-hugging flight paths. While cruise missiles can be detected by aircraft with "look down" radars (AWAC aircraft, for example), these were in relatively short supply from the United States, and located only in Alaska.[22] While Canada's CF-18s (and the US's F-35s) have this capability, the problem of cruise missile detection and engagement is frustrated by range and radar cross-section.

The new generation of Russian, as well as future Chinese, ALCMs has rendered the 1970s NWS technology obsolete. The new generation of weapons has a much longer range, with launch points located beyond the capability of the long-range NWS radars to detect, and the short-range radars are largely incapable of detecting faster-moving cruise missiles in flight. Nor do the fourth or fifth generations of fighters possess the range from FOLs to reach the LRA prior to their launch points unless supported by in-flight refuelling, which creates additional issues, especially availability and cost. What is needed today is extremely long-range detection capability that can spot any launch activity deep within Russian and Chinese territory.

The future is also likely to hold a new generation of cruise missiles travelling at very high speeds, including the possibility of hypersonic weapons, which creates other challenges for NORAD's aerospace missions.[23] In addition to the new generation of ALCM threats, North American and NORAD defence and deterrence requirements confront a new generation of long-range SLCMs. Russian, and in the future Chinese, SLCMs can threaten North America from deep in the North Atlantic and Pacific Oceans, a threat that simply did not exist at the time of NWS construction, creating significant surveillance gaps on the East and West Coasts of North America. With the collapse of the Intermediate-Range Nuclear Forces (INF) Treaty, NORAD and North America could face the threat of long-range, high-speed ground-launched cruise missiles (GLCMs) from the Russian Arctic.[24]

Alongside cruise missiles, the Russians and Chinese have developed hypersonic weapons, and these weapons blur the neat division between air and ballistic missile threats (see chapter 6 for more details). While NORAD possesses the early warning mission for both air-breathing and ballistic missiles, the assets supporting each component have long been separate. The NWS is strictly designed for the former. The American ballistic missile early warning network (BMEW), which primarily consists of three radars (in Clear, Alaska, Thule, Greenland, and Fylingdales, England), is designed for the latter. Hypersonic weapons can be launched from a rocket or can be powered by high-speed engines or "scramjets" that can manoeuvre, at very high speeds, to their destination.[25] This new threat and evolving technology suggests that it is time to integrate the two warning systems.

Overall, the challenges confronting North American and NORAD's defence and deterrence functions are much greater and more complicated than was the case in the 1980s at the time of the NWS's construction. What is required now is an integrated, multi-domain detection system; the new goal is for joint all-domain command and control (JADC2).

NWS RENEWAL

The NWS was built in the 1980s under the binational Air Defense Modernization Plan (ADMP) and completed in the early 1990s. The end of the Cold War and the collapse of the Soviet Union negated any requirement for further investment in the NWS or the FOLs. At the time, the NWS and FOLs were relatively new and, in the absence of any existential threat to North America, were adequate for NORAD's surveillance and general air defence missions. Neither NORAD's engagement in anti-drug operations nor its ONE missions after 9/11 required significant new investments relative to its external aerospace warning and control mission. 9/11 justified the new investments linking NORAD with internal, civil radar feeds. As for the NWS, even intelligence warnings of new, threatening Russian capabilities were insufficient to justify significant, major investments in modernizing the NWS, until the geopolitical environment transformed in 2014.

Understanding the complicated issues facing Canada and the United States in modernizing North American defence begins with the NWS, and the recognition that it is already obsolete relative to the capabilities of competitors, its location, and the threat environment. As such, the NWS is the first priority of what will be a relatively long modernization process. Although the Liberal Trudeau government recognized NORAD modernization and NWS renewal as priorities in its 2017 *Strong, Secure and Engaged* defence policy, it downplayed the urgency to replace the NWS, noting that the radars were still operational and would be until 2025 if not beyond.[26] No money was attached to NWS renewal in the 2017 defence policy of the 2018 *Defence Investment Plan*, nor in the 2019 *Defence Investment Plan Update*, and only in 2021 were initial, modest sums of money promised.[27] The lack of agreed-upon future architecture for the NWS, technological considerations, a desire not to create national anxiety about the state of the NWS, and other internal preferences for investment probably account for the hesitancy to confirm large dollar figures.

The United States, Canada, and NORAD activated their advice architecture. The 2019 *US Missile Defense Review* confirmed that homeland defence is the United States' primary focus.[28] Roughly around the same time, a Binational NORAD Steering Group (BNSG), focused on surveillance and research and development (R&D), and a Binational Committee on FOLs emerged. Dominated by functional military experts, both come "under" the PJBD and the MCC. In Canada, the Defence NORAD Steering Committee (DNSC) was established for internal coordination purposes. In the fall of 2019, the Canadian Continental Defence Policy Division (CDPD) was created within the Office of the Assistant Deputy Minister for Policy (ADMPOL). The CDPD has three focus areas: (i) domains and technology policy; (ii) NORAD policy; and (iii) capabilities and liaison. Appropriately, the CDPD's director is one of the co-chairs of the BNSG. Finally, in the wake of the 2019 federal election, the prime minister's mandate letter to the minister of National Defence (at the time Harjit Sajjan) stressed the priority of the NWS.[29]

Whether this active support from Canada for NORAD was motivated by a clear recognition of the status of the NWS, or some form of pressure from the US, or simply a perception that failure to move forward might lead to unwanted American pressure, is difficult to know. Nonetheless, North American defence clearly began to emerge as *a*, if not *the*, defence priority for both nations, and with it, NWS renewal as the top priority, even if there was no formal commitment of defence dollars until 2021.

While the cruise missile threat emanating from Russia is the primary driver for a new NWS, modernization is also a function of its existing location relative to the 2018 Canadian decision to "align" the Canadian Air Defence Identification Zone (CADIZ) farther north to match the full extent of Canadian Arctic territory. Prior to 24 May 2018, the CADIZ simply followed the lines of NWS radar positions stretching across roughly the middle of Canada's Arctic and down the coast of Labrador. Much of Canada's northern archipelago was far outside the CADIZ. Moving the CADIZ northward meant that there was now a "blind" area outside of the range of the NWS but within the new CADIZ.

The location issue is not solely related to the new CADIZ. In the past, with the air-breathing threat being projected almost exclusively over the Arctic Ocean, the NWS was conceptually separated from the other radar systems covering the approaches to North America. Today, however, given Russian LRA flight paths and the threat of SLCMs off both coasts, NWS renewal needs to be conceptualized and structured to detect threats from all coasts, if not for 360 degrees. This, in turn,

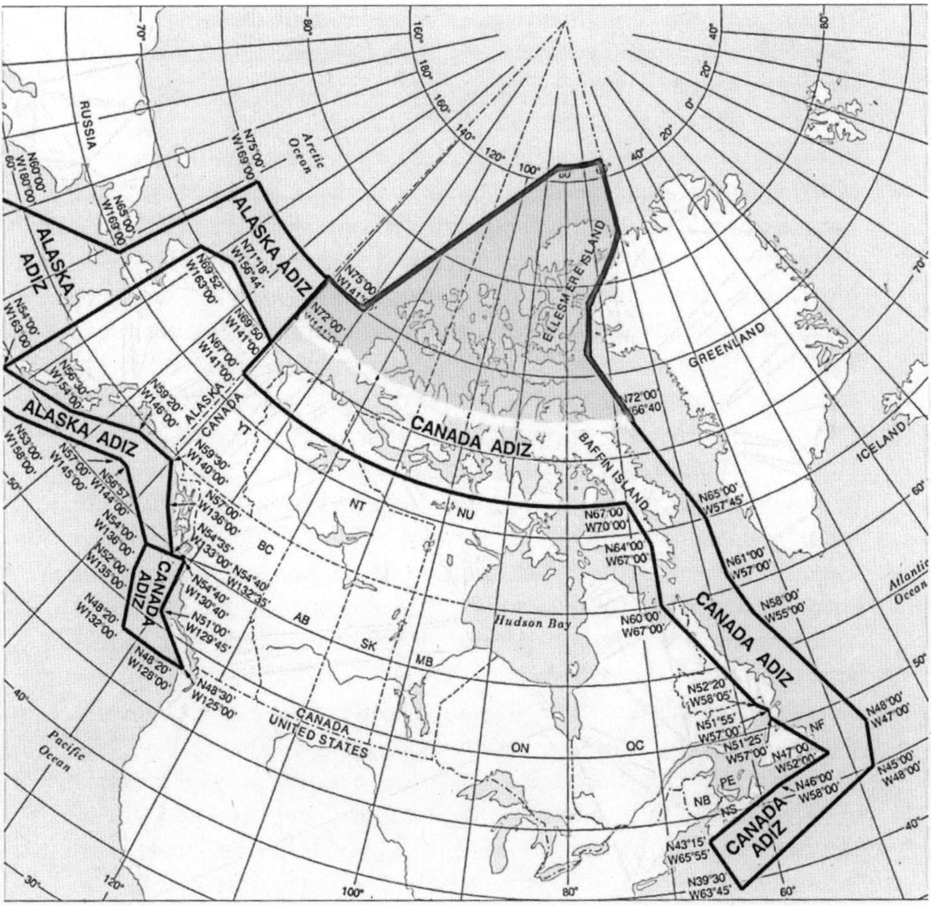

4.1 Aligned CADIZ

raises other issues for the "new" NWS, or perhaps what should be more appropriately labelled the North American Warning System (NAWS).

As noted above, the first issue concerns the inability of the existing radars to detect and track cruise missiles in flight. In other words, the simple replacement of the existing long- and short-range radars by new ones of similar capability are insufficient. Indeed, it is questionable whether new ground-based radars, notwithstanding potential new technologies such as quantum radar, will be able to detect cruise missiles in flight.[30] Certainly, very large and expensive long-range phased array or over-the-horizon radars may provide a solution (assuming the problem posed by atmospheric variations at high altitudes can be solved), but their costs and the difficulties of building such large infrastructure, especially with the melting permafrost in the Arctic, would likely be logistically and financially prohibitive.

Even so, these ground-based radars remain essential for aircraft identification, whether civil or military, at least for the time being. Moving part of the NWS north to meet CADIZ requirements is one option. This also links into the requirement to extend the life of the existing radars, given the time required to redesign (binationally or bilaterally), procure, and establish a new NWS. The existing radars' use will be extended for at least another fifteen plus years, at which time a final decision will be made on their future relative to other sensors developed and deployed to deal with the ALCM threat environment as they come online.

The ideal approach is "look-down" radars, which can be employed by aircraft such as AWACs and fifth-generation fighters,[31] which are high-demand/low-intensity assets for both the United States and Canada, and thus for NORAD. In addition, the employment of remotely piloted aircraft systems (RPAS), or drones, which can linger at high altitudes for long periods of time, are another potential option. Finally, the United States has experimented with high-altitude tethered aerostats possessing cruise missile detection and interception capabilities.[32]

Beyond ground- and air-based detection capabilities, there may also be a maritime-based solution to be considered, especially due to the potential requirement to track Russian and, in the future, Chinese nuclear-powered submarines with SLCM capabilities,[33] and possibly the employment of naval vessels with anti–cruise missile capabilities, notwithstanding the lack of year-round, ice-strengthened naval vessels.[34] Outer space offers another partial solution to the cruise missile threat, and particularly all-weather, day/night space-based radar. Canada's RADARSAT Constellation, with three identical earth observation satellites, along with RADARSAT II, provides wide-area surveillance of the North. However, the satellites do not possess the capability to track airborne moving targets, and the constellation needs to be expanded significantly to provide persistent, 24/7 coverage of the approaches to North America.[35] Nonetheless, future space-based assets should be able to contribute significantly to NORAD's aerospace warning mission.

Overall, no single-domain warning sensor or set of assets is likely to be sufficient to provide the necessary coverage and fidelity essential for NORAD's aerospace warning mission, especially over such a large expanse as the North American Arctic. Instead, each domain (land, air, maritime, cyber, and space) will likely provide a part of a "layered sensor grid for domain awareness," or effectively a "system of systems" approach.[36] This integrated "system of systems," in turn, confronts several major additional challenges related to existing and future technologies, the capacity to move and integrate large amounts of data from different sensors in the difficult Arctic communications environment,[37] and the upgrading of NORAD systems to ensure target discrimination and battle management through the future employment of machine learning and artificial intelligence (AI) capabilities. Overall, replacing the NWS with an NAWS is an essential element of NORAD modernization, but is only one of the threads in a Gordian knot of necessary changes and adjustments.

These challenges speak to the need for a binational or bilateral process, which will have to contend with resource limitations, the need to keep pace with future technologies, and differing levels of political interest. Moreover, the requisite technologies relative to the various domain sensors and system integrations are likely to emerge at varying points in time, such that the system's construction will require an incremental approach rather than waiting for the "perfect" system. Nor will the system likely reach some end date. Both the DEW line and NWS were "one and done" systems, employing existing technology and designed to last for decades. A new system, in contrast, is better understood as "never done," as it will need to be adaptable as technology continues to advance. Despite governments and bureaucracies that perceive investment and procurement projects as having start and end dates, with a straightforward linear process from R&D to operational deployment, the "new" NWS/NAWS will likely be nothing of the sort. Already, AI is being used to help analysts see more of what the NWS picks up but cannot identify. A DoD initiative called Pathfinder applies AI learning to the NWS feeds to detect patterns and identify objects far better than the naked eye. Such AI and machine-learning innovations are a vital part of the NWS renewal.

The future NAWS architecture should not be conceptualized in isolation from two other components of the NORAD mission suite. The first is the separation of the air-breathing from the long-range ballistic missile early warning missions. Although both are subsumed within NORAD's early warning mission, they have long been separate, practically speaking. With the emergence of hypersonic weapons, future technology will need to integrate ballistic missile warning with air warning as part of JADC2. The second is NORAD's aerospace control or air defence mission. The specific defence/intercept issues that are emerging are specifically examined in chapter 6. Here, the key issue relates to integrating interception capabilities into the early warning system, and with it the issue of FOLs.

As part of the 1970s ADMP, Canada developed a series of FOLs in the far north for dedicated NORAD air defence assets. These are located at Iqaluit, Nunavut; Goose Bay, Newfoundland and Labrador; and Yellowknife and Inuvik, in the Northwest Territories; while Resolute Bay, Nunavut is home to the Canadian Armed Forces Arctic Training Centre (CAFATC) housed with Natural Resources Canada's Polar Continental Shelf Program.[38] However, given the relatively short range of fighters and the wide expanses of the Arctic, these will require the co-deployment of air-to-air refuelling assets, which are in short supply, especially with the planned retirement of Canada's C-130 Hercules H model, which had been devoted to this mission.

Legacy FOLs are also under examination. Among additional locations under consideration are former World War II and early Cold War sites at Rankin Inlet in Nunavut; Gander, Deer Lake, and Stephenville (all in Newfoundland); and Churchill, Manitoba; as well as former US bases in Greenland. The committee also has representation from USEUCOM as a function of Greenland being within its area of responsibility and potential Russian cruise missile flight paths over and east of Greenland (and perhaps even farther east over Iceland) to North American targets.

The potential for more southerly positioned bases suggests that a defence-in-depth posture is being developed. During NORAD's annual VIGILANT SHIELD exercise in 2017, a US air defence National Guard unit was deployed to the NORAD base at North Bay, Ontario, suggesting that ground-based point defences are also under consideration. Of note, Canada does not possess this capability, although it is one of the investment priorities in *Strong, Secure and Engaged*, albeit identified for the defence of forward-deployed forces, not specifically for North America.

Overall, not only is the NWS renewal a complicated process, requiring new technology and advanced integrated surveillance and communications systems, but also the ALCM threat, in particular, has much wider investment implications that are essential to NORAD modernization. The final price tag is difficult to estimate, and this partially explains its absence in Canadian defence investment plans. Moreover, defining what is and is not NWS infrastructure under the existing cost-sharing agreement is another difficult question.

In the 1980s, Canada and the United States agreed to share the costs of building the NWS in Canada on a 40 per cent (Canada) / 60 per cent (United States) basis.[39] The agreement remains in place, but the details of what is and is not covered are unclear. There is no guarantee that this arrangement would extend to all future NORAD modernization or renewal projects or development in Canada. Given the multiple-domain sensors and JADC2 requirements, it is difficult to differentiate a strictly NORAD requirement from a requirement that serves other national purposes as well. For example, the need to modernize and upgrade infrastructure at CANR to absorb and exploit efficiently the large data flows as part of JADC2 initiatives would also benefit Canada's Joint Forces Air Component Commander and be of value to non-NORAD Canadian operations.[40] Space-based surveillance satellites, in the future, could support both NORAD and Canadian operations, including those overseas. Upgrades to the existing FOLs in the Canadian Arctic, which support NORAD, are vital to the local civilian communities. FOLs mean runways and additional infrastructure (such as fire-fighting equipment). In other words, the devil is in the details, and cost-sharing is likely to be a major focus of negotiations.

The Canadian Arctic component of the "new" modernized NORAD also raises additional questions regarding the process of moving from plans to operational capability. No longer can national defence operate in a vacuum in the Arctic. Indeed, the Arctic environment, both physical and political, represents another challenge for North American defence cooperation and NORAD. The decided pivot of the US administration to the importance of the Arctic via successive strategies, including the first-ever US Department of the Air Force's Arctic Strategy, cannot be dismissed as temporary. According to the strategy:

> Residing at the intersection between the U.S. homeland and two critical theaters, Indo-Pacific and Europe, the Arctic is an increasingly vital region for U.S. national security interests. The Arctic's capacity as a strategic buffer is eroding, making it an avenue of threat to the homeland, due to advancements by great power competitors. Additionally, it hosts critical launch points for global power projection and increasingly accessible natural resources.[41]

THE CANADIAN ARCTIC

The functional, technical military experts of NORAD and the wider CANUS North American defence relationship, including industry, are well aware of the difficulties and costs of building and maintaining defence infrastructure in the Arctic, especially given melting permafrost, severe storms, and extreme temperatures (increasingly at both ends of the thermometer). No matter the trajectory of climate change, the Arctic will remain a costly environment, especially for the development of ground-based assets. Access to the Arctic will likely remain limited from the summer to early fall months, and the movement of major equipment will be maritime-based. At the same time, maritime access for defence purposes will need to be sensitive to the requirements to resupply the local communities spread across the Arctic.

Beyond these physical challenges, organizational, bureaucratic, and political challenges are much greater and more complicated than in the past when the DEW line, NWS, and FOLs were constructed. All of these are related, in varying degrees, to climate change. Climate change is transforming the Arctic into a distinct theatre of defence and security operations. In the past, for NORAD, the Arctic was simply an avenue of potential air attack against major military, industrial, and population centres in the south. Today, the opening of the Arctic to maritime traffic, albeit not nearly at the levels often predicted for Canada, raises questions about security threats to the Arctic itself. In this context, Russian military developments in its Arctic are seen by some as a harbinger of a possible clash of arms in the Arctic zone.[42] While the likelihood remains relatively low, not least because it is hard to discern what objectives would be sought by Russia, especially as it has the most to lose in the Arctic, or by China through the employment of land and maritime forces, the possibility that an adversary might undertake "grey" zone operations (below the threshold of war) in the Arctic should not be discounted.[43] For example, using research vessels to gather additional intelligence, buying strategic mining assets, paying for needed infrastructure, spreading misinformation, and supporting proxy forces are examples of new methods of interference, "influence," and coercion.

As well, there are many non-military security threats that are emerging largely as a function of the opening of access to the Arctic to shipping. Even though these are primarily regulatory and constabulary in nature, they have defence and military implications as a function of the role of national armed forces responding to requests for assistance by civil authorities, or what are known in the United States as Defense Support of Civil Authorities (DSCA) operations. These missions, however, are a CJOC, not a NORAD concern, underlining the potential mandate overlaps that can surface as a result of the CJOC/NORAD/USNORTHCOM tricommand relationship.

Shipping, especially tourism and cruise ships, has increased in numbers and frequency in American and Canadian Arctic waters. A report by the Protection of the Arctic Marine Environment (a scientific working group of the Arctic Council) on shipping in the NWP notes a 44 per cent increase in the number of unique ships (from 112 to 160) and an increase in the gross tonnage of ships operating in the NWP between 2013 and 2019.[44] The requirement for enhanced surveillance, reconnaissance, and enforcement capabilities will also increase, including for surveillance of traffic movement, reconnaissance of specific vessel activities, and interception of vessels undertaking illegal activities, such as fishing, polluting, or drug trafficking. It makes little sense to develop separate systems for the military and civilian agencies. A layered sensing grid solution should provide improvements and information for military and civilian agency requirements, including tracking climate change. In particular, communication infrastructure in the Arctic is poor, and upgrades to defence communications to allow the transmission of large amounts of data will also help fill local community needs.

Similarly, both the military and civilian enforcement agencies face constrained and limited resources that dictate close cooperation. For example, the Royal Canadian Navy's Arctic and Offshore Patrol Ships (AOPSs) will likely find little to do on the purely defence side of the equation, but a great deal to do in support of civilian agencies. Cooperation with the United States is also vital. Like Canada's, American Arctic resources are limited. In the case of a major maritime disaster in the Arctic, whether in American or Canadian waters, cooperation will be essential. Neither nation is likely to be able to handle air or maritime disasters on its own. This also extends to Greenland/Denmark and is the basis for the *Agreement on Cooperation on Aeronautical and Maritime Search and Rescue in the Arctic* signed in 2011 by the eight Arctic states. There is also the matter of managing expectations. While the US military expects access to combat SAR, most initial SAR responses in Canada's Arctic are by civilian volunteers.

These civil-military and cross-border considerations raise serious questions about whether or not the CANUS governments are organized efficiently and effectively enough to meet the challenges that are emerging in the Arctic. There is no single government department or agency on either side of the border with the authority to oversee Arctic security. In the case of Canada, the prominent departments and agencies with different authorities include the CAF, the RCMP, the CCG, Transport Canada, DFO, Environment and Climate Change Canada, Public Safety Canada, Parks Canada, and the Yukon, Northwest Territories, and Nunavut territorial governments, as well as local governments and communities. In the case of National Defence, especially considering its aerial search and rescue (SAR) mandate, physical military presence is concentrated at Joint Task Force North (JTFN), located in Yellowknife, NWT (a relatively small, under-resourced command with responsibility for the entire Canadian Arctic), which coordinates with the 1st Canadian Ranger Patrol Group. Departmental coordination resides in the hands of a high-level interdepartmental committee.

On the American side of the equation, there is a similar web of government agencies, with one significant difference. The USCG has defence, constabulary, and regulatory authority, whereas in Canada, constabulary authority rests with the RCMP, and regulatory authority with Transport Canada and Fisheries and Oceans Canada. As for DoD, ANR serves as the Arctic capabilities advocate for the US military, but this places coordination responsibilities on a subcommand when the Arctic is divided among three regional combatant commands (USNORTHCOM, EUCOM, and INDOPACOM) and discounts the need for capabilities advocacy for Antarctica as well.[45] All of this suggests that the Arctic has always been an afterthought, a hot potato, assigned to various agencies as a function of their mandate and/or location. Seamless and integrated approaches to securing and defending the Arctic will, therefore, be hit and miss.

Given then the number of agencies that operate in the Arctic and the need for all of them to have access to information, the final NWS replacement architecture should be a dual-use (military-civil) capability. Whether the separate and distinct military and civil requirements can be easily harmonized, and the process by which civil requirements are taken into account, represents another challenge. Supporting NORAD's vital detection, deterrent, and defence requirements may be the primary driver, but civilian needs relative to the costs of building and operating in the Arctic cannot be ignored. This then raises a different cost-sharing issue: contributions from other government departments and agencies. For example, the platforms employed to support NORAD ground, air, maritime, cyber, and/or space defense will also support civil departments and agencies in Canada and the United States.

Whether a single, secure communication structure can support civilian and military needs simultaneously is a different question. The data vital for NORAD's mission suite are not necessarily the data vital to the mandates of other government departments and agencies, nor those required for meeting the needs of local communities. What will be needed are separate and distinct communication nodes capable of filtering data relative to distinct needs, something on the model of the RADARSAT Constellation structure. Here, the satellites are the responsibility of the Canadian Space Agency, and, in order to exploit the data for defence purposes, National Defence under Project Epsilon established two ground stations, with the possibility of a third in the future to be located in the Arctic.[46] In this model, each department, agency, or community will need to fund its own data-processing node, but the question remains as to who funds the platforms and/or the specific sensors themselves. Advances in nanosatellites (cubesatellites) may also assist with a division of the data needs of different actors, especially those of local hamlets.

Alongside these challenges, two others exist. First, environmental/regulatory requirements for infrastructure construction and removal are much more complicated today than in the past. Properly dismantling radar sites will add significant costs to the new system, and the costs of environmental cleanup are likely to fall strictly on Canada, outside of the cost-sharing arrangement with the United States.[47] Second, not least as a function of Canadian Supreme Court rulings, the Indigenous communities of the Arctic must be consulted and fully engaged in the development process. In the past, these communities were all but ignored. Certainly, the UNDRIP notes the need for militaries around the world to consult with Indigenous communities when conducting exercises or activities on Indigenous lands (which is most of the Canadian and US Arctic). Indeed, ensuring that environmental/regulatory issues are properly addressed in full consultation with local groups may be the most difficult, yet critical, part of the NWS renewal process.[48]

CONCLUSION

NORAD confronts a significant dilemma. The NWS, vital to the air component of its early warning mission, is obsolete. Its capacity to deter and defend against the existing and future threat environment is at issue. Urgent upgrades are needed but a one-for-one replacement is not the solution. Major technological, funding, bureaucratic and political factors represent significant obstacles to be overcome. At best, the renewal of the NWS will be incremental in nature, with the development of "gap fillers," that, in turn, will result in an integrated architecture built in pieces and from the bottom up.

At the same time, the North American defence "box," with NORAD at its centre, confronts the (re)emerging Arctic security environment with all of its challenges. Defence requirements can no longer be considered in isolation from multiple civilian authorities and local communities. This, in effect, speaks to the merger of two domains: the traditional aerospace defence domain of NORAD, and the Arctic defence and security domain, both lacking a centralized, overarching CANUS organizational structure. For now, the defence domain ostensibly resides beneath the tri-command structure consisting of CJOC, NORAD, and USNORTHCOM. The civil security side is much more complicated, informal, and arguably problematic, residing in cross-border agency-to-agency and internal inter-agency cooperation, with different mandates, authorities, and interests. And yet, the logic that led to NORAD's creation is present with the merger of these domains. Of course, the likelihood that either Canada or the United States will recognize the value of a binational organizational solution in the foreseeable future is very low. Immediate requirements and emergencies will dominate, and the obstacles to a binational solution seem too great at this time. Among these obstacles is Canada's Arctic sovereignty obsession, which implicitly posits the United States as the greatest threat, not least because of the managed NWP disagreement. Nonetheless, the Arctic will remain a region of great importance to North America that can no longer be cast as simply an avenue of approach.

5

Command and Control or Else?

In today's world, command and control (C^2) is usually, if not always, married to the concepts of communication, computers, intelligence, surveillance, and reconnaissance, and expressed as C^4ISR. Even so, C^2 is conceptually and practically distinct from the other five elements. C^2, in basic terms, outlines decision-making authority. The other items (communications, computers, and ISR) provide the inputs and outputs essential to the making and execution of decisions and orders. As combined inputs, they provide vital information, analysis, and transmissions essential to decisions. As outputs, they provide information for execution and feedback for subsequent decisions (the latter somewhat synonymous with control). On the surface, the concept of C^2 is relatively straightforward. It is the authority (command) to assign, allocate, and employ (control) forces under specified conditions.[1] In practice, it is complicated in a binational command structure. While control can be delegated, command remains exclusively with the commander.

C^2 is NORAD's primary function. NORAD has communication systems and computers vital to its warning and control missions, but where these transition from being national assets to binational ones is difficult to know. For example, the NWS is Canadian-owned, even though it was funded jointly by Canada and the United States on a 40/60 basis. It primarily supports the NORAD aerospace warning mission, but also serves national functions for Canada. Closely related, it is difficult to discern the point at which the communication systems moving NWS information transitions from a national asset supporting Canada to a binational NORAD asset. Nonetheless, ISR are all national in terms of ownership, reflecting NORAD's status as a supported command. Not only does

NORAD not possess any ISR assets, but its C² component cannot, at least in peacetime, task ISR assets, including in its maritime warning mission. Of course, the dual-hatted commander of NORAD can task US ISR assets as the commander of USNORTHCOM, but these are American-only assets, and are restricted to employment over American territory in the absence of an existing agreement with Canada.

In terms of its aerospace control (defence) mission, the commander of NORAD has C² authority over the defence assets dedicated to NORAD by Canadian and US senior command authorities, ostensibly the CDS and the SecDef.[2] In peacetime, these assets track and shadow (primarily) Russian long-range aviation assets approaching Canadian and American airspace. In wartime, their mission is to intercept and defeat these assets. As in the case of warning missions, the commander of USNORTHCOM can obtain C² over US land and maritime assets within USNORTHCOM's area of responsibility. Coordination with Canadian land and maritime assets, however, is a function of bilateral arrangements primarily between USNORTHCOM and CJOC. Finally, USNORTHCOM can also obtain C² over US air assets, but only within the context of its DSCA missions.

Overall, since its inception, NORAD'S C² envelope has remained relatively static and narrow in scope. Two recent developments, however, pose a challenge to NORAD C². The first is internal to the command and stems from the 2015 annual fall VIGILANT SHIELD-16 exercise, in which a new C² structure was employed under the initiative of its new commander, Admiral Gortney (USN) (2014–16). The second is external, and a function of the ongoing US development of JADC2. For the NORAD and USNORTHCOM commander, General VanHerck (USAF) (2020–present), the goal is for all-domain awareness to facilitate information dominance and decision superiority.[3] Both the internal and external factors have significant implications for NORAD modernization, as well as for the CANUS defence relationship in North America. Before examining these in detail, it is useful to place NORAD's C² within a general understanding of C² and its nature in the Canadian and American command structure.

CANADIAN, AMERICAN, AND NORAD C²

Command entails the authority to assign and allocate assets and personnel, and control is the process through which assets and personnel are employed. Both, in turn, are conditioned or limited in their

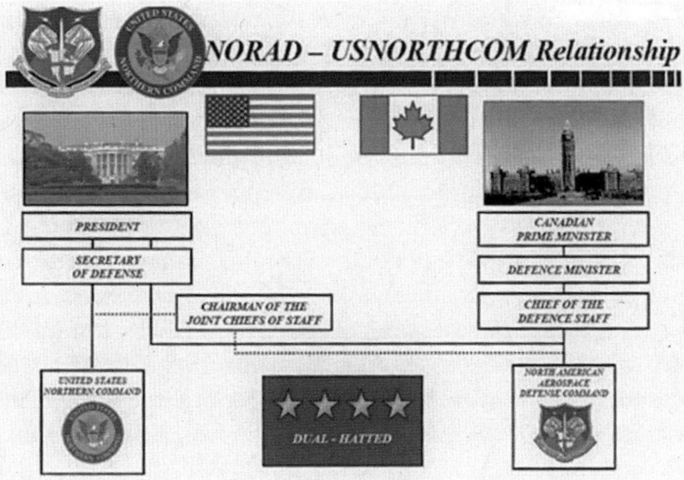

5.1 NORAD and USNORTHCOM command structure

scope based upon their location within an overarching vertical chain of command and a functional horizontal command structure. Vertically, overarching command authority is constitutionally set, and embodied in the position of commander-in-chief. In the case of Canada, the constitution vests the power of command in chief in the Queen of Canada, but in practice this authority is exercised by Cabinet, and by the prime minister specifically. (The Governor General's role as commander-in-chief isn't really in the chain of command. It is a ceremonial position. The Governor General's authority as the Queen's representative in all other matters, however, is not ceremonial.) In the United States, the commander-in-chief is the POTUS. Authority then devolves to the politically appointed cabinet representatives, namely the Canadian minister of National Defence (MND) and the SecDef. The chain of command continues with the senior military authorities – the CDS in Canada and the US commanders of the Combatant Commands. The Joint Chiefs of Staff (JCS) in the United States are not in the operational chain of command but are the principal military advisors to the POTUS, the SecDef, and the National Security Council. The CDS and his/her chiefs of the Canadian services are the principal military advisors to the Cabinet and prime minister. In NORAD's case, the NORAD commander reports to the CDS on the Canadian side and the SecDef on the American side. Note that the NORAD commander is the same rank as the CDS but there seems to be an unwritten rule of deference to the CDS on the part of the NORAD commander.

Although the vertical chains of command in both countries are generally similar, there are important differences, largely because of the significant disparity in size and capabilities between the CAF and the American military, and also the difference between the systems of government (a constitutional monarchy versus a republic). Both Canada and the United States possess a joint command structure at the operational level. Canada possesses a single joint operational command for both external and internal military missions not related to NORAD, called CJOC, and a functional command, Canadian Special Operations Forces Command (or CANSOFCOM). The United States, as set out in its UCP, has seven geographic combatant commands (AFRICOM, CENTCOM, EUCOM, INDOPACOM, NORTHCOM, SOUTHCOM, and SPACECOM) and four functional commands (CYBERCOM, Special Operations Command [SOCOM], STRATCOM, and Transportation Command [TRANSCOM]). In June 2021, the adjectives "geographic" and "functional" were dropped to de-emphasize the seams between the regional commands, but they remain helpful descriptors.

NORAD does not feature in the UCP (although it is identified as important) and NORAD is an asterisk to missions overseen by CJOC. And yet, NORAD is vital to both countries. Besides its uniqueness as a shared or binational command, it is simultaneously a functional and operational one. In terms of its warning missions, it has a universal area of operations (i.e., it can warn of threats emanating from anywhere in the world). In terms of its air control (defence) mission, it is geographically limited to North America, largely because of the limited reach of its assets, its defensive mandate, and USNORTHCOM's area of responsibility.

Beneath this first level or tier of command authority resides a welter of second-tier commands, with their own subordinate command tiers below them right down to the smallest unit within the respective military service structures. Within this complicated vertical structure, each level or tier is delegated geographic or functional command authority, usually spelled out in the terms of reference (TOR). For example, NORAD's TOR for its maritime warning mission explicitly prohibits NORAD from duplicating any existing national maritime warning assets.[4]

Interacting with the multi-layered vertical C^2 structure is a horizontal structure at various levels. This represents the distinction

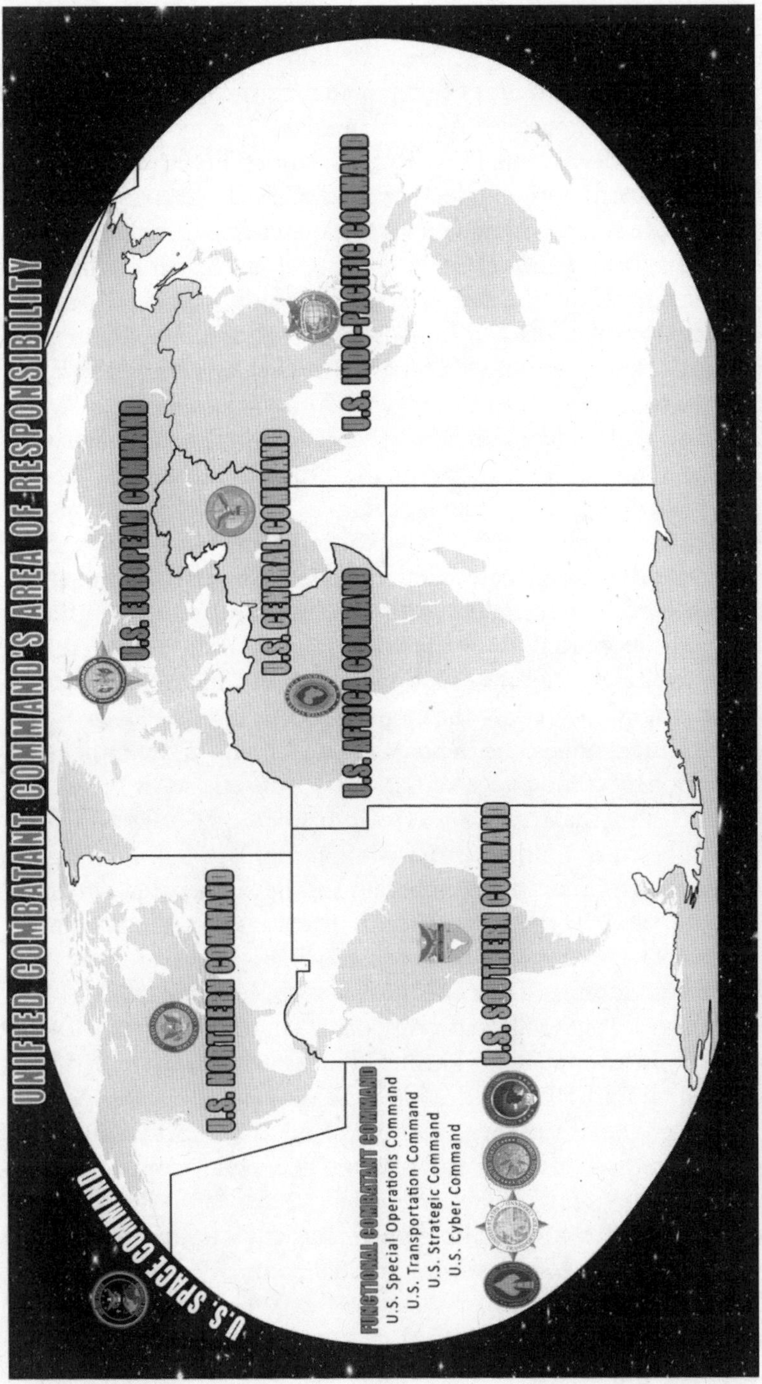

5.2 US UCP as of 1 April 2021

between force employers (those who are assigned personnel to complete missions) and force generators (those who recruit, train, and equip personnel). Although functionally distinct in terms of their authority and thus purpose, these commands are often linked together with a single- or dual-hatted (and sometimes triple- or even quadruple-hatted) commander. For example, the commander of the 1st Canadian Air Division (1 CAD) is quadruple-hatted. He/she is the force generator for airpower in the CAF on behalf of the commander of the RCAF (the overall force generator for CAF Air Forces). He/she is also the Canadian Joint Forces Air Component Commander (JFACC), the force employer for airpower in Canada and the rest of the world. In addition, this major-general is the commander of CANR, also as a force employer, and finally, he/she is also the commander for Search and Rescue operations in the Trenton Search and Rescue Region as force employer and generator (the latter under his/her 1 CAD hat).[5] Indeed, the CANR commander is unique among his/her NORAD regional commander peers, for the CANR commander is her/his own force generator and employer and can be both supporting and supported in his/her CANR role. No other NORAD region has that flexibility in terms of assigning assets and personnel, coordinating training, and calling for more assets.

In the United States, the lieutenant-general who is the Joint Force Air Component commander for USNORTHCOM and 1st Air Force commander is also the triple-hatted commander of CONR as a force employer based at Tyndall Air Base in Florida. The ANR commander is in the most difficult position because assets he/she needs are often held by INDOPACOM and sometimes by USNORTHCOM. The lieutenant-general of ANR (Joint Base Elmendorf-Richardson, Anchorage, Alaska) is also the commander of the Alaskan Command (USNORTHCOM), the commander of the Eleventh Air Force (Pacific Air Forces, INDOPACOM), and the commander of ANR. He/she is responsible for the integration of all military activities in the Alaskan joint operations area, synchronizing the activities of more than 21,000 active-duty and reserve forces from all services across two geographic commands.

Despite being (just) dual-hatted, the NORAD and USNORTHCOM commander as the NORAD commander is strictly a force employer. All force generation is completed by national commands and personnel are CHOPed over to NORAD. As USNORTHCOM commander he/she is both a force employer and generator.

A final important C^2-related distinction that emerges in NORAD discussions is between a supported and supporting command. Understanding this distinction depends upon what point within the overall command structure is engaged. Generically, force generators are conceptualized as supporting commands because they provide the forces employed operationally. In the case of NORAD, as an operational command and force employer, it is supported by ISR data generated from national assets and aircraft dedicated by each country's national command authority under specific conditions, and, at least for fighter-interceptors, placed on alert status. At the same time, however, NORAD, in terms of its maritime warning mission, is also a supporting command. Although not a "force" per se, its integrated tactical warning/attack assessment function supports both nations' national command authorities' decision-making.

In summary, NORAD is a force employer, and both a supporting and a supported command. The commander of NORAD may delegate control (as has been done to allow NORAD regional commanders to execute missions) but ultimate command authority rests with him or her. And yet, because it is a binational command, there is another level of complexity.

Reflecting its unique binational status, the top-level commands are also mixed between American and Canadian personnel, which extends further down the chain of command. Administrative command remains with national commands normally. For example, if a CAF officer requires disciplining because of bad behaviour while deployed to NATO HQ, it is his/her national command authority who decides on discipline, not NATO or the foreign commander who may have been his/her supervisor. In NORAD, the strict national lines for administrative control blur.

Although the NORAD Agreement only specifies that the commander and deputy commander cannot come from the same nation, in reality, the commander has always been a four-star American (general or admiral), and the deputy commander a three-leaf Canadian (lieutenant general). Moving down to the regional sub-commands, this division is replicated. CANR in Winnipeg is commanded by a two-leaf Canadian major-general, with the deputy a one-star American brigadier general. Interestingly, this brigadier general is also the deputy JFACC for Canada, which means he or she commands air assets in Canada and abroad. In turn, ANR, located in Anchorage, and CONR, at

Tyndall Air Force Base in Florida, have an American commander and a Canadian deputy, with one difference from CANR: the commander in each case is a three-star American lieutenant general and their Canadian deputy is a brigadier-general. This difference is largely a function of other considerations within the overall US command structure and the other "hats" that the American commanders assume.

In terms of its operational command authority for aerospace control (air defence), little changed until the late 2000s. The commander of NORAD, drawing from the interceptor assets committed to the command by the national command authorities, provides air tasking orders to the regional commands, which includes the possibility that Canadian NORAD interceptors will be tasked into one of the American regional commands and vice versa.[6] The regional commands (ANR, CANR, and CONR[7]) undertake the specific conduct of their respective air defence or battle management missions. The actual air defence of Canada and the United States maintain a national character; American planes could defend Canada, but under Canadian command, and vice versa. Overall, this structure is defined as centralized command and decentralized execution (or arguably control).

C² AND THE NEW COMBINED FORCES AIR COMPONENT COMMAND STRUCTURE

In 2015, under a new NORAD commander, Admiral Bill Gortney, the annual fall exercise VIGILANT SHIELD–16 was decidedly different from past years. He introduced and exercised a new commander, a Combined Forces Air Component Commander (CFACC), and sought to test the limits of the NORAD C² structure. This new structure was used in subsequent exercises.

The idea of a CFACC is not new. Indeed, in a theatre of operation, it is routine to establish component commanders to manage tactically the missions within a domain, allowing the commander to think strategically about the situation and its many domains. This same thinking led to the idea of a NORAD CFACC: someone to manage the air tasking orders over a very large operations area, leaving the NORAD commander to consider wider, strategic considerations.

In 2019, the CDS and the SecDef gave authority to consider such a position. One idea was for the CONR commander (a three-star based in Tyndall, Florida) to be double-hatted as the NORAD CFACC, and this was practised in at least one VIGILANT SHIELD exercise. However, there were further discussions about the additional personnel that would be required to have this function available and ready to implement immediately; to maintain the binational character of NORAD, the deputy would necessarily be Canadian. Instead, discussions turned to co-locating the NORAD CFACC staff with the N2C2 at NORAD HQ, requiring fewer additional personnel, already operating 24/7, and physically closer to the commander of NORAD should discussions be necessary.

In its simplest sense, the NORAD commander's air tasking authority is delegated or devolved to the CFACC. As best as can be discerned, the idea for the potential creation of a CFACC has little to do with clear problems or failures of the previous structure. 9/11, for example, was not a C^2 failure. While the C^2 had never been tested in combat situations, it had been regularly exercised over time. Instead, the CFACC was a product of three interrelated factors, and was largely internally driven.[8]

First, the demands on the NORAD commander have grown exponentially since 9/11, largely because of the ONE missions, the creation of USNORTHCOM, and the DSCA activities USNORTHCOM deals with, largely attributable to climate change. Prior to 2002, the commander's attention was narrowly focused on a single domain, and its aerospace warning and control missions. With the creation of USNORTHCOM, the commander's attention broadened extensively into two additional domains, land and maritime, with others also emerging (the cyber, information, and space domains), and the operational tempo increased significantly, especially as a function of repeated no-fail DSCA missions to deal with natural disasters. At the same time, USNORTHCOM, as one of the US combatant commands, faces increased demands from Washington, especially in terms of responding to Congressional oversight committees. Simply, divided attention and increased demands could overwhelm a commander seeking to manage both tactical and strategic considerations. A CFACC would enable the commander to focus attention on the strategic level, and in the parlance of the day, "look up and out, rather than down and in," as NORAD and USNORTHCOM commander General Robinson (2016–18) often noted.

Second, USNORTHCOM/NORAD stands out as a C^2 anomaly in comparison not only to the other combatant commands in the US UCP, but also to other national command structures. Key allies, with some variance, staff a Joint Force Air Component Commander (JFACC), and commonality in command structures facilitates interoperability for alliance and/or coalition operations overseas: i.e., what is known as a Combined (more than one nation) and Joint (more than one service) Force Air Component Command (CJFACC). Canada has a JFACC, for example – the 1 CAD commander, who is also the CANR commander.

Of course, for NORAD, the structure would have to be labelled a Combined Force, rather than a Combined and Joint one, for political reasons. "Joint" implies the involvement of several of the military services.[9] NORAD is an independent command, equal to USNORTHCOM, but "joint" suggests that land and maritime forces are also involved, which, in turn, could be interpreted (from the Canadian perspective) as NORAD assuming the status of the air arm of USNORTHCOM and therefore subordinate. The other issue is the mismatch of rank. One suggestion has been to dual-hat the NORAD J3 as the CFACC. The NORAD J3 (N/J3), however, is typically a Canadian and a MGen (one rank lower than a LGen). How can the CONR and ANR Lt Gens depend on the MGen to coordinate in a time of conflict? (For CANR, it would be a matter of coordination between peers.) The right rank is a consideration.

Finally, beginning with Admiral Gortney, and followed by his three successors (Generals Robinson, O'Shaughnessy, and VanHerck), all of the NORAD commanders had come from component command experience. Admiral Gortney had commanded naval operational forces in Operation Enduring Freedom (Afghanistan) and Iraqi Freedom in CENTCOM. General Robinson had been commander of Pacific Air Forces and Air Component Commander for USPACOM. General O'Shaughnessy had also been USPACOM's Air Component Commander. Although General VanHerck did not serve as a regional air component commander, he worked extensively at high levels as commander of the USAF's Warfare Center and at the Pentagon, where he was director of the Joint Staff before becoming the NORAD and USNORTHCOM commander. Their experiences, relative to the aforementioned NORAD C^2 conundrum help to explain the traction of the idea of a NORAD CFACC.

The development and exercising of a CFACC has not been an easy one, in part because it exists within a binational command. The decision to exercise the CFACC at Tyndall Air Force Base alongside CONR Headquarters was a function of several considerations. It was considered the site farthest and safest from the threat posed by Russian (as well as future Chinese) long-range aviation and cruise missiles, which would be vectored from the north to targets in the heart of the continent. Tyndall was also the only location that had the size and resources to host the CFACC. Neither of the other two, ANR or CANR, was large enough or possessed the resources to do so without major infrastructure investments. CANR, for example, would need an expanded Combined Air Operations Centre (CAOC). In contrast, the costs of new infrastructure at Tyndall would be borne entirely by the US, as per longstanding practices.

This does not mean that Canada faces no additional costs. At a minimum, additional Canadian personnel will be required for the CFACC should it materialize, and it is highly unlikely that this will be cost-neutral even if these personnel are transferred from Colorado Springs. In addition, the CANR CAOC will need significant upgrades to ensure its communication systems and bandwidth are sufficient to handle the information and data feed from a CFACC (not to mention other upgrades to the electricity and sewer systems that come with older buildings and the harsh Winnipeg climate). Of course, such upgrades are necessary, independent of the CFACC construct, as part of NORAD modernization (a priority for both governments). Whether these costs will be greater with a CFACC than without is difficult to estimate.

Beyond these considerations, there is also the requirement for a backup or redundant CFACC. This became clear when in 2018, Hurricane Michael shut down Tyndall. In addition, with a 360-degree threat vector today, Tyndall is vulnerable to sea-launched cruise missiles. Similarly, ANR is located closest to the threat origin and also resides on an earthquake fault line. In contrast to both, CANR, located at the centre of the continent and facing fewer climate change–related disruptions (for now), arguably offers a secure and safe location for at least the backup CFACC. As the backup, the Headquarters and CAOC will necessitate significant investments regardless, and this is likely to be also part of NORAD modernization.

A final consideration at the end of the day is whether a CFACC truly changes any of the internal issues surrounding C^2 from the past. After all, are not the three NORAD regions their own CFACC? LCol French asks a very important question:

> [D]oes the regional system still satisfy the intent of placing binational air defence under a single commander for which a continent-wide air defence battle can be properly waged or does

> NORAD run the risk of fighting three independent battles in three geographically diverse regions with competing limited resource requirements?[10]

Certainly, given the demands confronted by the dual-hatted NORAD and USNORTHCOM commander and the possibility that the commander could face multiple events at the same time, the logic for a CFACC holds. However, this does not necessarily mean that anything has changed relative to the regional commands. They will continue to act relatively autonomously to compete for the CFACC's attention and delegation of resources (air taskings), but with one significant difference. Instead of the single NORAD commander at arm's length making these decisions, now, with a potentially dual-hatted CFACC and "other" commander (J3 Operations? CANR? CONR? But likely not ANR, given the conundrum of two geographic commands), a potential conflict of interest emerges between the commitment to defend North America and the need to protect the region from which the CFACC hails.

Of course, as the CFACC idea matures and repeated exercises are undertaken, many of these issues could be sorted out, and the envisioned CFACC may well look different from its future iterations. One suggestion is that the CFACC reside in the NORAD HQ and turn the NORAD J3 side of the N2C2 into a true operations centre that can coordinate air tasking orders for the three NORAD regions. Regardless, organizations in general, and the military in particular, are constantly driven towards a single model and approach, and NORAD, as a combatant command (albeit rarely expressed or understood in those terms), was an anomaly that needed to be standardized. At the same time, the CFACC structure does potentially provide an indication of what a multi-domain NORAD C^2 might look like, and this is significant relative to other external pressures emanating from within the United States.

NORAD C^2, MODERNIZATION, AND THE UCP

Several years ago, the concept of JADC2 emerged from within the Pentagon. The return to great power competition and the need for speed meant that DoD was searching for maximum information in minimal time. JADC2 is the DoD's concept to connect sensors from all of the military services – Air Force, Army, Marine Corps, Navy, Coast

Guard and Space Force – into a single network.[11] All combatant commands are expected to move toward this vision "as the Department's existing command and control architecture is insufficient to meet the demands of the [2018] National Defense Strategy (NDS)."[12] For USNORTHCOM, it is consistent with, or the logical outgrowth of, the new multi-domain North American threat environment. At the same time, reflecting the CFACC conundrum, other US combatant commands effectively exercise JADC2, albeit in a multilateral, bilateral, or coalition relationship. As such, the NORAD/USNORTHCOM/C^2 structure, with or without a CFACC, remains an anomaly. NORAD remains a single-domain C^2 arrangement (notwithstanding its maritime warning mission), whereas USNORTHCOM is a tri-plus-domain arrangement entailing maritime, missile defence, and land (the latter for DSCA). The same situation holds for CJOC, although it is not geographically constrained. It possesses authority for all Canadian military operations at home and abroad, except for those associated with North American air defence or under CANSOFCOM.

As commander of NORAD, General VanHerck (USAF) (2020–present) is focusing on a chain of outcomes that includes domain awareness (for NORAD in the aerospace and maritime domains), information dominance, and decision superiority rather than JADC2 specifically (although the chain and JADC2 endeavour to achieve similar outcomes). This is not surprising given that JADC2 implies operational all-domain authority, which requires a fundamental transformation of the CANUS North American defence relationship from a single binational and multiple bilateral structures to an integrated all-domain binational structure. Such a big step is, at least for the time being, a "bridge too far," given its implications for a range of military service interests and preferences, and larger political considerations usually surrounding sovereignty concerns, especially in Canada. Hence, the chain eliminates fears that JADC2 might be misinterpreted as a signal about the real objective of NORAD modernization – similar in some ways to the fears that the stand-up of USNORTHCOM led to misplaced beliefs that NORAD had simply become its air arm.

Information dominance simply eliminates this fear, is consistent with NORAD's multi-domain warning missions (air, space, and maritime), and reflects its status as a supporting command. In other words, information dominance largely equates to the status quo, and also places a marker related to the scope of NORAD modernization, if not outright setting the boundary of NORAD modernization as infor-

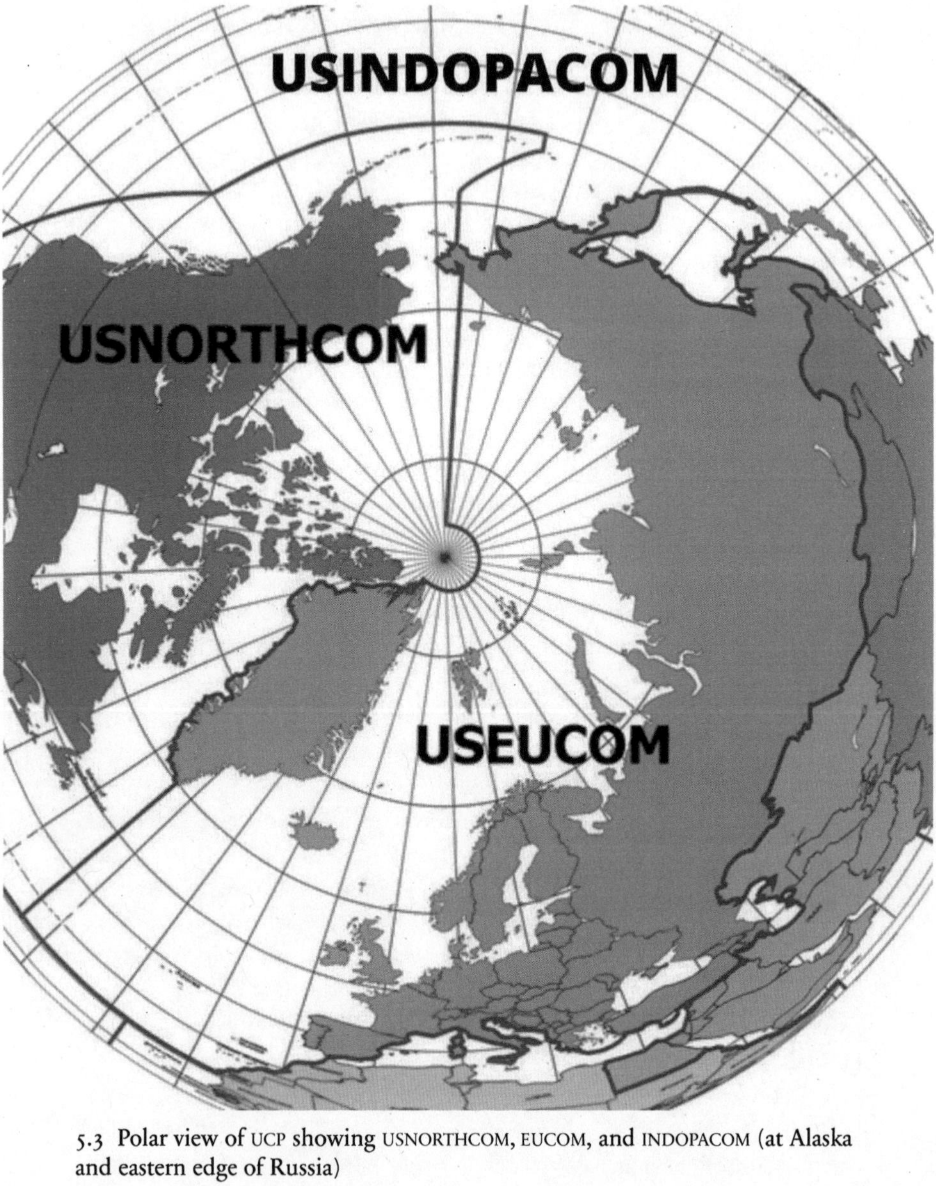

5.3 Polar view of UCP showing USNORTHCOM, EUCOM, and INDOPACOM (at Alaska and eastern edge of Russia)

mation acquisition, transmission, and analysis. Effectively, NORAD modernization is all about communication, computers, intelligence, surveillance, and reconnaissance (especially integrating such data from other combatant commands and allies),[13] not C^2. Unfortunately, as laid out in previous chapters, NORAD modernization entails, or should entail, much more.

As originally identified by the BPG in its final report,[14] the C^2 structure and NORAD's place within it creates numerous seams, which may be manipulated by an adversary. In this context, NORAD has a global area of operations as a function of its warning missions. However, its control mission is regional and geographically specific as a function of the interception capabilities assigned to it. In other words, NORAD is simultaneously a functional and a regional command, unique in terms of its place in both the Canadian and US command structures.

Successive commanders have emphasized the importance of being able to strike at the launch platforms or "archers," rather than the more difficult task of defeating the missiles or "arrows." However, the capacity and authority to do so reside with other commands. Canada does not possess the capabilities to undertake such missions, the plans to acquire such capabilities, or the political will to do so. Even USNORTHCOM, which does have access to such capabilities, is regionally constrained to its area of responsibility. Thus, ironically, NORAD's responsibility for the aerospace control (air defence) of North America in the new threat environment is ceded to other US commands. For example, EUCOM is the lead for Russia even though NORAD deals with Russian sorties regularly. In practical terms, this means that USEUCOM and USINDOPACOM possess an aerospace control mission for North America in the case of the "archers," and pass on the mission for the "arrows" to NORAD. These C^2 seams are, in turn, problematic because of geographic mission interpretations and priorities. A useful example is USEUCOM and its link to NATO relative to the placement of Greenland in its area of operation.

Although Greenland geographically and perhaps culturally (given that Inuit peoples reside in Canada, the United States, Greenland, and Russia) is nearer to North America, it is European because of its political relationship within the Danish realm. Perceptually, the defence and security needs of Greenland are synonymous with those of Europe, not North America. Greenland's place and role within USEUCOM's AOR, as well as military resources assigned to it per se, are determined by thinking about war in Europe. Greenland's significance has long been, at least from a Eurocentric viewpoint, the western end of the Greenland-Iceland-United Kingdom (GIUK) gap or maritime chokepoint (which now also includes Norway). See figures 3.1 and 5.3.

The North Atlantic, in this context, is the home of three interrelated yet distinct threat environments and responses. The first is as an avenue for the Russian Northern Fleet seeking to threaten the backdoor of Europe, relative to the likelihood that conflict or war with Russia will occur in Eastern Europe. The second is the threat posed by Russian naval infiltration south of the GIUK gap to the sea lines of communication that would bring reinforcements from North America to Europe. The final is the threat of Russian long-range aviation, including cruise missiles, transiting down or along Greenland's east coast headed for North American targets. Dealing with these threats is under the authority of USEUCOM, which by virtue of its AOR is focused on Europe, not North America.

The response to the first two threats, especially from US naval thinking, is to move naval assets quickly north to strike at the Russian Northern Fleet (the "archers"), before they infiltrate farther south to strike or to reach launch points. The response to the third, however, is problematic because of the naval focus and location of the threat in the western reaches of the North Atlantic. The Navy, and thus USEUCOM, is seeking the decisive offensive battle. The long-range threat, whether from ballistic or cruise missiles from air-, land-, or sea-based "archers," is a defensive mission. In this case, capabilities to undertake the two related yet distinct missions are not limited. Choices in a crisis or war will have to be made, and theoretically USEUCOM's choices are likely to be different from NORAD's and USNORTHCOM's. This is the essence of the C^2 seam problem.

In the early years of the Cold War, several US military facilities were located in Greenland, as well as Newfoundland, but the latter were all closed over time and most of the Greenlandic US facilities as well. Today, as part of NORAD modernization and the examination of FOLs, old Greenland and Newfoundland bases are being re-examined. While the latter are not an issue for NORAD given that Newfoundland is part of Canada, Greenland is not. NORAD has had no relationship with Greenland in the past (notwithstanding Thule Air Force Base as part of the ballistic missile early warning network, although its existence is thanks to a Denmark-US bilateral agreement).

In contrast, USNORTHCOM's AOR, and thus authority, extends five hundred nautical miles into the Atlantic (well short of the launch points of air- and sea-launched cruise missiles), and reaches to the northern and southern tips of Greenland. While future air bases in Greenland might be assigned to USNORTHCOM in a revised UCP, it possesses no aerospace control mission. This is NORAD's alone as an independent command, as embedded in the NORAD Agreement and NORAD's recognized place within the UCP. To date, however, NORAD and Canada have not engaged Greenland/Denmark in discussions on developing a formal control relationship, which would have implications relative to the existing binational agreement.

Of course, with Greenland in EUCOM's AOR, C^2 coordination provides a possible, albeit clunky, solution. Assets assigned to one command as directed by the respective command authorities can be transferred to another. In the past, for example, naval air defence assets have been transferred to NORAD command, and USNORTHCOM can directly access US naval assets via US Fleet Forces. US Fleet Forces serves as the maritime component command for USNORTHCOM as US Naval Forces Northern Command (NAVNORTH). Given the relationship between NORAD and USNORTHCOM, one would presume such a transfer could be relatively seamless. However, the extent to which this scenario has been exercised in the context of NORAD VIGILANT SHIELD exercises is difficult to know. Maritime participation over time has been relatively mixed and limited.[15] With the re-establishment of the US 2nd Fleet (under US Fleet Forces Command in 2018) and its colocation with a new NATO Joint Force Command Norfolk,[16] it would seem the USEUCOM/USNORTHCOM blending of assets and AORs is potentially in the works. The commander of the 2nd Fleet is also commander of the Allied Joint Force Command Norfolk and reports to US Fleet Forces Command, which reports to USNORTHCOM, and 2nd Fleet headquarters resides within USNORTHCOM's AOR at Norfolk, Virginia.

This introduces another problematic command seam. Simply, the NORAD/USNORTHCOM and USEUCOM seam meets the USN and RCN command seams. As noted in chapter 3, the USN and RCN have a long history of close cooperation reaching back to World War II. The RCN is able to integrate its frigates into American aircraft carrier task forces, thereby coming under American command. A Canadian rear admiral can serve (and indeed has served) as vice-commander of the re-established 2nd Fleet, reflective of the close RCN/USN relationship, but this position could be filled by a number of foreign exchange officers. Of course, relationships within the 2nd Fleet are on a bilateral footing, and it is difficult to know, following the experiences of World War II and the Cold War, if the national naval command authorities are divided on a geographic basis, with the RCN responsible for the northern reaches of the west Atlantic and the USN the southern, with the division line ostensibly an eastward projection of the CANUS border. Regardless, this historical cooperation was premised largely on a single mission: to protect the sea lines of communication from North America to Europe to ensure the supply of personnel and material for the war in Europe. In meeting this mission, the primary task was anti-submarine warfare, which the RCN embraced. The importance of the transatlantic link, which is strengthened by foreign exchange officers embedded in US forces for NATO cohesion, is still paramount but often overlooked.

Today, however, this experience, in some senses, is obsolete for two primary reasons. First, a major war today against a peer competitor is largely "come-as-you-are." With the possibility of escalation to nuclear weapons in the background, the emphasis on prompt global strike capabilities is key. Modern high-tech weapons systems cannot be quickly produced, as was the case during World War II. A major war is likely to be over long before reinforcements are developed and deployed. In other words, the primacy of sea lines of communication between North America and Europe is largely a thing of the past, notwithstanding its lingering significance in the minds of USEUCOM and NATO. For commerce and trade, however, sea lines of communication are becoming even more important, as the temporary blockage of the Suez Canal by the container ship *Ever Given* in March 2021 made clear. Supply chains were affected for weeks, creating cascading price and supply problems for manufacturers, retailers, and consumers. To be clear, the mandate of the 2nd Fleet and Joint Force Command Norfolk does not specifically include convoy protection, but the idea persists.

Second, as former NORAD and USNORTHCOM commander General (ret) O'Shaugnessy and Brigadier General Fesler argue, a key vulnerability, and thus prime adversarial target, is extant forces in the homeland preparing to transit to Europe.[17] These assets can be targeted by long-range stand-off weapon systems, especially air- and sea-launched cruise missiles. As air-breathing systems threatening targets in North America, they fall under NORAD's command authority. With the limited range of fighter interceptors, notwithstanding existing and future Army ground-based point defences assigned to NORAD, the primary response is naval air defence systems. If these need to be transferred to NORAD command, and thus will need to be planned and exercised, the logic of unity of command suggests that naval authority, and hence the relationship between the USN and RCN relative to the Atlantic, should fall under NORAD, transformed into a binational one, with the implementation of a Combined Forces Maritime Component Command. As these will also require, as mentioned above, Army ground-based point defences, effectively what emerges is the requirement for a Combined and Joint Forces Command within NORAD authority.

Although this discussion focuses on the Atlantic seams, similar issues exist in terms of the Arctic and Pacific. In the former case, the area is shared geographically by NORAD, USNORTHCOM, USEUCOM, and USINDOPACOM. The latter involves only USINDOPACOM. NORAD is likely to remain a defensive, reactive command, not least because Canada is unlikely to support any shift into an offensive mission, notwithstanding the fact that Canada does not have the capabilities to undertake an offensive mission relative to the "archers." With cruise missiles and hypersonic weapons (the "arrows"), NORAD needs to acquire command authority, relative to the "arrow" launch points, to undertake a coordinated all-domain defence of North America.

A final C² consideration is the likelihood that, in the near future, the US will revise its UCP, with direct attention focused on seams and gap issues. For example, many of USNORTHCOM's maritime capabilities are held by INDOPACOM. This is awkward given that USNORTHCOM is the Arctic capabilities advocate for the US military, but EUCOM remains the "lead" for the Arctic.

Nevertheless, NORAD, as an integral part of the UCP, should be a focus of attention. With the emphasis today on global threats and global responses, this could lead to a radical reshaping of the UCP. In this regard, Canada will have little choice but to react. Two options present themselves. The first, as discussed above, is to expand NORAD's mission and C² suite, even though it would remain primarily an aerospace control mission with all-domain authority. The second may well be the marginalization of NORAD, and in the process, NORAD being pushed downward in terms of status within the command structure; in that scenario, NORAD may well end up as a simple appendage to, for example, USNORTHCOM to remain the air element therein. The reason there has not been a major change in the UCP since 9/11 (other than a few shifts of the seams and dropping the adjectives "geographic" and "functional") is likely because the consequences of Great Power competition and the vulnerability of the homeland are only just now coming to light. NORAD and USNORTH-

COM may finally emerge from the backwaters of the command plan. With this increased attention, the seams and gaps, as they relate to USNORTHCOM's AOR, are coming into greater focus, which inevitably draws attention to NORAD.

CONCLUSION

C^2 is a subject that academics normally eschew and leave to the practitioners. But as this chapter outlines, C^2 is fundamental to the raison d'être of commands and the relationships between commands, which can expand or limit tactical and strategic options. It matters, for example, that NORAD is a force employer and both a supporting and supported command. This means NORAD owns no assets (other than the NWS) and is completely dependent on what the national authorities see fit to assign to it. As both a supported and supporting command, this means that NORAD is supported by ISR data generated from national assets and aircraft dedicated by each country's national command authority, under specific conditions, and, at least for fighter-interceptors, how many are placed on alert status. At the same time, however, NORAD, in terms of its maritime warning missions, is also a supporting command. The creation of a CFACC could change the focus of the NORAD commander. And changes to other commands, be they in terms of AORs, reporting relationships, or mandates, create knock-on effects for the entire UCP and therefore the role of allies and partners. This is all before one layers the complication of NORAD as a binational command, which requires the commander to think in terms of North America and not Canada vice the United States, notwithstanding her or his other hat as the USNORTHCOM commander with a very different mandate and relationships with civilian agencies.

DoD's new vision for JADC2 now opens the door for a reimagination of the formerly stovepiped organization of commands and commanders in domain-specific silos. While, on paper, it makes sense to connect sensors from all of the military services, practically speaking, this assumes no service rivalries, egos, or resource fights. Before the war in Ukraine in 2022, the joke within the naval world was that the most likely conflict in the North Atlantic would not be with the Russians and NATO, but turf/resource battles between the newly established 2nd Fleet and its EUCOM counterpart, the 6th Fleet. In the rush to achieve the JADC2 vision, NORAD becomes an obvious outlier and complication. How is it possible to achieve JADC2 with a command that is limited to one and a half domains and needs to manage national caveats? Option one is to keep it that glaringly exceptional command that few people understand and appreciate. Option two is to let it disappear and/or be absorbed by the United States. There are signs that, given new attention to the homeland, USNORTHCOM and NORAD may receive more attention from the other commands and from politicians. That being said, in times of Great Power competition and a changing threat environment, patience has never been a virtue, but sustained attention to North America is exactly what is needed.

6

The "New" Aerospace and Space Domains

The idea of an aerospace domain emerged in the late 1950s and was quickly adopted by the US military in general, and the USAF in particular. It simply referred to the merger of two distinct domains, air and space, and was reflective of organizational interests stemming from the emergence of rocket or missile technology providing access to outer space. This new technology raised the question of which military service would take responsibility for space following the bruising debate on the division of air assets between the US Army and USAF.[1] In employing the term "aerospace" the USAF laid a natural claim to outer space, and, of course, to the resources that came with this claim. Moreover, since it already possessed control over the US long-range strategic bomber fleet, which was then the core US strategic deterrent, it was logical to add responsibility for the US long-range intercontinental ballistic missile suite as the second part of what would become the US strategic deterrent triad.[2]

Canada was the third country to place a satellite in orbit, in 1962.[3] Canada's engagement in military outer space looked promising until the release of the 1967 Chapman Report on the status of space research in Canada, which emphasized a "civil science and civil applications" approach to space.[4] It wasn't until 2011 that the CAF appointed a Director General (DG) Space (an RCAF brigadier-general) responsible for CAF space capabilities, including the acquisition of space systems (force development), the management of the space cadre (force generation), and operations (force employment).[5] The lack of attention by the CAF to space can be explained by the fallout from the Chapman Report, declining defence spending, the desire to protect traditional core capabilities, and the fight against unification, which occupied the military's attention in the 1960s and 1970s. Moreover, in the early years, military space was synonymous with nuclear weapons and strategic nuclear deterrence – a non-starter for Canadian governments that continues to this day, even though NORAD is essential to early warning of incoming missiles, facilitating US strategic deterrence.

By default, Canada's involvement in military space fell to NORAD, especially after NORAD acquired the ballistic missile warning mission in the 1960s. Even so, NORAD's TOR mentioned only the air domain. Although some discussions emerged prior to the 1968 NORAD renewal about replacing the term "air" in NORAD with "aerospace," this change did not occur until the agreement renewal in 1981. Despite the name change, there was no significant impact on NORAD's mission suite. Roughly two decades later, the USAF dropped the concept of "aerospace," and replaced it with "air and space,"[6] but NORAD continues to have "aerospace" in its name.

Today, however, evidence strongly suggests that air and space are slowly but inevitably merging into a single aerospace domain as envisioned long ago. On the civil side, this is evident with the development of SpaceX's reusable Falcon 9 rocket and on-orbit maintenance capabilities. A full merger of air and space still awaits new propulsion technology that would enable the smooth and cost-effective transit of vehicles between the two domains. On the military side, the ongoing development of manoeuvrable hypersonic weapons has raised the need to merge air and ballistic missile defences. It is this requirement that has direct implications for NORAD's core aerospace warning and control mission on functional grounds. The air/space merging, as a consequence of these weapons, is likely to drive future binational cooperation, not unlike the recognition of the need to warn of maritime threats to North America.

In order to understand this evolving process, it is useful to examine the nature of this somewhat "new" domain relative to the evolution and the state of Canadian and American involvement in military space, and the place of NORAD in it. In light of this evolution, the analysis of hypersonic weapons development examines two key issues confronting the future of North American defence integration: ballistic missile defence and the weaponization of outer space. While both appear as fundamental barriers to future integration, the expansion of NORAD's responsibilities makes functional sense.

THE "NEW" AEROSPACE DOMAIN

Understanding the nature and implications of the "new" aerospace domain can be somewhat confusing. The 1981 NORAD agreement and its terms of reference define NORAD's two traditional missions, aerospace warning and aerospace control. The former includes both air and space, although the assets supporting each are distinctly different in several ways. The latter is restricted to the air domain and is more accurately called air control.

The air warning assets primarily reside in the NWS.[7] In addition, there are nationally owned and funded radars in northern Alaska, down part of the West Coast of Canada, and on the coasts of the continental United States and the Mexican border that feed into NORAD, providing it with 360-degree coverage of North America. In addition, since 9/11, NORAD is also supported by national civilian radar feeds from the FAA and NAVCanada.

The space warning assets, usually translated as "ballistic missile warning" assets, are almost exclusively American. They entail a constellation of infrared satellites in geosynchronous orbit (GEO) and polar orbit (PO), designed to detect ballistic missile launches.[8] In addition, through the development of heat plume data bases, the type of ballistic missile can be quickly characterized upon launch.[9] The initial launch data from these assets then serve to cue the US ground-based phased array radars located at Clear (Alaska), Thule (Greenland), Fylingdales (United Kingdom), Cape Cod (Massachusetts), Cavalier (North Dakota), and Beale (California). As a function of the parabolic flight path of ballistic missiles, these radars provide tracking information and potential target locations, and, when combined with initial satellite data, enable NORAD assessors to decide whether North America is under attack, and if so, to characterize the nature of the attack; this is known as integrated tactical warning/attack assessment. Combined, these systems form what is termed the Ballistic Missile Early Warning System (BMEWS).

In addition to the primary ballistic missile warning mission, the BMEWS's radars also track objects in space in conjunction with the US Space Surveillance Network (SSN), which includes radar and optical tracking assets located around the globe. These combined assets track

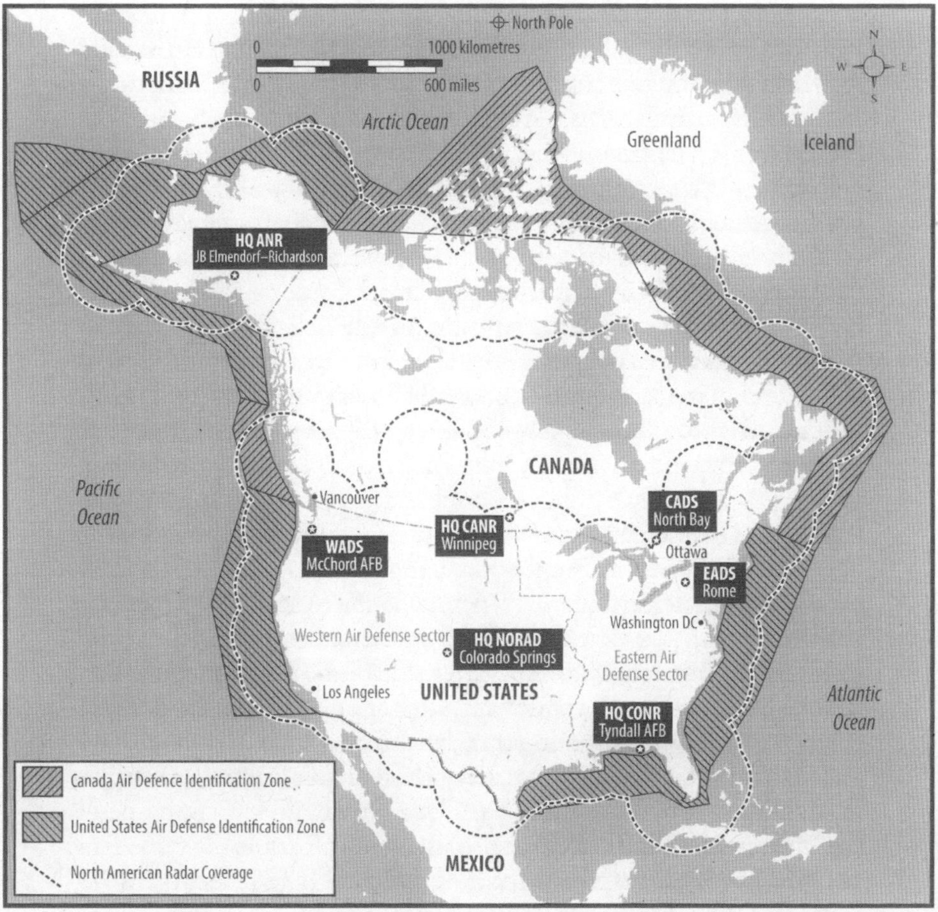

6.1 North American Aerospace Defense Command: Command-Control HQ and radar coverage. Map created by Mike Bechtold.

all objects in orbit around the earth to a minimum size of 10cm (approximately the size of a baseball). Canada contributed two ground-based optical sensors decades ago, and in 2013 launched a space-based optical sensor called Sapphire into low earth orbit (LEO), dedicated to observing satellites in geosynchronous orbit. Overall, the BMEWS/SSN data is fed into the NORAD assessment process primarily to ensure that de-orbiting satellites and material are not mistakenly interpreted as ballistic missile warheads.

In terms of the aerospace control mission, NORAD's only mission is air control or air defence. As noted in chapter 1, both Canada and the United States dedicate air defence assets, on a yearly basis, to the NORAD Command. NORAD has no ballistic missile control mission. Prior to the development and deployment of ballistic missile defences, this control mission belonged to the United States via its strategic nuclear retaliatory forces as part of the US strategic deterrent. Since the stand-up of a limited continental BMD system in 2004, and the Canadian non-participation decision (discussed below), the two continental ballistic missile defence sites at Clear, Alaska and Vandenberg, California are strictly under USNORTHCOM's command, although NORAD's ballistic missile warning function is linked to them.

Reflecting these differences, there are two operations directors in the NORAD and USNORTHCOM Command Center. While NORAD and USNORTHCOM integrate key staff positions (for example, the J2 intelligence position serves both NORAD and USNORTHCOM [N-NC/J2]), there are separate directors of Operations for NORAD (N/J3) and for USNORTHCOM (NC/J3), reflective of the different mandates.

In terms of integration on the space side of the equation, Canadian NORAD personnel are seconded to monitor and analyze the ground-based BMEWS radars. In addition, Canadian NORAD personnel have served directly on the US space side of the equation, such as at Schriever Air (now Space) Force Base outside of Colorado Springs, home of the United States' premier space defense unit. Following the Canadian decision not to participate at the governmental level in the 1980s US Strategic Defense Initiative (SDI) research program (otherwise known as "Star Wars"), Canadians were barred from access to the Space section in the Cheyenne Mountain Headquarters, and from access to classified US space intelligence.[10] It would seem Canada's participation in the space domain, while important, can be constrained by politics.

The "separateness" of air and space is also found at the national level. NORAD, as the binational aerospace component of the CANUS defence relationship, has a binational aerospace warning role and a defensive response role. Any North American offensive air/ballistic missile components remain unilaterally within the control of the United States in the conventional and nuclear realms. Conventional strike forces located in North America are strictly American and are primarily assigned to USSTRATCOM, not least because Canada lacks such capabilities. Naturally, nuclear forces are also strictly American.

Space is given bilateral attention by Canada and the United States. NORAD had been the primary access point for Canadian military positions associated with the space domain because of NORAD's ballistic missile warning mission and the fact that Canada had no national military space program until recently. NORAD's central role for Canada in military space was further cemented with the stand-up of USSPACECOM in 1985. The Space commander was dual-hatted as the commander of NORAD. In 2002, however, USSPACECOM was disestablished, and its mission suite assigned to USSTRATCOM. As a result, NORAD was de-linked from US military space.[11]

Subsequently, CANUS military space relations evolved into a bilateral arrangement, propelled forward by three developments on the Canadian space side. First was the development by the Canadian Space Agency (CSA) in 1990 and the launch of its first earth observation radar satellite (RADARSAT I)[12] in 1995, followed by RADARSAT II in 2007, and then the deployment of an additional three RADARSATs in 2019 (RADARSAT Constellation) equipped with an Automated Identification System (AIS) for ships. These programs have been of significant military value to the United States and to other allies. The RADARSAT Constellation, located in polar orbit, is primarily conceptualized (or publicly sold) as a national sovereignty asset to provide wide-area surveillance of the Canadian Arctic. However, since satellites in polar orbit can overfly all parts of the globe, it can thereby provide potentially valuable surveillance in support of military operations overseas as well, specifically because of its all-weather, 24/7 surveillance capabilities.

Second, as noted above, Canada entered into the space surveillance world with its first dedicated operational military satellite in 2013 – the optical Sapphire satellite – making a significant contribution to the US Space Surveillance Network. Finally, DND signalled its seriousness about space by establishing a new Director-General group for space, replacing a lower-level Directorate of Space Development (DSPACED), and assigned operational responsibility for Canadian military space to the RCAF.[13]

These three developments, but especially Canada's space assets, were highly valued by the United States. A Canadian military liaison position was established at Vandenberg Air Force Base in California (renamed Vandenberg Space Force Base on 14 May 2021). The Canadian liaison joined British and Australian liaison representatives on the basis of bilateral agreements, but they would be subsequently tied into the Five Eyes (Australia, Canada, New Zealand, United Kingdom, and United States) multilateral intelligence arrangement. For the time being, DND's preference has been to keep the arrangement on a strictly bilateral path, not least for sensitive political reasons, as discussed below.

Overall, the concept of aerospace, as applied to NORAD, is really a misnomer. The relationship between NORAD and the wider CANUS defence setup has, for all intents and purposes, been an air and space one. This reality, however, is about to be put to the test with the development of hypersonic weapons.

FUTURE NORAD CHALLENGES: HYPERSONICS

Hypersonic weapons are a class of weapons systems that travel at speeds around Mach 5, or 6,000 kilometres per hour (1.7 kilometres per second).[14] There are two types: hypersonic glide vehicles (HGVs) and hypersonic cruise missiles (HCMs).[15] HGVs are launched by a rocket and then glide to hit their target. HCMs are powered by a ramjet or scramjet engine. Both are the developmental focus of the United States, China, and Russia, could be armed with nuclear warheads (although the United States is considering only conventional weapons for now), and operate at an altitude between 30 and 100 kilometres in sub-orbital space.[16] Most importantly, both are manoeuvrable in flight, in contrast to ballistic missile warheads, which have a predictable parabolic flight path and transit at much higher altitudes, with long-range missiles cutting through orbital space.

Hypersonic weapons are the successor to the research and development of manoeuvrable re-entry vehicles (MARVs) of the 1970s, undertaken in conjunction with the development of multiple independently targeted re-entry vehicles (MIRVs). Their similarity is found in their purpose: to defeat ballistic missile defence (BMD) systems. Once the Soviet Union and the United States moved away from missile defence (then known as anti-ballistic missiles, or ABMs) and signed the 1972 ABM Treaty, the strategic requirement for MARVs disappeared, supported by significant technical and cost barriers.[17] With the development and deployment of BMD systems, the requirement to defeat these systems emerged, and hypersonics became the solution, at least according to pronouncements made by Russian President Putin.[18]

Hypersonic weapons, especially HGVs, which are the primary focus of Russia, present significant challenges to North American defence and NORAD. First of all, they cannot be clearly classified as either a ballistic missile warhead or an air warhead. They are capable of manoeuvring both outside and inside the atmosphere. Second, identifying, tracking, and cueing intercept defences against these extremely high-speed, low-profile, manoeuvrable weapons is extremely difficult for current radar systems which are designed against either exo-atmospheric or endo-atmospheric threats, but not both. Finally, intercept defences also reside in an either/or domain. The US ground-based mid-course phase BMD system is designed to intercept ballistic missile warheads in outer space, high above the altitude of hypersonics. Air defences, whether air, maritime, or ground-based, are designed to intercept threats in the atmosphere, well below the altitude of hypersonics, until they descend.

Technology does exist to confront the challenge of hypersonics. Existing radar technology, as well as optical and infrared sensors, and possibly the development of quantum radar, are likely to prove highly effective once optimized for hypersonics. However, the architecture of supporting systems does not exist. The primary northern BMEWS radars, for example, required for tracking hypersonics in their sub-orbital phase, are located on the periphery of the continent, looking up and out, with the exception of the phased array radar system at Cavalier, North Dakota. Once the warheads fly over the BMEWS radars, they cannot be tracked by the system. Civilian inward-facing ground-based radars, linked into NORAD since 9/11, are optimized for subsonic flight, and likely lack the power and fidelity to track hypersonics in sub-orbital or atmospheric flight. Space-based sensors provide a possible solution and are in the initial development phase in the United States.[19]

On the intercept side, the US Theater High Altitude Area Defense (THAAD) system, designed against medium- and intermediate-range ballistic missiles and deployed at Guam and Hawaii, has the potential to intercept hypersonics, although the speed of the interceptor missiles may need to be upgraded. Relatedly, high-altitude air defences also offer a solution. However, both are only capable of providing a point defence capability with limited defensive coverage. Given the ability of hypersonics to cover a large, relatively unpredictable geographic swath of targets, a large number of systems are required just to defend potential high-priority targets.[20] The possible re-constitution of the 1980s air-launched anti-satellite system is another possible solution, one that could also be acquired for Canada's new fighter.[21] Whether ground- or air-based, part of the solution is also likely to require significant forward-deployed systems, especially in the Canadian Arctic, to provide a layered defence.

Overall, hypersonics need to be understood as a simultaneous ballistic missile and air threat. The NWS and NORAD modernization, as discussed in chapter 4, has to be able to integrate detect-and-defend capabilities against long-range cruise missiles and hypersonics – a daunting and costly challenge. Missile and air defences need to be merged to deal with the reality of the "new" aerospace domain, as does the C^2 function, which is divided between USNORTHCOM (missile defence) and NORAD (air defence). Of course, this means that the Canadian policy not to participate in missile defence becomes an issue.

NORAD AND THE BALLISTIC MISSILE DEFENCE CONUNDRUM

If the United States proceeds to integrate air and missile defence in response to the development of hypersonic weapons, Canada's non-participation policy on ballistic missile defence (BMD) becomes problematic. The neat conceptual, structural, and operational arguments that underpinned this policy are collapsing, and with this collapse, NORAD's relevance becomes a major consideration. This is evident with the tension, if not paradox, of Canadian defence policy.

In the 2017 White Paper *Strong, Secure and Engaged* (*SSE*), the Liberal Trudeau government announced that it would not change its non-participation policy on ballistic missile defence as announced in 2005 by the Liberal Martin Government. *SSE* also established NORAD modernization as a priority even though no details or funding commitments were included. However, NORAD modernization will entail much more than simply a renewal of the NWS or strictly air defence capabilities (i.e., the replacement of the CF-18 interceptor). Indeed, NORAD modernization will entail a myriad of changes including a rethink of forward operating locations in the Arctic and new communication systems. Key will be a functional response to the implications of the air and space domain merger driven by the development of hypersonic weapons, and ongoing US initiatives designed to integrate air and missile defence. These steps are necessary if NORAD is to remain the central venue for CANUS continental defence cooperation. One way or another, future Canadian governments will have to come to grips with this new strategic reality, or face NORAD's marginalization and confront US unilateralism in the defence of North America with few, if any influence opportunities.

In all fairness, it was potentially premature in the roughly two-year process of drafting *SSE* that the defence policy world would foresee this new strategic reality and its implications for Canadian BMD policy and NORAD. While certainly Canadian and US intelligence were aware of ongoing research on hypersonic weapons, when the technical obstacles to actual operational deployment would be overcome remained an open question. Governments are also rarely willing to commit funds to a *what if* proposition, and, in the case of Canada, more immediately pressing and costly capability modernization requirements (such as the CF-18 interceptor replacement and the national shipbuilding strategy) mitigated against bringing forward yet another new requirement.

Moreover, NWS renewal is a costly requirement, and agreeing on a way forward with the United States, a priority. Simply put, the drafters of *SSE*, like those of all past White Papers, had to be sensitive to what the current political traffic would bear, including funding, in order to be successful. Hence, vagueness and ambiguity become *best practice*, thus explaining references to, but no detail on, NORAD modernization.

Regardless, the future of NORAD is at the centre of the merging air and space domains, as it has always been in Canadian policy considerations from the beginning of the BMD issue in the 1960s.[22] What is different this time, however, is the prospects of isolating NORAD and its current aerospace mission suite from BMD. Technology and strategic contexts are forcing the convergence of the two.

Technology dictated a clear separation between air and space requirements and capabilities. The first generation of US missile defence, the Safeguard anti-ballistic missile system, consisted of relatively short-range, nuclear-tipped, terminal-phase interceptors.[23] They possessed a limited defensive footprint, and could only defend a small area, such as a city or military target.[24] The system, including its supporting long-range radar, could only be deployed in close proximity to a potential target.[25] In contrast to the air part of NORAD's aerospace missions, Canada and Canadian territory were strategically irrelevant to ABMs. While some Canadian defence and NORAD officials were concerned about the future of ballistic missiles rendering air defence obsolete, these concerns quickly evaporated with American reassurances and the linking of NORAD's ballistic missile warning mission to the ABM system.[26]

US President Reagan's 1983 SDI was simply a missile defence research program, and thus had no operational relevance to NORAD and its future. Similarly, the next two programs, President George H.W. Bush's Global Protection Against Limited Strikes (GPALS) and President Clinton's National Missile Defense (NMD), also never moved beyond the research and development phase. It was only following President George W. Bush's decision in December 2002 to proceed with the operational deployment of a ground-based mid-course phase missile defense system (GMD) that Canada's longstanding missile defence policy of prevarication became problematic for NORAD.

Before the Canadian "no," the government agreed to the American request to link NORAD's ballistic missile warning mission into the new GMD system in August 2004. This acted as a significant buffer for NORAD to the subsequent non-participation decision. Canada aided with the warning via NORAD, but USNORTHCOM retained sole decision-making power to defeat an incoming missile with the GMD system and had no mandate requiring the United States to protect Canada.

In addition, GMD's strategic purpose made Canada's position on missile defence marginal, if not irrelevant, to the United States, thereby further insulating NORAD from any fallout from the Canadian "no." The system promised to provide limited but full continental defence coverage from its two operational sites in Alaska and California. Its strategic purpose is to defend against the growing long-range ballistic missile threat posed by North Korea. The flight path of these missiles negates any need for interceptors or supporting radars to be stationed in Canadian territory in order to defend the continental United States. This strategic reality partly explains the US rejection of the Canadian proposal to link participation with the assignment of GMD command and control to NORAD in negotiations held in 2003–04. All the United States really needed was to link ballistic missile warning into the system, and this, as noted above, was easily agreed to by Canada via NORAD, as had been done during the brief life of the Safeguard ABM system.

Even if a third GMD site is built in the northeastern United States, designed to defend against future ICBM threats from Iran in particular, little is likely to change for NORAD and for Canada. The third site will likely require a forward-deployed tracking and cueing radar, and Canadian territory is the obvious and logical location.[27] However, a radar site in eastern Canada can be easily integrated into the NORAD warning mission, and support not just the US third site, but also NORAD's space tracking mission. In other words, Canada can participate without participating, and this setup can remain in place as long as Canada and Canadian territory are not vital for US strategic interceptors. Whether the United States would informally commit to defending Canada under these conditions is a politically and strategically moot question for NORAD and its future, as the decision to defeat a missile via the GMD would remain a USNORTHCOM (i.e., a US-only) decision.

Today, however, the strategic implications of hypersonic weapons, and to a lesser degree future nuclear-powered cruise missiles, fundamentally change US strategic continental defence requirements, and with them, NORAD requirements. Air defence and ballistic missile defence radars need to be integrated into a system of systems to deal with the transition of a missile threat into an air threat, and this process is underway in the United States. Similarly, air defence and missile defence interceptors also need to be integrated. Their integration in turn requires the merger of operational command and control, rather than their separation, as is evident in the current NORAD and USNORTHCOM Command Center. This, in effect, is the new strategic reality, driven by new technology, and is at the centre of NORAD modernization.

Certainly, it might be possible for CANUS military planners and designers, especially within NORAD, to find a solution that sustains, artificially, the separation of air and space relative to NORAD modernization. This will require a willingness, especially on the part of the US military in general, and the USAF, USNORTHCOM, and the rest of the combatant commands under the UCP in particular, to accept this artificiality. In this context, relative to the strategic importance of Canadian territory, the United States can simply ignore Canada. However, such a work-around is likely to be militarily dysfunctional and relegate Canadian involvement, engagement, access, and influence to a limited, tactical, and traditional anti–cruise missile role.

History provides a useful example in this regard. In the wake of Prime Minister Brian Mulroney's 1985 decision not to participate officially in SDI research in response to the US invitation to all of the NATO allies, Canada was excluded from a range of high-level strategic planning committees, including those that impacted on NORAD's missions, and the informal Canadian NORAD exemption to US *no foreign eyes* intelligence and briefings was revoked. Similarly, beginning in the late 1990s, Canadian NORAD positions in key space billets were downgraded to the margins, and Canada's ability to obtain vital information on the issues surrounding potential Canadian participation in the US BMD program from the US Ballistic Missile Defense Organization (BMDO), and subsequently from its successor, the US Missile Defense Agency (MDA), was limited.[28]

Nonetheless, strategically, a work-around is possible as a function of the importance of ground-based radars deployed across the Canadian north as part of the system-of-systems requirement for the defence of North America, and thus the defence of the continental United States. Similarly, forward-deployed cruise missile interceptors also remain necessary, which may, in the future, also require surface-to-air capabilities.

NORAD interceptors, as a function of their relatively short-range reach, are unable to strike at cruise missile launch platforms from all areas of Russia, for example. NORAD's aerospace control mission requires anti–cruise missile capabilities, which are also essential to deal with hypersonic weapons, especially once they enter and manoeuvre in the atmosphere. In other words, NORAD's control mission becomes a cruise missile defence mission, which should logically include hypersonic intercept capabilities during their sub-orbital phase. Conceptually, depending upon the labelling and branding of the mission, traditional ballistic missile defence could be kept at arm's length if the US wants to do so.

Failure to move forward in this regard will have dramatic implications for NORAD. At a minimum, Canada and Canadian NORAD personnel are likely to be excluded from high-level US strategic planning venues. The C^2 structure and processes, embodied in an American/Canadian commander and Canadian/US deputy commander within the NORAD command structure, become extremely problematic. The Canadians would not be able to obtain access to US *aerospace* planning and decision-making, rendering the commander–deputy commander relationship dysfunctional.

This also means that there will be pressure to end integration of the NORAD/USNORTHCOM Command Center. Canada and NORAD could be pushed to the margins. NORAD might simply revert to a warning mission suite in which Canada outsources aerospace defence to the

US; after all, USNORTHCOM's area of responsibility includes Canada. To what extent the United States would inform Canada via NORAD or bilaterally of its operational plans to defend North America from the merged air and space domains becomes the key functional question. Alternatively, Canada could invest significant funds to contribute to the defence of North America, including cruise and hypersonic missile defence.

Of course, these considerations will compete with concerns that altering Canadian policy on BMD, and fully engaging in the "new" aerospace domain, carries with it significant new investment demands. These, in turn, potentially put at risk other investment priorities, especially in the wake of the economic impact of the COVID-19 pandemic and inflation. Yet, history suggests that the United States will be flexible and understanding of Canadian budgetary constraints, as evident in the various funding arrangements concerning NORAD.

In the end, Canada faces stark choices: find an arrangement to undertake missile defence or relegate NORAD to the margins of the CANUS defence relationship and lose the key access point for Canadian influence opportunities in the defence of North America. The answer seems obvious, except for one other political policy/functional issue that is brought into play by the merger of the air and space domains: outer space itself.

NORAD AND THE OUTER SPACE CONUNDRUM

Under NORAD and USNORTHCOM commander General Robinson (2016–18), the PJBD instructed NORAD to break what was to be a holistic study of the Evolution of North American Defence into its constituent domain components (land, maritime, cyber, etc.). Aerospace and outer space were to be considered separately. Yet, the separation of the aerospace and space domains is arguably artificial and problematic for the defence of North America, and NORAD's place within it. Certainly, significant differences exist as a function of physical principles and technological requirements, notwithstanding the absence of a legally defined altitude boundary line between national air and international outer space.[29]

Operationally, the main difference in terms of the merging of the air and space/aerospace and outer space domains is the primary defence interest of concern. The aerospace defence domain is directly concerned with weapon systems that transit through space, including sub-orbitally, on their way to terrestrial targets; outer space is faced with direct threats to orbital assets, i.e., satellites of vital strategic, operational, and economic value. The air, ground, sea-based, and potentially space-based assets necessary to defend against aerospace threats are also capable of threatening orbital assets. This conundrum has been one of the underlying issues related to existing Canadian policy on BMD.

Satellites, as a function of their fixed orbital path, their size, and the relative ease of tracking them, are highly vulnerable targets.[30] Both China and the United States have employed direct-ascent BMD interceptors in an anti-satellite role. In 2007, China destroyed its own defunct weather satellite in LEO.[31] In 2008, the United States employed its Aegis sea-based interceptor to destroy its own intelligence satellite, which had failed to reach orbit and threatened to spread toxic material over a wide area upon re-entry.[32] Russia, in contrast, has not tested or employed its BMD capabilities in a anti-satellite role, although there is little doubt that its existing BMD systems are also capable in this regard.[33]

For NORAD, this represents another potential barrier to engaging in an integrated response to hypersonic threats, and to the merger of air and missile defence, in two ways. First, this raises the spectre of the weaponization of outer space. Second, it shifts NORAD from a strictly defensive function to potentially an offensive one as well.

The concept of the weaponization of outer space is problematic. There is no formal legal definition of an outer space weapon, except for the Article IV prohibition of the 1967 Outer Space Treaty (OST) on placing nuclear or other weapons of mass destruction in orbit.[34] However, other WMD are neither defined nor identified. Generally, such weapons are understood to be chemical or biological. However, one must consider what else might fall into this category in the future: for instance, a large satellite that was purposefully de-orbited and targeted against a city or against other satellites, or a space-based electro-magnetic pulse weapon. Since a satellite could be purposely de-orbited, whether labelled a weapon of mass destruction or not, one can conceptualize that space is already weaponized, even though there are no orbiting satellites dedicated to this purpose.

There is also no clear definition of or consensus on weapons in outer space. For some, drawing on the Article IV prohibition, a space weapon must be in orbit and, at a minimum, complete a single orbit.[35] Weapon systems transiting through outer space or sub-orbital space, such as ICBMs and hypersonics, are not space weapons per se. Nor would any terrestrial weapon system (whether air-, land-, or sea-based) capable of striking targets in space be considered a space weapon. In this case, the expansion of NORAD's mission suite into the space side of aerospace control appears unproblematic.

However, what may be unproblematic functionally is likely to be deeply problematic politically for NORAD, especially for Canada. Canadian governments, regardless of political stripe and in contrast to the United States, are directly opposed to the weaponization of space. It is a fine line between defining weaponization as only dedicated systems deployed on-orbit and defining weaponization as any system capable of striking objects orbiting in space, especially in the absence of a formal international agreement or treaty. Whether future Canadian governments would be able or willing to withstand the political fallout from seeking to make this distinction is an open question.

Related, terrestrial weapon systems, as noted above, can serve both defensive and offensive purposes. If NORAD acquires the mandate and capabilities to defend against the hypersonic threat, it would then also possess the capabilities to launch offensive anti-satellite strikes. In other words, hypersonics, driving the merger of air and missile defences, are also blurring the long-held, albeit problematic, differentiation between defence and offence. In some ways, this is no different from the blurring of defence and offence that resides in the air and maritime domains as well, evident in the "archers vs. arrows" distinction. Going after the "archers" can be a defensive strategy as well as an offensive pre-emptive one.

At the same time, there are also organizational issues at play. The CANUS military space relationship is a bilateral one and does not include all of the elements of military space. This enables both countries to decide which areas of military space are open to cooperation. It enables Canada to keep within the defensive, non-kinetic area of military space, and the United States to keep Canada out of highly sensitive areas of military space. In some ways, it is simply the modernized version of Canada's arm's-length relationship with both the US strategic nuclear deterrent and the BMD program. In both cases, Canada, through NORAD, participates in the warning and attack assessment component, but the response side rests solely with the United States.

With the creation of the US Space Force in 2019, there may be new and complicated connections for Canada and NORAD to space. While largely a force generator, the US Space Force may be assigned responsibilities that are within NORAD's purview. In many ways, the new Space Force is simply a structural re-labelling of the longstanding internal division within the USAF between its strategic missile and space elements and traditional air-breathing elements – i.e., between the missiliers and the pilots.

Nevertheless, the Space Force serves to complicate not only the existing CANUS bilateral military space arrangement, but also responses to the hypersonic threat environment, and, with it, NORAD as the logical, functional command for hypersonic defence.

CONCLUSION

NORAD's warning mission has long been engaged in both the air and space domains. Hypersonics may require a new suite of sensors to be integrated into a modernized North American early warning system of systems. Even if Canada makes the unlikely decision to stand aside from the hypersonic intercept mission, Canada's participation in NORAD can continue on the warning side, as it did in the case of BMD. Few problems arose when NORAD was linked to the US ABM Safeguard system or the US-only GMD system. The real problem is the control side of NORAD's mission suite. Here, the possibility of NORAD marginalization looms large.

Canada faces a similar situation as it did in the late 1940s and 1950s. The United States will take whatever steps are necessary to ensure its own defence. Today, it is not long-range aviation bombers per se that are the problem, but cruise missiles and hypersonic weapons. Developing and deploying anti–cruise missile capabilities will simply be an extension of NORAD's existing aerospace control mission, whether air-launched or ground-based area and point defences. Hypersonics, however, are highly problematic given their speed, manoeuvrability, and thus unpredictable trajectory.

As manoeuvrable weapon systems in both sub-orbital and air space, hypersonics are a new type of cruise missile, separate and distinct from ballistic missiles and thus BMD. Canadian potential future capabilities to intercept hypersonics in sub-orbital space may provide Canada with the capability to intercept satellites, at least in low earth orbit. From here, it is a relatively small step to BMD itself. As BMD in past Canadian debates became linked to the weaponization of space, so too could anti-hypersonic capabilities.

With the United States on the path to integrating air and missile defence (hopefully to be called cruise missile defence), Canada faces increasing pressure to engage, lest it cede its defence against hypersonics to unilateral American decisions. The NORAD aerospace control mission will quickly become irrelevant if this happens. In this outcome, the United States will continue to defend Canada, but with little, if any, Canadian input.

As for outer space, it can remain a separate control domain in which Canada and NORAD remain in a strictly defensive posture. Eventually, however, this bridge will also have to be crossed.

7

Cyber, Land, and Where To from Here for NORAD

2017 was an important year for NORAD. At the first summit meeting between Prime Minister Trudeau and President Trump in February, NORAD modernization was placed on the agenda. In their joint statement, the leaders confirmed: "The North American Aerospace Defense Command (NORAD) illustrates the strength of our mutual commitment. United States and Canadian forces jointly conduct aerospace warning, aerospace control, and maritime warning in defence of North America. We will work to modernize and broaden our NORAD partnership in these key domains, as well as in cyber and space."[1] Roughly three months later, the PJBD agreed that a NORAD-led EvoNAD study was needed, but recommended that NORAD break it into six packages that would study each domain in turn. The domains in order are air, maritime, cyber, aerospace, space, and land, as well as future domains, such as the information domain, where mis-, mal- and disinformation campaigns are waged. In June, the Government of Canada released the 2017 Defence White Paper *Strong, Secure and Engaged*. In it, NORAD modernization was referenced eleven times, including a hint that NORAD might be expanded, and that Canada intended "to engage the United States to look broadly at emerging threats and perils to North America, across all domains, as part of NORAD modernization."[2]

The commitment to NORAD modernization was reiterated at the first video meeting of Prime Minister Trudeau and President Biden on 23 February 2021. In their joint statement, they announced: "The Prime Minister and the President agreed to expand cooperation on continental defense and in the Arctic, including by modernizing the North American Aerospace Defense Command (NORAD) … They directed their Ministers of Foreign Affairs and National Defence and Secretaries of State and Defense to meet in a 2+2 Ministerial format to further coordinate our joint contributions to collective security."[3] The devil is, of course, in the details, of which there are few.

In the background, both governments are exploring their needs and options. The military and policy planning staffs in NORAD, Ottawa, and Washington, DC, plus a host of unseen national and bilateral committees and working groups, defence research scientists, the MCC, and industry are involved. Exactly what is part of modernization efforts remains unclear. Everything from new infrastructure (including extending runways at Arctic FOLs), machine learning, artificial intelligence, training, new command and control structures, more sharing of information, and a new approach to continental defence are included. NORAD modernization is no longer a narrowly focused endeavour as it was when the DEW line was upgraded to the NWS in the 1980s. Today, NORAD resides in a more complicated geopolitical, technological, and organizational environment.

The ultimate goal for the USNORTHCOM and NORAD commander is to have all-domain awareness to facilitate information dominance and decision superiority.[4] For these goals to be achieved, Canada and the United States will need an integrated, 360-degree, all-domain system-of-systems. The NORAD modernization of the 2020s has potentially significant implications for the nations' armies and navies beyond the simple struggle for resources. More broadly, it also touches on the interests and preferences of a range of other civil security agencies and government departments, as well as local communities, especially in the Arctic, whose voices cannot be ignored. Finally, NORAD has always been attended by politics, especially associated with the binational agreement's renewals of the past. This time, however, the politics of NORAD modernization are likely to be much more problematic because of the range of actors involved, and the integration and defence cooperation required.

Naturally, the nature and extent of integration is difficult to predict, and numerous different outcomes are possible, ranging from the minimalist, in which the status quo remains, to the maximalist, in which NORAD evolves into an all-domain binational North American Defence Command. Certainly, the maximalist option is not likely in the immediate future, and beyond a few voices on the margins, it is not likely in the minds of policy-makers, most probably because of the incredible costs and because other issues (such as pandemics) push NORAD issues to the side. Nor, however, is the minimalist scenario likely either, given the reality of the new, all-domain threat environment, the response to which will either drive NORAD forward or push it backward to irrelevancy and to the margins. The status quo is simply no longer viable.

Avoiding irrelevancy is the focus of this final chapter on the future of NORAD, with an examination of the functional requirements for a modernized NORAD. The ultimate evolution that includes expanded NORAD mission suites and greater North American binational integration is likely to be gradual, similar in many ways to the process that created the original North American Air Defense Command. When North American air defence cooperation began after World War II, no one on either side of the border thought that the outcome would be a unique, binational command. In a similar vein, driven by functionality, NORAD modernization will likely set in motion a long process towards full defence binationalism.

In examining the beginnings of this long-term process, it is useful to examine the two domains that are most unlikely to be subject to a binational outcome in the foreseeable future, and yet part of the EvoNAD study: cyber and land (which just fizzled). Each domain, for different reasons, clearly illustrates the challenges that confront binationalism. Subsequently, the analysis examines the primary organizational and political barriers to an integrated binational all-domain warning and control NORAD, which will likely make this a slow and gradual integration process. Finally, the discussion turns to examine the potential scope of NORAD modernization in the context of functionalist requirements. In the end, our analysis borrows from Prime Minister Mackenzie King's 1942 quip about conscription: binationalism if necessary, but not necessarily binationalism.[5]

CYBER AND LAND

On the surface, merging the cyber and land domains into a single discussion seems problematic. Cyber and land are obviously distinctly different domains, with different characteristics, properties, processes, and actors. Cyber is a non-physical domain in which large amounts of information and data are transmitted and processed at relatively high, if not near-real-time speeds.[6] Land is a physical domain of geographic features, infrastructures, and people that move at a relatively slow speed, and sometimes not all. Cyber is immaterial, land material.

Yet, in the case of North American defence cooperation and NORAD, these domains are similar in many ways. Neither resides within the traditional mandate of defence and the armed forces in North America. Both domains primarily operate in the security policing world, exclusively under the jurisdiction of civil departments and agencies, notwithstanding the military's responsibility for its own cyber systems and networks. Both the Canadian and US militaries lack the authority to undertake such constabulary missions: the Canadian military by virtue of the National Defence Act and the US military by virtue of the 1878 *Posse Comitatus* Act.[7] In both domains, the militaries act as second responders, responding to "requests for assistance" (Canada) or providing "defense support of civil authorities" (US). Neither military sees itself as undertaking constabulary functions, nor desires to do so.

In some ways, the cyber and land domains can be thought of in terms of NORAD's maritime warning mission. As discussed in chapter 3, the implementation of that new mission faced major barriers. None of the maritime civil security actors greeted NORAD with open arms. Instead, they saw NORAD as an interloper, possessing none of the knowledge or experience vital to understanding the civilian maritime domain. NORAD was an air force institution, and aerospace and maritime were entirely distinct domains. NORAD, residing at the end of the maritime intelligence chain, was also simply seen as irrelevant and redundant even though it provided a valuable impetus for greater national and bilateral inter-agency cooperation. NORAD's new role helped to bring the formerly stovepiped, multi-agency maritime security world together to avoid the possibility of NORAD taking over. NORAD's maritime warning function is still not well known and remains undervalued, but now that it has been established, few would argue for its removal.

All of the challenges faced by NORAD when it was assigned a maritime warning mission exist for the cyber and land domains as well. While NORAD officials have quietly argued for entering into the cyber domain, beyond ensuring that its cyber requirements are secure from outside access and interference, such a mission confronts resistance from not only the dominant civil security departments and policing agencies, but also the private sector. Much of North American critical infrastructure resides in the private sector, and for a variety of reasons, including proprietary rights, private companies are wary of military interference in their cyber security. Moreover, an overt, lead military role is likely to generate deep suspicions within the public as a whole in terms of "militarizing" a civilian public domain. For some time, civil rights groups have been deeply concerned about the activities of intelligence and counter-intelligence agencies in monitoring the cyber world and spying on their own citizens.

In both domains, the military, as a second responder, needs to be aware of and prepared to respond to a major human-made or natural disaster, in which, for example, a cyber attack shuts down the Northeast integrated electrical power grid, or a major earthquake in the Northwest destroys the Vancouver-Seattle corridor.[8] Both scenarios would be devastating for both Canada and the United States, given their deep economic and energy integration.

Both militaries have significant experience responding to major natural disasters, and each country has provided military assistance to the other. Bilateral agreements and protocols exist for the provision of cross-border support, and these are updated as part of the "lessons learned" process.[9] In addition, planning and exercises for the provision of military support and assistance to civil authorities also occur. However, the extent to which the first responders are directly engaged in such planning and exercises, and likewise the involvement of the military in civilian exercises, is difficult to know. If the maritime warning world is any indication, prior to NORAD's entrance into the domain, and certainly prior to 9/11, the warning-to-response worlds (the left and right sides of bang) of cyber and land are highly stovepiped and divided on civil-military lines. Moreover, beyond virtual exercises and varying degrees of non-military engagement, cross-border disaster relief exercises are notably absent. In other words, everyone in the disaster response world may recognise the threat, plan, and exercise responses in their own stovepipes, but ensuring an efficient, effective, coordinated, quick response via cross-border and cross-agency planning and exercises appears missing.

Perhaps there is a lesson to be learned from the COVID-19 pandemic. Notwithstanding long-time warnings from the medical field and the recognition, for example, by the Paul Martin government in 2006 that pandemics were part of a new international threat environment, and despite the Severe Acute Respiratory Syndrome (SARS) and Ebola outbreaks, neither the Canadian nor American governments were adequately prepared for COVID-19.[10] Nor is there any indication, given the trans-border nature of viruses, that any significant discussions were held between the two countries on a coordinated response prior to the COVID pandemic.

NORAD is not a second responder. Instead, in terms of CANUS defence cooperation, it is located in the bilateral relationship between USNORTHCOM and CJOC. Certainly, NORAD is exposed to support missions as the third leg of a tri-command relationship and by virtue of the integrated NORAD and USNORTHCOM relationship. Nonetheless, NORAD is an outsider looking in. Even with the possibility that air-based surveillance and reconnaissance may be vital to surveying a disaster area, such a response would be primarily national. NORAD command has no authority to task surveillance and reconnaissance assets, as none are committed to NORAD, notwithstanding its ONE mission. Of course, this might change in the future in relation to developing and implementing an all-domain warning system, but until then, NORAD has no role to play.

The cyber domain is somewhat different from land. NORAD, along with USNORTHCOM, for example, participates in the USCYBERCOM-led military cyber event conferences.[11] Otherwise, NORAD is not engaged in the cyber defence/security world, beyond ensuring that its own networks are secure. CANUS cooperation remains bilateral under the lead of the Department of Public Safety (Canada) and the DHS (United States). One can envision a potential role for NORAD based upon its maritime warning mission, whereby it receives a North American cyber domain common operating picture and provides an additional set of "eyes" on potential threatening cyber events. However, this remains unlikely, unless, as in the case of maritime warning, a major cyber event with significant repercussions for both countries occurs, and the attack is found to be a function of an intelligence-sharing failure.

A final consideration for NORAD relative to both domains resides in the political world, surrounding the emotionally charged concept of sovereignty. This is more pronounced in the land domain. The 1960s witnessed major Canadian sovereignty concerns regarding Canadian culture being overwhelmed by US culture, which led to several policy initiatives to protect the Canadian cultural industry, including, eventually, the internet world. Even so, the cyber-cultural link has not been a major political issue per se, although its potential to become one does exist, and could well be triggered if NORAD were to acquire a cyber security role for North America.

The same cannot be said of the land domain. Sovereignty remains, especially in Canada, a sensitive issue. Even though both countries have provided each other with military assistance in response to domestic requirements according to existing bilateral arrangements, these are generally and purposely not well-publicized. While the Canadian media regularly reports occasions when Canada has provided assistance to the United States, such as in the case of Hurricane Katrina or fighting wildfires, the same is not the case when the United States provides assistance to Canada. Few media outlets publicized the US provision of strategic airlift to move generators into eastern Ontario and Quebec in response to the 1998 ice storm. Any hint of shifting land cooperation from a bilateral to a binational agreement, whether through NORAD or some alternative arrangement, is simply a non-starter politically.

In the end, the cyber and land domains are simply a "bridge too far" for a binational solution, notwithstanding a functional logic. No Canadian government, at least for the time being, is prepared even to contemplate such a step in the context of land and sovereignty, barring a major catastrophe that may serve as a forcing function.

NORTH AMERICAN DEFENCE MODERNIZATION AND BARRIERS TO BINATIONALISM

The cyber and land domains, in particular, demonstrate most clearly the primary barriers to a fully integrated, all-domain, binational solution to North American defence and security cooperation. These, of course, are also present in the other domains beyond NORAD's current mission suite. They also underpin the problem of defining the meaning and scope of North American defence modernization, and NORAD's place within it. If the 2017 Canadian Defence White Paper, *Strong, Secure and Engaged*, and the 2021 Trudeau-Biden joint statement are any indication, NORAD modernization is simply one part of North American defence modernization. Where binational modernization ends and bilateral modernization begins, however, cannot be fully discerned, at least for now.

Years prior to *Strong, Secure and Engaged*, and to the formal recognition of the new international threat environment, modernization was relatively simple and straightforward, at least from a Canadian perspective; the NWS would reach the end of its serviceable life in approximately 2025. The existing short- and long-range radars across the Canadian Arctic and down the coast of Labrador needed to be replaced. The complication of the decision to "align" the Canadian

Air Defence Identification Zone (CADIZ) farther north on 24 May 2018 to cover the entire Canadian Arctic archipelago meant that the NWS at approximately 70°N was too far south. Still, the thinking was that the NWS needed "renewal," but not necessarily one-for-one replacement (see figures 4.1 and 6.1).

The scope of modernization has grown exponentially, and with it, the costs, although they are still not fully determined, nor is the scope of the 60-40 US-Canada cost split, largely associated with changes to the NWS, clear. With the DoD's focus on JADC2[12] (and expected of all military commands), the reimagined NWS will likely be joined by space, maritime, and additional land- and air-based assets. The existing radars, whose life will be extended to 2035 and possibly beyond, may well be replaced with larger and more expensive over-the-horizon radars, or first-generation quantum radars. The communication systems for NORAD will also need to be modernized to handle and move much larger amounts of data more quickly. Artificial intelligence (AI) is already helping analysts see more of the data that the NWS detects but that existing algorithms cannot interpret. Through a US military and industry-led initiative called Pathfinder, AI is helping analysts see more patterns of activities collected by the NWS radars with more acuity.[13] The Government of Canada has also launched a public-private partnership entitled the All-Domain Situational Awareness (ADSA) science and technology program to research new surveillance technologies,[14] and Defence Research and Development Canada is exploring options including maritime-based sensors such as Canadian Arctic Underwater Sentinel Experiment (CAUSE), which is part of a larger project titled the Northern Watch Technology Demonstration Project (NWTDP). And with RADARSAT Constellation on-line, and other space programs, such as the Canadian High Arctic Ionospheric Network, coming to fruition, additional valuable information and technology could be a boon for NORAD – if it can manage all of the information and execute missions successfully. Like drinking from a fire hose, more is not always better.

The regional NORAD commands (ANR, CANR, and CONR) also require significant investment and modernization, especially to ensure the interoperability of Canadian and American capabilities and to ensure they will be able to receive and analyze all of the information that will come with JADC2. Finally, the FOLs in the Arctic (such as at Iqaluit and Inuvik) need infrastructure investments, and new FOLs may need to be built. All of these are daunting and costly challenges to varying degrees, especially in the Arctic.

These NORAD modernization activities all fit within existing mission suites and can be conceptualized as the status quo. Beyond lie two other possible components, one grounded within its warning mission and the other in its control mission, linked together by the new all-domain threat environment. Expanding the warning components is probably the simplest. NORAD already possesses both the air and ballistic missile/space warning missions, and integrating them as a function of the hypersonic weapon threat is a relatively simple and logical (functional) step forward. Similarly, integrating NORAD's existing maritime warning mission with the air and space domains does not appear to be problematic either. Adding cyber and land is somewhat problematic, although the maritime warning mission provides a template for NORAD's engagement in these two domains. Overall, were NORAD modernization to include the adoption of an integrated all-domain warning role, grounding it upon an integrated single North American common operating picture appears a reasonable option.

The control side of the equation is, however, much more problematic, even in the case of its traditional aerospace control mission. Successive NORAD commanders, reflecting dominant American strategic thought, repeatedly emphasize the requirement or preference to intercept launch platforms ("archers"), rather than delivery systems ("arrows"). Given the long-range cruise missile threat, this would require a significant upgrade in NORAD intercept capabilities, which Canada neither possesses nor plans to acquire. Nor is it likely that the United States would assign such capabilities to NORAD, since they are currently assigned to USSTRATCOM and the USAF Global Strike Command. Such capabilities would also transform NORAD from a purely reactive defence command into an offensive, preemptive command. No Canadian government is likely to agree to such a posture, nor is it likely to accept forward-deployed, long-range offensive strike forces on its territory.[15] Nor is it likely that the United States would agree to share such a command. Allies are recognized as vital to the US strategic posture, but the offensive decisions remain with the United States.

Alongside this barrier is the question of the US integration of air and missile defence. As discussed in chapter 6, this raises the thorny issue of ballistic missile defence (BMD), which also filters into the space domain, given its anti-satellite capabilities. A workaround is possible. NORAD's control mission is transforming into a cruise missile defence mission, which will also entail hypersonic weapon defences. The US ground-based, mid-course BMD system at issue, located in Alaska, does not possess the capability to intercept either cruise missiles or hypersonics. In other words, the two can be conceptually separated, leaving Canada's non-participation in BMD policy in place.

Whether or not the United States would be amenable to such a solution and whether the Canadian government could sell the distinction domestically remains to be seen. At the same time, other US-theatre BMD systems, such as THAAD, may be refined to deal with hypersonics. With the adoption of additional ground- and air-based intercept systems necessary to confront both cruise and hypersonic weapons, Canada would have to participate for NORAD to continue its aerospace control mission. This could entail ground-based intercept deployments on Canadian soil, for either area or point defence purposes.[16] Beyond the additional costs this would entail for NORAD modernization, deploying ground-based interceptors on Canadian soil is not likely to be an easy sell politically, if past problematic Canadian debates on BMD participation are any indication.

Beyond the aerospace control side of the equation, expanding into the maritime control domain, regardless of the functional logic, will meet with significant naval opposition. Navies in general, and the USN and RCN in particular, continue to guard their independence. While the commander of USNORTHCOM has authority over US NAVNORTH and naval air defence assets can be assigned to NORAD command, and the USN and RCN work together closely, going forward to the logical endpoint of a binational maritime control mission in the form of a NORAD Combined Forces Maritime Component Command will meet with resistance. It would require, at a minimum, a dictate from above à la maritime warning, and even then, strict parameters on NORAD's role are highly likely. This does not mean, however, that modernizing the CANUS maritime relationship is not a possibility. Rather, it is likely to be a "last viable option" scenario, given that services are often reticent to be reorganized and adapt to the exceptional coordination demands of a binational arrangement.

Beyond the military services, there is no shortage of civil security agencies, as well as other government departments, different layers of government, and non-governmental actors, which all have a stake (to varying degrees) in NORAD and North American defence modernization. This structural and political reality makes even the simplest element of modernization complicated. This, in turn, will become more pronounced as the costs of modernization begin to emerge.

While the Canadian and US governments have pledged new money for modernization, what specific funds will be assigned given the consequences of the COVID-19 pandemic and other economic pressures remains unclear.[17] Both defence departments and the military services will watch to see if the costs of modernization affect existing and other planned investment priorities, especially overseas requirements, which are typically preferred over "homeland" defence. The probability that many within the departments will see modernization as a zero-sum game is high. This extends further into the potential impact of modernization investments on other government departments, which are also likely to perceive spending in relative terms. In theory, though, NORAD modernization efforts in the Arctic (if spent wisely and with dual civilian-military use in mind) may benefit communities and other departments. Overall, as the nature, scope, and costs of NORAD and North American defence modernization are revealed, organizational and bureaucratic push-back is likely to grow.

How these barriers are managed will depend on the priority attached to modernization by both governments, especially in the United States. Depending upon the nature and pace of post-pandemic economic recovery, modernization is unlikely to receive much government attention for some time, except for the odd statement and reassurance that NORAD still matters. In the case of Canada, rarely has defence ever been a major political priority. Russia's agression against Ukraine in 2022 has helped to shift attention to homeland defence, but will this attention be sustained? As for the United States, where defence *is* a political priority, the Biden administration has many international defence and security issues, such as international fallout from the pandemic, as well as China, Russia, and Iran, among others, not to mention internal political gridlock, which are likely to dominate government attention. Climate change, too, is a growing priority that will complicate any infrastructure projects, especially in the Arctic. Melting permafrost, soil erosion, more violent and frequent storms, and changing ecosystems are but a few of the challenges. As such, the modernization process will be driven from the bottom up, having already begun at the functional level, and rising through the intra- and interdepartmental layers until the government finally confirms the processes and policies. In other words, the functional solution(s) that emerge initially will be massaged and altered in the process of obtaining intra- and interdepartmental consensus. Of course, at every stage, there will be changes reflective of different understandings and beliefs about what the political traffic will bear. Neither government is expected to intervene to direct the process as it unfolds, leaving the details of NORAD and North American defence modernization largely undefined and to the discretion of technocrats.

In the case of Canada, however, this process will be significantly informed and affected by perceptions within the defence world of the significance the United States attaches to modernization, as well as how the United States comes to define modernization. The greater priority attached by the United States, the greater the priority in Canada. This is not to suggest that the United States will dictate the outcome to Canada, nor will the CANUS defence relationship be abandoned if Canada fails to respond in a meaningful way. Throughout the post–World War II era of CANUS defence cooperation, significant differences, as especially evident on the BMD file, have had no appreciable impact on the overall relationship, and certainly have incurred little punishment from the United States. US officials are well aware of and highly sensitive to the realities of Canadian defence politics. Nevertheless, the fear that the United States could respond negatively is a helpful excuse to garner Canadian attention and action.

Finally, informing this process, which has yet to surface publicly, is one politically and emotionally charged concept: sovereignty. On the one hand, the process that led to the creation of NORAD was a functionally driven, bottom-up one, which attracted little if any public or political attention. It was only *post facto* that the NORAD agreement came under scrutiny and attack, often expressed in terms of the loss of Canadian sovereignty. Each subsequent renewal repeated this pattern, more or less. Indefinite renewal in 2006 eliminated the specific focus on the Agreement, but both North American and NORAD modernization could reawaken the sovereignty question, arguably more pronounced in Canada, but potentially also present in the United States.

The meaning of sovereignty has long been debated within the academic and epistemic community, and no consensus truly exists. Nor does this debate have much relevance within the reality of politics, especially within Canada. Rather, sovereignty is largely understood at the political level in Canada in two forms.[18] The first is the idea of sovereignty as the ability of the government to control its territorial space. This is typically argued by the political right. Here, NORAD enhances Canadian sovereignty in drawing from American resources to enhance Canadian control of its territory as a function of, for example, the NWS and US contributions to its establishment to provide surveillance and thus control of vast Canadian territory. The second form is the idea of sovereignty as independence or autonomy from foreign (read: US) interference. This is typically the concern of the political left. In this case, deepening and broadening CANUS defence integration will be opposed on grounds of undermining Canadian independence from the American behemoth. The sovereignty-as-control versus sovereignty-as-independence camps are deeply entrenched in Canada, and unlikely to be shaken by the academic debate surrounding the definition of the word. Simply, the camps' different interpretations of sovereignty are, in reality, a political/emotional mask hiding the longstanding debate in Canada about the nation's relationship with the United States. Both sides, however, tend to ignore the Indigenous employment of the concept of sovereignty as extending beyond borders to the rights they have to be involved in decisions regarding the military use of their land.[19]

The UNDRIP reaffirms the right of Indigenous peoples to be consulted when their land is the subject of exploitation or military use.[20] The CAF and the US armed forces are now more aware of their responsibility to consult with Indigenous peoples, especially with respect to exercises and new infrastructure in the Arctic. Certainly, no-one will tolerate another environmental disaster like those resulting from old DEW line sites leaching toxic chemicals into the ground. Any new infrastructure projects must consider their impact on the environment, and opportunities for the local population to benefit from the infrastructure through dual-use functionality and/or job opportunities.

THE FUTURE OF NORAD

Barriers aside, the path to binationalism and an integrated all-domain North American Defence Command seems, at least in terms of functional theory, to be logical. Contingent, unpredictable events and political decisions can change the future of CANUS North American defence cooperation and limit the depth and breadth of defence integration. Regardless, North American defence generally, and NORAD modernization specifically, cannot avoid setting the foundation for future binationalism, given the extent of CANUS integration in many issue areas (including energy grids, critical infrastructure, and supply chains, for example).

In the context of the new geopolitical environment, the development of advanced, offensive military technologies has eliminated the relative sanctuary of North America. As well, the neat, simple, and exclusively air threat domains of the Cold War are no longer. The notion that one domain is the exclusive purview (turf) of a single service has been eroding over time and this largely unrecognized fact is driving a binational solution forward.

In effect, defence integration has been an ongoing process even though the term "integration" has not been specifically ascribed to it. Functionally driven defence integration (i.e., technical solutions to a problem) is evident with respect to continental defence both internally and externally. Internally, it has entailed the slow, gradual breaking down of inter-service domain barriers via the promotion of cooperation and the effective and efficient employment of resources for operational campaigns under the concept and doctrine of jointness. Jointness is simply another word for integration.[21]

Externally, functionally driven defence integration is evident with the dominance of coalitions and alliances entailing overarching command structures, planning, training, and interoperable military technology, of which multinational NATO and binational NORAD are exemplars. This is the concept and doctrine of combined forces.

While many factors have contributed to this slow process toward greater defence integration, another driver is the changing nature of deterrence and warfighting requirements as a result of new technology. Military technologies, such as the development of airpower, ballistic missiles, nuclear weapons, and now hypersonic weapons, rapidly eroded the properties of space and time. What is more, grey zone tactics and mal- and disinformation campaigns can further advance competitors' intentions. Deterrence and war have truly became global, and thus the protection provided by geography and distance have disappeared. War has similarly shrunk the time available to states to mobilize and deploy their military capabilities. War can now occur in "real time" with little, if any, advance warning or pre-deployment positioning of assets, personnel, or resources. Situational awareness has also steadily approached real-time because of the range of high-tech surveillance and reconnaissance technology, along with the capacity to accumulate, analyze, and move larger and larger amounts of data at high speeds, now significantly enhanced by the emergence of AI and machine learning.

As a result, all states, even the great powers, no longer have the luxury of time and space. As a product of technological developments, war is now fundamentally "come as you are." Time does not permit states to mobilize or convert production processes to mass-produce military assets. Time-consuming procurement practices, especially for Canada, generate a significant gap in technological applications, with deployed military capabilities lagging significantly behind cutting-edge (often private-sector-generated) technology. Furthermore, given the continuing rise in costs of military systems, few states can afford to maintain and possess the full range of capabilities across all domains. Combined, these forces drive integration.

Exploiting technology in the context of the shrinking of time and space places an onus on technological expertise – the functional experts or technocrats vital for a modern, efficient and effective defence. The traditional image of soldiers, sailors, and aircrew, with their service-based identities, has evolved into a joint identity based upon technical commonality. An information technology engineer does not need a service-based identity. Rather the capability and end goals are germane. Technology, generally, has no service identity.

With technology, defence becomes the world of the functional, as its complexities can only be understood, developed, and exploited by the technical experts, both military and civilian. These include not just highly trained engineers and technicians, but also planning, training, and operational experts vital to the application of force. In the complicated defence world, it also extends to the top of defence organizations seeking to manage such a complex entity and translate resources into efficient and effective operational capabilities to meet the range of demands placed on the military by governments.

The complexity and intricacies of modern defence are largely beyond the knowledge and understanding of political leadership faced with a dizzying mélange of competing political priorities. Certainly, the political world sets the basic parameters of defence, and the defence world is well attuned to the political limits of integration and what the political traffic will bear. Nonetheless, this reality drives defence integration forward from the bottom up. In the case of NORAD, the functional air defence technocrats on both sides of the border who drove CANUS air defence cooperation forward shared much in common despite their national identities, and this led to the functional logic of shifting the nature of cooperation from bilateral to binational integration, albeit limited to a single domain.

There is also the need for transnational integration when dealing with combined forces. Plans need to be developed and exercised with allies. These necessities in turn drive the need to integrate training regimes to promote and ensure interoperability beyond just the equipment. In the process, national militaries come to develop a transnational character, even though their national identities do not disappear, and, in many cases, such as NATO, remain strong and dominant.

In the case of NORAD, its Canadian and American personnel come to acquire a nascent North American identity, without entirely shedding their national ones. Even when returning to a national posting, North America does not entirely disappear. For example, there is no NORAD liaison officer in CJOC because there is no need for one per se. NORAD input is simply present as a function of CJOC personnel who have served in NORAD. This is similar, although far less developed, across the broad area of military personnel exchanges between Canada and the United States, although based upon not a geographical but rather a service-based identity.

Arguably, functionally driven defence integration, informed and supported by common political interests is farther along in the case of Canada and the United States in a NORAD and continental defence context than within a NATO one. In both the CANUS and NATO cases, its legal and political foundation is based on the 1949 Treaty of Washington. Bilateralism, and in the case of NATO, multilateralism, requires a large number of MOUs to manage the requirements and needs of collective defence. Only in the North American case does a unique binational arrangement exist, and even then, a considerable number of bilateral arrangements are required.

Bilateralism (or multilateralism) and binationalism are not different in kind. Rather, they differ in degree relative to defence integration.[22] In both cases, the agreements contain the ability of each state to terminate the relationship, usually with notice. The uniqueness of the NORAD binational relationship is the product of many factors, of which geography is at the core. Canada and the United States share the continent and both countries recognized and accepted (long ago) the reality that the defence of North America was indivisible, harkening back to Roosevelt's 1938 Kingston Declaration.[23] To defend Canada means to defend the United States and vice versa. This, in turn, is reinforced by common language, heritage, economic integration, and political and popular culture, notwithstanding significant, but arguably marginal, differences. Note, however, that further North American defence integration is not a step towards political integration. Even as North American defence modernization moves toward greater integration, this is unlikely to spill over into greater CANUS political, economic, or social integration, for example.

Although one of the principles of Canadian defence is to always operate in coalitions, and to work with the United States when dangerous combat-related overseas commitments and operations are at stake, an integrated North American Defence Command does not mean that Canada would join every and any US overseas military engagement. Throughout the history of NORAD, Canada has made independent decisions on whether to engage or not, such as during the Vietnam War and the 2003 Iraq War. NORAD has not affected the ability of Canadian governments to act independently overseas, and Canadian decisions have had little effect on NORAD. There is no reason to expect that this would change should North American defence integration proceed, nor is there a substantive reason to expect that the United States would pressure Canada to join in overseas operations because of NORAD.

NORAD's authority is derived from an agreement between two sovereign states out of national self-interest. The NORAD commander reports to the national command authorities and the scope of command is determined in cooperation between these two authorities. Each national command authority retains the right to withdraw its authority within the terms of the agreement. In addition, as per the authority granted to the NORAD command, elements supporting NORAD remain national, and the execution of its missions as a function of its regional command structure is also national. Canadian air space is under a Canadian command in this sense.

In other words, the national reality remains at the core of the uniqueness of the binational NORAD in the world of defence cooperation. Neither Canada nor the United States can truly dictate to the other. Rather, each seeks to influence the other in meeting their common national interests via consensus-building. Respecting sovereignty remains the foundation of NORAD.

Finally, the North American defence integration process, since its air defence beginnings, has been in both countries' national interests. Canada is vital for the defence of the United States, and not just because of its "real estate." Likewise, the United States is a vital contributor to Canada's ability to control and defend its sovereignty and contribute to the defence of the United States. Neither can optimally deal with its homeland defence requirements without the other. This alone provides the foundation for further defence integration in response to the changing threat environment.

The final consideration is for new partners in NORAD, especially Mexico, an independent Greenland, and perhaps others. So long as Greenland is part of the Danish realm, it will remain squarely in EUCOM's AOR and outside of NORAD. However, given the importance of Thule Air Base and refuelling capabilities in Nuuk for both the RCN and the USN, it would be a natural fit in the USNORTHCOM AOR and as part of a possible trinational arrangement with NORAD.

The other partner to consider in the future is Mexico. Physically part of North America and within USNORTHCOM's AOR, Mexico could help defend against air threats emanating from the south. While Mexican liaison reps are present in USNORTHCOM, and despite attempts at a trilateral security partnership, there is still unease on the part of all three countries about operating trilaterally, let alone trinationally. And while Canada (jealously?) guards its special relationship with the United States, it is likely that Canada, in the future and through NORAD, will come to accept liaison officers from other states with particular functional expertise.

CONCLUSION

An air of inevitability is one thing; inevitability is something else. There is nothing assured in the future of North American defence cooperation and there is no shortage of possible futures. NORAD could be frozen in time, and North American defence modernization may proceed on a bilateral track. NORAD could expand into an all-domain warning command, while its air control command remains unchanged. NORAD could also expand to integrate North American maritime control, with this as the end state. NORAD could become a fully integrated, all-domain North American Defence Command. Among these possible futures, there also exist numerous different combinations and options.

There is, however, little likelihood that North American defence will be re-nationalized. If NORAD could withstand the disappearance of its fundamental rationale with the end of the Cold War and the collapse of the Soviet Union, and could survive the failure that was 9/11, it will continue "in perpetuity."

The process that is likely to unfold will not be straightforward, simple, or quick. The aforementioned barriers are not simply going to go away, and overcoming them will not be easy. Nonetheless, the status quo is no longer viable. Change will occur, and change is more likely than not to be in the direction of an expanded NORAD, even if its end state is unpredictable. Thus, to return to the introduction, the end state will be binationalism if necessary, but not necessarily binationalism, as the future of North American defence cooperation unfolds.

Future changes to NORAD will be driven by technical experts, as they have been throughout the history of NORAD and as predicted by functionalism. And similar to the past, profound changes in the global environment (be it the end of the Cold War or 9/11 or new peer competitors and technology) have shifted political attention to this binational agreement, if only in fits and spurts. While agreements to fund capabilities and approve broad-stroke outcomes of the Command require political attention, NORAD will remain dependent on its military experts if it is to continue and adapt in perpetuity.

APPENDIX 1

List of NORAD Commanders and Deputy Commanders

NORAD Commanders

Name	*Dates*
Gen Earle E. Partridge, USAF	12 September 1957 – 30 July 1959
Gen Laurence S. Kuter, USAF	1 August 1959 – 30 July 1962
Gen John K. Gerhart, USAF	1 August 1962 – 30 March 1965
Gen Dean C. Strother, USAF	1 April 1965 – 29 July 1969
Gen Raymond J. Reeves, USAF	1 August 1966 – 31 July 1969
Gen Seth J. McKee, USAF	1 August 1969 – 30 September 1973
Gen Lucius D. Clay, USAF	1 October 1973 – 29 August 1975
Gen Daniel James Jr, USAF	1 September 1975 – 5 December 1977
Gen James V. Hartinger, USAF	1 January 1980 – 29 July 1984
Gen Robert T. Herres, USAF	30 July 1984 – 5 February 1987
Gen John Piotrowski, USAF	6 February 1987 – 30 March 1990
Gen Donald J. Kutyna, USAF	1 April 1990 – 29 June 1992
Gen Charles A. Horner, USAF	30 June 1992 – 12 September 1994
Gen Joseph W. Ashy, USAF	13 September 1994 – 26 August 1996
Gen Howell M. Estes III, USAF	29 August 1996 – 14 August 1998
Gen Richard B. Myers, USAF	14 August 1998 – 18 February 2000
Gen Ralph E. Eberhart, USAF	18 February 2000 – 5 October 2004
Adm Timothy J. Keating, USN	5 November 2004 – 23 March 2007
Gen Victor E. Renuart Jr, USAF	23 March 2007 – 19 May 2010
Adm James A. Winnefield Jr, USN	19 May 2010 – 3 August 2011
Gen Charles H. Jacoby Jr, USA	3 August 2011 – 5 December 2014
Adm William E. Gortney, USN	5 December 2014 – 13 May 2016
Gen Lori J. Robinson, USAF	13 May 2016 – 24 May 2018
Gen Terrence J. O'Shaughnessy, USAF	24 May 2018 – 20 August 2020
Gen Glen D. VanHerck, USAF	20 August 2020 – Present

NORAD Deputy Commanders

Name	*Dates*
Air Marshal C. Roy Slemon	12 September 1957 – 14 August 1964
Air Marshal C.R. Dunlap	15 August 1964 – 25 August 1967
Air Marshal William R. MacBrien	26 August 1967 – 22 January 1969
LGen Frederick R. Sharp	23 January 1969 – 14 September 1969
LGen Edwin M. Reyno	15 September 1969 – 31 August 1972
LGen Reginald J. Lane	1 September 1972 – 1 October 1974
LGen Richard C. Stovel	2 October 1974 – 15 September 1976
LGen David R. Adamson	16 September 1976 – 17 August 1978
LGen Kenneth E. Lewis	18 August 1978 – 24 June 1980
LGen Kenneth J. Thorneycroft	25 June 1980 – 25 May 1983
LGen Donald C. Mackenzie	26 May 1983 – 10 August 1986
LGen Donald M. McNaughton	11 August 1986 – 11 August 1989
LGen Robert W. Morton	11 August 1989 – 2 August 1992
LGen Brian L. Smith	3 August 1992 – 1 August 1994
LGen J.D. O'Blenis	2 August 1994 – 7 August 1995
LGen L.W.F. Cuppens	8 August 1995 – 7 April 1998
LGen G.E.C. Macdonald	8 April 1998 – 8 August 2001
LGen Kenneth R. Pennie	8 August 2001 – 14 July 2003
LGen Eric A. Findley	14 July 2003 – 2 August 2007
LGen J.J.C. Bouchard	2 August 2007 – 10 July 2009
LGen Marcel Duval	10 July 2009 – 15 August 2011
LGen Thomas J. Lawson	15 August 2011 – 4 September 2012
LGen Alain Parent	4 September 2012 – 1 July 2015
LGen Pierre St-Amand	1 July 2015 – 20 July 2018
LGen Christopher J. Coates	20 July 2018 – 21 July 2020
LGen Alain Pelletier	21 July 2020 – Present

APPENDIX 2

The NORAD Agreement

Agreement Between the Government of Canada and the Government of the United States of America on the North American Aerospace Defense Command

E105060

THE GOVERNMENT OF CANADA AND THE GOVERNMENT OF THE UNITED STATES OF AMERICA, hereinafter referred to as "the Parties,"

RECALLING their longstanding partnership of binational cooperation in the defense of North America through participation in the North American Aerospace Defense Command (NORAD);

CONVINCED that such cooperation is a proven and flexible means to pursue shared goals and interests, remains vital to their mutual security, and is compatible with their national interests as the architecture of North American defense and national defense in their respective countries continues to evolve, including the establishment of Canada Command and United States Northern Command;

NOTING that this cooperation is conducted within the framework of the North Atlantic Treaty and is an important element of their contribution to the overall security of the NATO area;

MINDFUL that in the years since the first NORAD Agreement was concluded on May 12, 19 58 [*sic*], NORAD, as a distinct command, has evolved to address the continuing changes in the nature of the threats to North America and that it will need to continue to adapt to future shared security interests;

RECOGNIZING that, despite arms reduction agreements, large nuclear arsenals still exist, deliverable by strategic ballistic missile, cruise missile or long-range aircraft capable of striking North America;

RECOGNIZING further that, despite non-proliferation and counter proliferation endeavors, efforts by others to acquire nuclear weapons, other weapons of mass destruction, and their means of delivery pose a major security challenge;
AWARE of dramatic changes in the geostrategic environment and in the threats to North America, as illustrated by the terrorist attacks of September 11, 2001, in terms of the nations, non-state actors or terrorist groups that might choose to challenge North American security, the symmetry and asymmetry of the weapons and methods they could employ, and the transnational and global nature of these threats;
ACKNOWLEDGING that space has become an important dimension of national interest and has become an increasingly significant component of most traditional military activities, and that a growing number of nations have acquired or have ready access to space services that could be used for strategic and tactical purposes against the interests of Canada and the United States;
REALIZING that a shared understanding and awareness of the activities conducted in their respective maritime approaches, maritime areas and inland waterways, including the capacity to identify vessels of potential interest, are critical to their ability to monitor, control, and respond to threats so that their shared security is ensured;
RECOGNIZING that the non-military air and maritime activities associated with drug trafficking and other illegal transnational activities are a threat to their national security; and
DESIRING to ensure that their respective and mutual defense requirements are met in the current and projected geostrategic circumstances;
HAVE AGREED as follows:

ARTICLE I – NORAD MISSIONS

1. The primary missions of NORAD in the future shall be to provide:
   a. Aerospace warning for North America;
   b. Aerospace control for North America; and
   c. Maritime warning for North America.
2. For the purposes of this Agreement:
   a. "Aerospace warning" consists of processing, assessing, and disseminating intelligence and information related to man-made objects in the aerospace domain and the detection, validation, and warning of attack against North America whether by air-

craft, missiles or space vehicles, utilizing mutual support arrangements with other commands and agencies. An integral part of aerospace warning shall continue to entail monitoring of global aerospace activities and related developments. NORAD's aerospace warning mission for North America shall include aerospace warning, as defined in this paragraph, in support of United States national commands responsible for missile defense.

b. "Aerospace control" consists of providing surveillance and exercising operational control of the airspace of Canada and the United States. Operational control is the authority to direct, coordinate, and control the operational activities of forces assigned, attached, or otherwise made available to NORAD.

c. "Maritime warning" consists of processing, assessing, and disseminating intelligence and information related to the respective maritime areas and internal waterways of, and the maritime approaches to, Canada and the United States, and warning of maritime threats to, or attacks against North America utilizing mutual support arrangements with other commands and agencies, to enable identification, validation, and response by national commands and agencies responsible for maritime defense and security. Through these tasks NORAD shall develop a comprehensive shared understanding of maritime activities to better identify potential maritime threats to North American security. Maritime surveillance and control shall continue to be exercised by national commands and, as appropriate, coordinated bilaterally.

ARTICLE II – GOVERNING PRINCIPLES

Based on a common appreciation of the circumstances described and of the experience gained since the inception of NORAD, the following principles shall govern the organization and operation of NORAD:

a. Commander NORAD, or Deputy Commander NORAD in the absence of Commander NORAD, shall be responsible to the Government of Canada communicating through the Chief of the Defense Staff of Canada and to the Government of the United States through the Chairman of the Joint Chiefs of

Staff of the United States. Commander NORAD and Deputy Commander NORAD shall each remain subject to their respective country's applicable national laws, policies, and directives. Commander NORAD shall function in support of the aerospace warning, aerospace control, and maritime warning missions that have been approved by the authorities of the Parties for the defense of North America, and conduct information operations supportive of NORAD missions.

b. Commander NORAD and Deputy Commander NORAD shall not be from the same country, and each of their appointments must be approved by both Parties. During the absence of Commander NORAD, command shall pass to Deputy Commander NORAD.

c. The NORAD Headquarters and NORAD Command and Operations Centers shall be composed of integrated staffs with representatives assigned by the Parties. Non-NORAD activities within Cheyenne Mountain Operations Center and other commands providing support to NORAD missions may include NORAD-assigned personnel, as appropriate, to perform NORAD duties. NORAD-assigned personnel performing NORAD duties in other commands may be called upon to support the mission of that command, as appropriate.

d. The financing of expenditures connected with the integrated headquarters of NORAD and in support of NORAD-assigned personnel at other Canadian and U.S. commands to perform NORAD missions shall be arranged by mutual agreement between appropriate agencies of the Parties.

e. NORAD shall include such forces as are specifically made available to it by the Parties to fulfill its missions. The authority of Commander NORAD over those forces and resources is limited to operational control as defined in Article I, paragraph 2b. Temporary reinforcement from one area to another, including the crossing of the international boundary, to meet operational requirements is within the authority of commanders having operational control. Additional Canadian and United States resources may be designated by the respective Parties to provide support to NORAD, including through cooperative arrangements with other commands and agencies.

f. No permanent changes of station of forces assigned, attached or otherwise made available to NORAD operational control will be made without the approval of the national authority of the Party concerned. The basic command organization for the Parties' respective defense forces, including administration, discipline, internal organization, and unit training, shall be exercised by national commanders responsible to their national authorities.

g. Plans and procedures to be followed by NORAD shall be formulated and approved by the Parties and shall be capable of rapid implementation in an emergency. Any plans or procedures recommended by NORAD that bear on the responsibilities of civilian departments or agencies of the two Parties shall be referred by the appropriate military authorities to those departments or agencies for action as appropriate.

h. Arrangements shall be maintained to ensure effective sharing, between the Parties, of information and intelligence relevant to the NORAD missions.

i. The "Agreement between the Parties to the North Atlantic Treaty Regarding the Status of Their Forces," signed in London on June 19, 1951, shall apply to activities under this Agreement.

j. The Parties acknowledge the importance of sound environmental practices. Without prejudice to the Parties' rights and obligations, environmental issues related to activities undertaken in connection with this Agreement shall be reviewed in the Permanent Joint Board on Defense.

k. The North Atlantic Treaty Organization shall continue to be kept informed through national NATO policy staffs, or other designated representatives, of arrangements for NORAD's role in the defense of North America.

l. Terms of Reference for NORAD shall be updated expeditiously following the entry into force of this Agreement and consistent with the foregoing missions and principles set out for NORAD. Changes in the Terms of Reference, including the addition of other aspects of the missions heretofore identified, shall be made by agreement between the Chief of the Defense Staff of Canada and the Chairman of the Joint Chiefs of Staff of the United States, with approval of higher national authorities as appropriate, provided that the changes are in consonance with the principles set out in this Agreement.

ARTICLE III – REVIEW AND AMENDMENT

1. The Parties shall meet to review this Agreement and consider possible amendments, under a mutually agreed mechanism, at least every four years or at the request of either Party.
2. This Agreement may be amended in writing at any time upon agreement of the Parties.

ARTICLE IV – FINAL PROVISIONS

1. This Agreement shall enter into force upon an exchange of diplomatic notes in which the Parties notify each other of the completion of any necessary internal procedures. Upon entry into force, this Agreement shall supersede the agreement on the North American Aerospace Defense Command done by Exchange of Notes on 28 March 1996, renewed on 16 June 2000, and amended on 5 August 2004.
2. Implementation of this Agreement shall include the updating, as required, of the NORAD Terms of Reference and other relevant instruments needed to facilitate NORAD missions. The Parties may conclude such further arrangements as necessary to advance the objectives and purposes of this Agreement, including mutual support arrangements with other commands and agencies.
3. Either Party may terminate this Agreement upon twelve months' written notice to the other Party.

IN WITNESS WHEREOF, the undersigned, duly authorized to that effect by their respective Governments, have signed this Agreement. DONE at Ottawa, on 28th day of April, 2006, in duplicate, each in the English and French languages, each version being equally authentic.

Gordon O'Connor
For the Government of Canada

David H. Wilkins
For the Government of the United States of America

Notes

ACKNOWLEDGMENTS

1 Centre for Defence and Security Studies, "NORAD Reports," University of Manitoba, https://umanitoba.ca/centres/cdss/papers/2201.html (accessed 25 September 2021).
2 University of Manitoba, "NORAD 60th Anniversary Conference," video, 3:19:38, https://digitalcollections.lib.umanitoba.ca/islandora/object/uofm%3A3024025.
3 University of Manitoba, "NORAD Files," https://digitalcollections.lib.umanitoba.ca/islandora/object/uofm%3Anoradfiles?display=uofm_list (accessed 25 September 2021).

INTRODUCTION

1 We mean a triptych in the sense of three works that can be appreciated both separately and together. Joseph Jockel wrote his book first, followed by Richard Goette, who deliberately concentrated on the decisions made in the years before NORAD was operational. We made a conscious decision to focus on events after the signing of the NORAD Agreement in perpetuity to limit overlap with Jockel's excellent work. The three books have a decidedly Canadian lens to the subject matter, which is consistent with the fact that interest in NORAD is higher in Canada (especially among the few academics who study NORAD) than in the United States.
2 Richard Goette, *Sovereignty and Command in Canada-US Continental Air Defence: 1940–1957* (Vancouver, BC: UBC Press, 2018). Note Joseph Jockel

also wrote an excellent book on the origins of NORAD. See Joseph Jockel, *No Boundaries Upstairs: Canada, the United States and the Origins of North American Air Defence 1945–1958* (Vancouver, BC: UBC Press, 1987).

3 Joseph Jockel, *Canada in NORAD, 1957–2007: A History* (Montreal and Kingston: McGill-Queen's University Press, 2007).

4 Charles Pentland, "Functionalism and Theories of International Political Integration," in *Functionalism: Theory and Practice in International Relations*, edited by A.J.R. Groom and Paul Taylor (London: University of London Press, 1975), 9–24, 15.

5 David Mitrany, *A Working Peace System: An Argument for the Functional Development of International Organization* (New York: Oxford University Press, 1944), 35.

6 USNORTHCOM's area of responsibility includes air, land, and sea approaches and encompasses the continental United States, Alaska, Canada, Mexico, and the surrounding waters out to approximately 500 nautical miles. It also includes the Gulf of Mexico, the Straits of Florida, and portions of the Caribbean region including The Bahamas, Puerto Rico, and the US Virgin Islands. The commander of USNORTHCOM is responsible for theatre security cooperation with Canada, Mexico, and The Bahamas.

7 In Canada, the preferred term is "pan-domain command and control." Different terms and language are examples of the national caveats each country navigates as part of the binational command.

8 National Commission on Terrorist Attacks Upon the United States, *The 9/11 Commission Report: Final Report of the National Commission on Terrorist Attacks upon the United States* (Washington, DC: US Government Printing Office, 2004).

CHAPTER ONE

1 Joseph Jockel, *Canada in NORAD, 1957–2007: A History* (Kingston, ON: McGill-Queen's University Press, 2007); Joseph Jockel, *No Boundaries Upstairs: Canada, The United States and The Origins of North American Air Defence, 1945–1958* (Vancouver, BC: UBC Press, 1987); Richard Goette, *Sovereignty and Command in Canada-US Continental Air Defence, 1940–57* (Vancouver, BC: UBC Press, 2018); Michael Keane, *The Night Santa Got Lost: How NORAD Saved Christmas* (Washington, DC: Regnery Kids, 2015); Gordon A.A. Wilson, *NORAD and the Soviet Nuclear Threat: Canada's Secret Electronic Air War* (Toronto: Dundurn, 2011); Marian Gilmore and Iris Talmadge, *NORAD The North American Air Defense Command* (New York: Dodd, Mead, 1967); Kenneth Schaffel, *The Emerging Shield:*

The Air Force and the Evolution of Continental Air Defense, 1945–1960: NORAD, Dew Line, SAGE, BOMARC, SAC, Early Warning Systems, Radar Fence, Atom Bomb Impact (Washington, DC: Office of Air Force History, 1991); David F. Winkler, *Searching the Skies: The Legacy of the United States Cold War Defense Radar Program* (Langley, VA: United States Air Force Air Combat Command, June 1997); Daizo Sakurada, *Canada and Its American Alliance: NORAD in Focus* (Tokyo: Keiso Shobo, 2021); and North American Aerospace Defense Command Office of Command Historian, *A Brief History of NORAD* (Colorado Springs, CO: NORAD, 31 December 2013), https://www.norad.mil/Portals/29/Documents/A%20Brief%20History%20of%20NORAD%20(current%20as%20of%20March%202014).pdf.

2 Initially, the 1958 Agreement established ten-year renewals. The first renewal of the Agreement came in March 1968. The time frames were changed and subsequent revisions, renewals, and extensions to the binational Agreement came in: May 1973; May 1975; May 1980; March 1981 (when the name was changed to "North American Aerospace Defense Command"); March 1986; April 1991; March 1996 (when NORAD's missions were redefined as aerospace warning and aerospace control for North America); June 2000; and May 2006 (when the Agreement was signed in perpetuity and a maritime warning mission was added).

3 As part of the indefinite renewal, the NORAD Agreement established a three-year evaluation process and a six-month notification period should either party decide to terminate the agreement.

4 In contrast to the United States, where annual national security strategy documents are produced largely in secret with only rare references to NORAD, Canadian governments undertake a defence review process culminating in a White Paper infrequently but usually at the beginning of a new government's tenure. Since the first White Paper in 1964 (Pearson Liberal), there have been only six Defence White Papers, each shortly following the formation of a new government: 1971 (Trudeau Liberal), 1987 (Mulroney Conservative), 1994 (Chrétien Liberal), 2005 (Martin Liberal), 2008 (Harper Conservative), and 2017 (Trudeau Liberal).

5 Government of Canada, "Defence Investment Plan: 2018," https://www.canada.ca/en/department-national-defence/corporate/reports-publications/defence-investment-plan-2018.html (last modified 5 May 2021).

6 The government allocated $163.4 million over five years for NORAD modernization research and development, and $88.8 million over five years for sustainment of existing NORAD-related continental and Arctic defence capabilities. Government of Canada, *Budget 2021: A Recovery*

Plan for Jobs, Growth and Resilience (Ottawa: Government of Canada, 2021), 289–90, https://www.budget.gc.ca/2021/pdf/budget-2021-en.pdf.

7 In the context of *SSE*, the DND Assistant Deputy Minister for Policy (ADMPOL) established a new Director-General (DG) for Continental Defence Policy to focus on three areas connected to North American and NORAD defence modernization: (i) NORAD Policy, (ii) Domains and Technology Policy, and (iii) capabilities and liaison.

8 The co-chairs are appointed by the prime minister and president, and report directly to them on all matters related to continental defence and security. The PJBD also includes Department of Homeland Security and Public Safety Canada representatives to consider critical security as well as military cooperation. It held its 238th meeting in 2019 in Ottawa and its 239th in June 2021. See Andrea Charron, *The Permanent Joint Board on Defence: How Permanent and How Joint? Celebrating 80 Years of Cooperation* (Winnipeg: Centre for Defence and Security Studies, University of Manitoba, 25 February 2020), https://umanitoba.ca/centres/media/The-Permanent-Joint-Board-on-Defence-final-workshop-report_2020.pdf.

9 Of the Canadian deputy commanders, only one has ascended to become Chief of the Defence Staff: General Tom Lawson. On the US side, most commanders retire after serving as NORAD commander. General Myers (NORAD and US Space Command commander 1998–2000) was the exception, becoming the fifth vice- and then the fifteenth chairman of the Joint Chiefs of Staff (2001–05).

10 During the early stages of NORAD's operational existence, Canadian and American land-based air defence surface-to-air missile systems were also committed to NORAD command, and naval air-defence assets could also be assigned as needed. In the new threat environment, both may again be committed to NORAD command.

11 RCN officials were posted to NORAD in the wake of 9/11 with the creation of the NORAD binational planning cell, followed by the binational planning group (BPG).

12 Whereas US FAA representatives are present at NORAD headquarters, NAVCanada and Transport Canada do not have personnel present.

13 US General Lori Robinson (USAF, commander of NORAD and USNORTHCOM 2016–18) is the only woman ever to serve as commander at any level within the NORAD command team. There has never been a woman commander or deputy for any of the three NORAD regions and never a Canadian woman deputy commander of NORAD.

14 The roots of EvoNAD can be traced back to General Jacoby's (USNORTH-

COM and NORAD commander 2011–14) omnibus NORAD Next study, which was scaled back due to resource limitations. General Robinson (2016–18) subsequently launched EvoNAD. EvoNAD aimed to review the threat vectors in six domains (air, aerospace, space, maritime, cyber, and land) and to think at least twenty-five years into the future. NORAD modernization essentially replaced this study which just seemed to fizzle.

15 Government of Canada, *Debates*, III, March 30, 1939, 2420 as reprinted in David Beatty, "The 'Canadian Corollary' to the Monroe Doctrine and the Ogdensburg Agreement of 1940," *The Northern Mariner / Le Marin du nord* 1, no. 1 (January 1991): 3–22, 4–5, https://www.cnrs-scrn.org /northern_mariner/vol01/tnm_1_1_3-22.pdf.

16 "Joint Statement by the Governments of Canada and of the United States of America Regarding Defence Co-operation Between the Two Countries," E100977 CTS 1947 No. 43. The Ogdensburg Declaration is found in the Appendix. See https://www.treaty-accord.gc.ca/text-texte .aspx?id=100977.

17 "Exchange of Notes Between Canada and the United States of America Providing for the Continuation of the Principles of the Hyde Park Declaration into the Post-war Transitional Period, with Special Reference to the Problem of Reconversion of Industry," E103749 CTS 1948 No. 1. The Hyde Park Declaration is found in the Appendix. See https://www.treaty-accord.gc.ca/text-texte.aspx?id=103749.

18 Richard Goette provides an excellent and detailed history of the steps leading to NORAD, as does J.J. Jockel. See Goette, *Sovereignty and Command*; Jockel, *No Boundaries Upstairs*.

19 Stephen Harris, "Early Warning Radar," *Canadian Encyclopedia*, https://www.thecanadianencyclopedia.ca/en/article/early-warning-radar (last modified 4 March 2015); Roy Fletcher, "Military Radar Defence Lines of Northern North America: An Historical Geography," *Polar Record* 26, no. 159 (October 1990): 265–76.

20 "Document 119. Principles to Govern the Future Organization of and Operation of the North American Air Defense Command: Notes Exchanged at Washington by Canadian Ambassador to the US (Robertson) and Acting Secretary of State (Herter), 12 May 1958." Found in US Department of State, *American Foreign Policy: Current Documents, 1958* (Washington, DC: US Department of State, 1962).

21 "Agreement Between the Government of Canada and the Government of the United States of America Concerning the Organization and Operation of the North American Air Defence Command (NORAD) 1958," E101015 CTS 1958 No. 9, https://www.treaty-accord.gc.ca/text-

texte.aspx?id=101015. The 1981 NORAD Agreement changed the command's name from the North American "Air" Defense Command to the North American "Aerospace" Defense Command.

22 The North Atlantic Treaty, 4 April 1949, Article 5. "The Parties agree that an armed attack against one or more of them in Europe or North America shall be considered an attack against them all and consequently they agree that, if such an armed attack occurs, each of them, in exercise of the right of individual or collective self-defence recognised by Article 51 of the Charter of the United Nations, will assist the Party or Parties so attacked by taking forthwith, individually and in concert with the other Parties, such action as it deems necessary, including the use of armed force, to restore and maintain the security of the North Atlantic area. Any such armed attack and all measures taken as a result thereof shall immediately be reported to the Security Council. Such measures shall be terminated when the Security Council has taken the measures necessary to restore and maintain international peace and security."

23 In part, NORAD was sold by Prime Minister Diefenbaker as a NATO commitment, reflecting his predilection towards the British Commonwealth. Likewise, in the 1980s, Prime Minister Pierre Trudeau argued that the agreement to allow US testing of air-launched cruise missiles (ALCMs) in the Canadian north was part of Canada's NATO commitment. In reality, the testing also served to test NORAD defences against a Soviet ALCM attack.

24 Today, there is a United Kingdom liaison officer in Colorado Springs, but this officer is formally attached to USNORTHCOM, not NORAD. Additionally, annual staff talks are held between the United Kingdom and NORAD/USNORTHCOM.

25 Land-based point defences or surface-to-air (SAM) sites, which included the controversial Canadian BOMARC defences, were dismantled by the 1970s.

26 Jockel, *No Boundaries Upstairs*.

27 As an example, in 2007, the US F-15 fleet was grounded due to an accident. To fill the gap in ANR capabilities, Canada deployed CF-18s. The Canadian Press, "Canadian Fighter Jets Temporarily Fill in for U.S. Air Defences," *CBC News*, 27 November 2007, https://www.cbc.ca/news/canada/north/canadian-fighter-jets-temporarily-fill-in-for-u-s-air-defences-1.635315.

28 For example, two large ICBM fields were located in North Dakota at Grand Forks and Minot, which hosted two B-52 bases. The eastern field and the Grand Forks B-52s, upgraded to host B-1B bombers in the

1980s, were eliminated as part of the Strategic Arms Reduction Treaty (START 1) in 1991. The western field, consisting of 100 Minuteman 3 ICBMs and strategic bombers, remains operational. In addition, the remaining US ICBM fields, permitted under the New START agreement (2010), are located in Montana, Wyoming, Colorado, North Dakota, and Nebraska. See National Park Service, "Minutemen Missiles on the Great Plains," 20 October 2020, https://www.nps.gov/articles/minuteman-missiles-on-the-great-plains.htm.

29 For an excellent discussion of the 1968 renewal, see Joel Sokolsky, "Changing Strategies, Technologies and Organization: The Continuing Debate on NORAD and the Strategic Defense Initiative," *Canadian Journal of Political Science* 19, no. 4 (December 1986): 751–74. Note especially 756–7, and also Jim Fergusson, *Canada and Ballistic Missile Defence 1954–2009: Déjà Vu All Over Again* (Vancouver, BC: UBC Press, 2010), 45–9.

30 BMEWS consists of two integrated systems, the Defense Support Program (DSP) of infrared satellites in geosynchronous orbit (modernized with a new generation of satellites in polar orbit) designed to identify missile launches, and the series of ground-based radars located at Fylingdales (United Kingdom), Thule (Greenland), Clear (Alaska), Beale (California), Cape Cod (Massachusetts), and Cavalier (North Dakota), which are cued by DSP to locate and track incoming IC/SLBMs. As a function of this mission, NORAD is responsible for tracking objects in earth orbit, supported by the American Space Surveillance Network (SSN), to which Canada contributed a space-based optical sensor (Sapphire) in 2013. BMEWS radars were American and none were placed on Canadian territory. For details, see James Fergusson, "The NORAD Conundrum: Canada, Missile Defence, and Military Space," *International Journal* 70, no. 2 (June 2015): 196–214.

31 In contrast to the original funding arrangement, the NWS was funded on a 60% (US) / 40% (Canada) arrangement. See "Financial Responsibilities: point 12" in "Exchange of Notes Constituting an Agreement Between the Government of Canada and the Government of the United States of America on the Modernization of the North American Air Defence System," E101003 CTS 1985 No. 8, https://www.treaty-accord.gc.ca/text-texte.aspx?id=101003. There is no guarantee that such a fund arrangement will be used in forthcoming renewal projects of the NWS.

32 It has been generally estimated that a Soviet ICBM first strike would take approximately 30 to 35 minutes to reach their ICBM/SAC bomber targets in the continental US. NORAD officials had roughly 7 to 10 minutes to

provide an assessment of whether North America was under attack. With roughly less than 5 to 10 minutes from an NCA decision to launch US ICBMs and its strategic bomber fleet, this provided the US NCA, the president, roughly 15 to 18 minutes to decide to launch before Soviet ICBMs would strike their targets.

33 The complexity of strategic nuclear deterrence, and its various iterations over the Cold War, are beyond the scope of this study. The best overview remains Lawrence Freedman, *Deterrence* (Cambridge: Polity Press, 2004).

34 Lieutenant Colonel Stephen Blair, "NORAD: Is the Sky the Limit?" (MA thesis, Canadian Forces College, Defence Studies, 2006), 27, https://www.cfc.forces.gc.ca/259/290/292/286/blair.pdf.

35 House of Commons, Standing Committee on External Affairs and National Defence (SCEAND), "Minutes of Proceedings and Evidence," no. 57, First Session of the Thirty-Third Parliament, 1984–85–86, 20–1.

36 Ibid.; R.B. Byers, *Canadian Security and Defence: The Legacy and the Challenges* (London: International Institute for Strategic Studies, 1986), 28.

37 For an excellent review of the American influence on Canadian Forces thinking, see Jamie Nelemans, *The Canadian Forces and American Military Influence, 1963–1989* (MA thesis, Lakehead University, Department of History, 2013), 91–134, https://knowledgecommons.lakeheadu.ca/bitstream/handle/2453/535/NelemansJ2013m-1b.pdf?sequence=1&isAllowed=y.

38 Government of Canada, *SCEAND: Order of Reference Respecting* NORAD, *Issue no. 48* (Ottawa: Government of Canada, 21 November 1985), in evidence from Mr Bill Robinson, 6.

39 Department of National Defence, *Challenge and Commitment: A Defence Policy for Canada* (Ottawa: Department of National Defence, 1987), 18.

40 NORAD Office of the Command Historian, *A Brief History of* NORAD *as of 31 December 2013* (Colorado Springs, CO: NORAD Office of History, 2013), 7, https://www.norad.mil/Portals/29/Documents/A%20Brief%20History%20of%20NORAD%20(current%20as%20of%20March%202014).pdf.

41 The 1991 renewal of the NORAD Agreement included cooperation on the aerial surveillance necessary to counter aerial drug-smuggling activities.

42 Department of National Defence, Policy Group, *The 1994 White Paper on Defence* (Ottawa: Department of National Defence, 1994), ch. 5, https://publications.gc.ca/collections/collection_2012/dn-nd/D3-6-1994-eng.pdf.

43 Joel Sokolsky, *Canada, Getting It Right This Time: 1994 Defence White Paper* (Carlisle, PA: US Army War College, 1995), 8.

44 Government of Canada, *NORAD 1986: Report of the Standing Committee on External Affairs and National Defence February 1986* (Ottawa: Government of Canada, 1986).

45 The DPSA entails the waiver of the Buy American Act for defence products from Canada to the United States, and the treatment of Canadian defence firms as American in DoD procurement processes, in return for a Canadian commitment to purchase American defence goods in terms of offshore acquisitions. See Tom Jenkins, *Canada First: Leveraging Defence Procurement through Key Industrial Capabilities; Report of the Special Adviser to the Minister of Public Works and Government Services* (Ottawa: Public Services and Procurement Canada, February 2013), https://www.tpsgc-pwgsc.gc.ca/app-acq/amd-dp/samd-dps/eam-lmp-eng.html; Jeffrey Collins, *Defence Procurement Canada: Opportunities and Constraints* (Ottawa: Canadian Global Affairs Institute, 2019), https://www.cgai.ca/defence_procurement_canada_opportunities_and_constraints.

46 Nils Ørvik, "Defence Against Help: A Strategy for Small States?" *Survival* 15, no. 5 (1973): 228–31, 230, and Nils Ørvik, "Canada Security and 'Defence against Help,'" *International Perspectives* 26, no. 1 (May/June 1983): 26–31, 29.

47 Ørvik's three cases are Norway, Sweden, and Finland, with Norway and Finland non-aligned prior to World War II, and the respective German invasion and Soviet invasion in 1940. Sweden remained in a posture of armed neutrality until its 2022 announcement of its intention to join NATO. Ørvik's reference to Canada was simply to make the case for increased Canadian defence spending. For a detailed analysis of the inapplicability of Ørvik's "defence against help" thesis, see Andrea Charron and James Fergusson, "Defence against Help: The Wrong Theory for the Wrong Country at the Wrong Time," in *Canadian Defence Policy in Theory and Practice*, edited by Thomas Juneau, Philippe Lagassé, and Srdjan Vucetic (Ottawa: Palgrave Macmillan, 2019), 99–118.

48 This is embedded in the functionalist/neo-functionalist case concerning global warming, which cannot be resolved on a national basis.

49 Stein labels the result of cooperation leading to the creation of the International Civil Aviation Organization (ICAO), located in Montreal, Canada, as a negative international regime. Common rules and procedures, as a function of technical considerations, were required to avoid the possibility of air collisions as a result of different national rules and

procedures. From a functionalist/neo-functionalist perspective, all states had a common interest to ensure air safety, and this, in turn, demanded an apolitical technical solution, relying upon the technical experts. See Arthur A. Stein, "Coordination and Collaboration: Regimes in an Anarchic World," *International Organization* 36, no. 2 (1982): 299–324.

50 Thirty minutes is employed as it is roughly the flight time of an ICBM from launch from the Soviet Union/Russia to its target or vice versa. See note 32.

51 See for example Richard Goette's explanation of the command-and-control compromises and disagreements as they related to the US defence of Newfoundland during World War II. Goette, *Sovereignty and Command*, 86–105.

CHAPTER TWO

1 Lieutenant-Colonel Stephen T. Blair, "NORAD: The Sky's the Limit?" (MA thesis, Canadian Forces College, Defence Studies, 2006), 35; House of Commons, Standing Committee on National Defence and Veterans Affairs, *Minutes of Proceedings and Evidence*, 23 March 2000, http://www.parl.gc.ca/infocomdoc/36/2/NDVA/Meetings/Evidence/ndvaev24-e.htm.

2 National Commission on Terrorist Attacks upon the United States, *The 9/11 Commission Report: Final Report of the National Commission on Terrorist Attacks upon the United States*. (Washington, DC: US Government Printing Office, 2004), 17–18.

3 Ibid., 20. There was a small delay before the call to NEADS was made to confirm information.

4 Ibid., 21.

5 Ibid., 25–6.

6 Ibid., 29.

7 The DEFCON system goes from 5, the lowest state of readiness, to 1, war is imminent or has started.

8 National Commission on Terrorist Attacks, *The 9/11 Commission Report*, 31.

9 Multiple US news stories, documentaries (especially from *PBS*, *FrontLine*, *History Today*, and others) provide details on the whereabouts of key US personnel, but there are fewer sources for the whereabouts of Canadian decision-makers. Consequently, and because the authors are Canadian, we focused on Canadian leaders.

10 CPAC, "Timeline: 9/11 and Canada," 11 September 2018, http://www.cpac.ca/en/cpac-in-focus/timeline-9-11-and-canada/.
11 YELLOW RIBBON was the name given to Canada's operation to host stranded airline passengers from around the world as US airspace closed. The operation was made famous by the Broadway musical "Come From Away," which tells the story of 7,000 passengers hosted by citizens in Gander, Newfoundland, and the exceptional hospitality they experienced.
12 CPAC, "Timeline: 9/11 and Canada."
13 Many Canadians, however, stayed in place. Author Andrea Charron, at the time, was posted to the Netherlands as a military spouse. Military personnel and embassy staff posted there remained in place with no instructions whatsoever.
14 National Commission on Terrorist Attacks, *The 9/11 Commission Report*, 44.
15 Ibid.
16 Joseph Jockel, *Canada in NORAD 1957–2007: A History* (Montreal and Kingston: McGill-Queen's University Press, 2007), 168. As Jockel notes, Diefenbaker would have approved enthusiastically, having often justified NORAD as the North American NATO contribution.
17 Ibid., 167.
18 Edward J. Drea et al., *History of the Unified Command Plan: 1946–2012* (Washington, DC: Joint History Office, Office of the Chairman of the Joint Chiefs of Staff, 2013), 81, https://www.jcs.mil/Portals/36/Documents/History/Institutional/Command_Plan.pdf.
19 In 1946, it was referred to as the Outline Command Plan.
20 Goldwater–Nichols Department of Defense Reorganization Act 1986, Public Law 99-433, 1 October 1986, https://history.defense.gov/Portals/70/Documents/dod_reforms/Goldwater-NicholsDoDReordAct1986.pdf.
21 "Joint forces" concerns integrating national services (Air Force, Army, Navy) into a holistic command structure. "Combined forces" relates to integrating allied forces together. Thus, NORAD should be understood as combined forces, evident in the development of a Combined Forces Air Component Commander (CFACC) in NORAD as discussed in ch. 5. The ideal in an alliance setting is Combined and Joint Forces Commands, as found in NATO's rapid reaction forces.
22 In 2019, USPACOM was renamed USINDOPACOM to reflect the importance of India.
23 "Unified Command Plan, Extracts from Joint Military Operations

Department (NWC2021A)" (Newport, RI: US Naval War College, September 1999); and Lt Commander Robert C. Buzzell, *Homeland Security and the Unified Command Plan* (Newport, RI: Joint Military Operations Department, Naval War College, 1 February 2002).

24 USEUCOM had had responsibility for most of Africa since the end of World War II. USAFRICOM was declared fully mission-capable on 1 October 2008. As a vestige of the EUCOM legacy, USAFRICOM's headquarters remain in Germany.

25 Drea et al., *History of the Unified Command Plan*, 81, 84. See also Philippe Lagassé, "A Common 'Bilateral' Vision: North American Defence Cooperation, 2001–2012," in *Game Changer: The Impact of 9/11 on North American Security*, edited by Johnathan Paquin and Patrick James (Vancouver, BC: UBC Press, 2014), 193–212.

26 CPAC, "House of Commons Proceedings: September 17, 2001," https://www.cpac.ca/episode?id=01c78d74-80f0-4959-b110-50fccc9996c5 (accessed 20 September 2021).

27 Ibid. In Part 1 (1:50:50 to 1:51:35), a speech by Minister of Foreign Affairs John Manley mentions how Canada's commonalities (values and ideas, security) with the United States bind the two states together (NORAD directly mentioned). In Part II (0:03:20 to 0:04:10), Minister of National Defence Arthur Eggleton explains that Canada is committed to NORAD as it is partners with the United States in the defence and surveillance of North America (NORAD directly mentioned); (0:07:50 to 0:08:50) the minister continues by reinforcing that Canada, along with the United States, is advancing in the defence of North America (NORAD not directly mentioned); and (0:35:10 to 0:36:10) Canadian Alliance MP and Senior Defence Critic Leon Benoit reminds the House that the 9/11 attacks highlight the importance of Canada's defence commitments to NATO, NORAD, the UN, and other alliances forces (NORAD directly mentioned).

28 Donald Rumsfeld, *Known and Unknown: A Memoir* (London: Penguin Group, 2012).

29 Quoted in Joseph Jockel, *Canada in NORAD 1957–2007*, 179, taken from *Proceedings of the Standing Senate Committee on National Security and Defence*, Issue 14, 6 May 2002.

30 Lagassé, "A Common 'Bilateral' Vision," 193–212.

31 Michel Chossudovsky, "Canada's Sovereignty in Jeopardy," *Global Policy Forum*, 17 April 2007, https://archive.globalpolicy.org/empire/intervention/2008/0817canada.htm.

32 Joel Sokolsky and Philippe Lagassé, "Suspenders and a Belt: Perimeter

and Border Security in Canada–US Relations," *Canadian Foreign Policy Journal* 23, no. 3 (2006): 15–29.

33 US Northern Command, "About USNORTHCOM," https://www.northcom.mil/About-USNORTHCOM/ (accessed 20 September 2021).

34 The concept of separate yet inseparable is drawn from the literature around the defence relationship between the EU and NATO. See Viktoriya Fedorchak, *Understanding Contemporary Air Power* (London: Routledge, 2020).

35 The N2C2 is fully integrated, except for J3 (Operations). There is a N/J3 = NORAD Joint Operations Directorate and NC/J3 = USNORTHCOM Operations Directorate. NATO countries use the continental staff system to identify functions via letters and numbers. 1 = personnel, 2= intelligence, 3 = operations, 4 = logistics, 5 = plans, 6 = signals, 7 = training, 8 = finance, 9 = civil-military relations. C = combined (multiple nations), J = joint (multiple services), N = NORAD, NC = USNORTHCOM.

36 In December 2002, President George W. Bush announced that the United States would proceed to deploy a continental BMD site at Fort Greely, Alaska, setting the fall of 2004 as its operational date. In the summer of 2004, after the collapse of negotiations with Canada, the governments agreed to allow NORAD to provide its early warning assessments (ITW/AA) to USNORTHCOM. See James Fergusson, *Canada and Ballistic Missile Defence 1954–2009: Déjà Vu All Over Again* (Vancouver, BC: UBC Press, 2010).

37 Under CDS Hillier (2005–08), the Canadian command structure was reorganized, first with the creation of CANCOM in 2005, followed by the creation of Canada Expeditionary Command, Canada Operational Support Command, and Canada Special Operations Forces Command (CANSOFCOM). In 2012, primarily for resource reasons, and with the exception of CANSOFCOM, the commands were merged into the Canadian Joint Operations Command (CJOC).

38 See Fergusson, *Canada and Ballistic Missile Defence 1954–2009*.

39 The mood generally toward the United States was sour, given its decision to invade Iraq illegally in 2003 and initial reports that the war on terror in Afghanistan was killing more Afghan civilians than Taliban. David Pugliese, "Missile Defence," *Bulletin of the Atomic Scientists* 61, no. 4 (July /August 2005): 14–16, https://journals.sagepub.com/doi/pdf/10.2968/061004004.

40 One wonders how much Canada owes to then-Chief of the Joint Chiefs of Staff Myers, as former NORAD commander, for tempering Rumsfeld's frustration with Canada as a potential brake on his decisions vis-à-vis continental defence.

41 Merrie Schilter-Lowe, "Keating Becomes NORAD and USNORTHCOM Commander," North American Aerospace Defense Command, 5 November 2004, https://www.norad.mil/Newsroom/Article/578046/keating-becomes-norad-and-usnorthcom-commander/.
42 Layne Karafantis, "NORAD's Combat Operations Center: A Distinctly Cold War Environment," *Information and Culture* 52, no. 2 (2017): 139–62, 157.
43 Lagassé, "A Common 'Bilateral' Vision," 193–212; Fergusson, *Canada and Ballistic Missile Defence*, 4–5; Binational Planning Group, "Executive Summary," *Interim Report on Canada and the United States* (CANUS) *Enhanced Military Cooperation* (Colorado Springs, CO: Binational Planning Group, 13 October 2004); The White House, *National Security Strategy Report* (various dates but especially 2002), see http://nssarchive.us/.
44 National Security Strategy Archives, "National Security Strategy Reports," various dates but especially 2002, http://nssarchive.us/ (last modified March 2021); Government of Canada, *Security and Open Society: Canada's National Security Policy* (Ottawa: Government of Canada, 2004), http://publications.gc.ca/site/eng/259263/publication.html. The Security and Prosperity Partnership of North America (SPP) was launched by the leaders of Mexico, Canada, and the United States in March 2005. It aimed to improve cooperation and information-sharing for the purpose of increasing and enhancing security and prosperity in the three states. It simply ceased to be in 2009.
45 USSPACECOM was merged with USSTRATCOM in 2002. STRATCOM is now responsible for strategic deterrence, global strike, and operating the Defense Department's Global Information Grid. It also provides a host of capabilities to support the other combatant commands, including strategic warning; integrated missile defense; and (global) command, control, communications, computers, intelligence, surveillance, and reconnaissance (C^4ISR).
46 In the case of the United States, the military cannot engage in policing, except under a declared national emergency by the president, as a function of the 1878 *Posse Comitatus Act*. While both the Canadian and American Coast Guards have such authority (the CCG in a very limited capacity related to safety and fishing violations), the US Coast Guard (USCG) can function under either Title Ten, which assigns it to the Department of Defense, or Title Fourteen, where it functions as a civil agency under the Department of Homeland Security.
47 The 1947 *National Security Act* restructured the American defence and

intelligence world, leading to the merger of US intelligence agencies into a single body responsible for external threats, the Central Intelligence Agency (CIA). It also led to the establishment of a centralized body within the executive branch, the National Security Council, and the United States Air Force (USAF). See https://www.cia.gov/library/readingroom/docs/1947-07-26.pdf.

48 For a review of DHS nearly twenty years after its creation, see Chappell Lawson, Alan Bersin, and Juliette Kayyem, eds., *Beyond 9/11: Homeland Security for the Twenty-First Century* (Cambridge, MA: MIT Press, 2020).

49 The first IBET had been established several years prior to 9/11 in response to the trafficking of marijuana across the British Columbia–Washington border.

CHAPTER THREE

1 Statistics provided by US Department of Transportation Maritime Administration (MARAD). See US Department of Transportation Maritime Administration, "U.S. Waterborne Foreign Container Trade by U.S. Customs Ports 2000–2017," 24 October 2018, https://www.maritime.dot.gov/data-reports/data-statistics/us-waterborne-foreign-container-trade-us-customs-ports-2000-%E2%80%93-2017.

2 Department of Public Safety and Emergency Preparedness Act, S.C. 2005, c. 10, https://laws-lois.justice.gc.ca/eng/acts/P-31.55/page-1.html. Thinking about the need for such a department had been in the works as a result of Y2K in 1999, but the real impetus came after 9/11. This department was part of a government-wide reorganization including separating Customs from the Revenue Agency and the position of the solicitor general (under which the RCMP and other security-related departments resided) was replaced by the minister of Public Safety and Emergency Preparedness Canada. See Christopher Murphy, "'Securitizing' Canadian Policing: A New Policing Paradigm for the Post 9/11 Security State?" *The Canadian Journal of Sociology* 32, no. 4 (Winter 2007): 449–75, doi:10.2307/20460665.

3 USNORTHCOM has 9 suborninate commands: US Special Operations Command, North; US Marine Forces Northern Command; US Fleet Forces Command / US Navy North; Air Forces Northern (First Air Force); US Army North; Joint Task Force North; Joint Task Force Civil Support; Alaskan Command; and Joint Force Headquarters National Capital Region.

4 The US NMIO was created in 2009 by the director of National Intelli-

gence to coordinate maritime intelligence integration, facilitate information sharing, and advance national-level maritime domain awareness. See NMIO "background" at https://nmio.ise.gov/.

5 The CANUS BPG was created in 2002 by the *Enhanced Military Cooperation Agreement* and was headed by Canadian LGen Eric Findley. The deputy was US Lt Gen Joseph Inge. The co-directors represented the Canadian Navy and USN. Bi-National Planning Group, *Interim Report on Canada and the United States (CANUS) Enhanced Military Cooperation* (Colorado Springs, CO: Bi-National Planning Group, 13 October 2004), https://www.hsdl.org/?view&did=461253._The BPG explored the changes in concepts, policies, authorities, organization, or technology needed to facilitate improved military cooperation between CANUS. Canada had already issued its new National Security Policy (April 2004). The United States issued its version later in the year. See *National Security Presidential Directive NSPD-41 Homeland Security Presidential Directive HSPD-13: Maritime Security Policy* (Washington, DC: 21 December 2004), https://www.hsdl.org/?view&did=462647. Both referenced the need for improved security in the maritime domain. The final report of the BPG on enhanced military cooperation was issued 13 March 2006.

6 The "Royal" designation was returned to the Canadian Navy in 2011.

7 Although the USCG has defence functions under Title 10 of the US Federal Code, and policing functions under Title 14, the CCG has only safety and regulatory authority, which thus confines the scope of their cooperation.

8 While early articles suggest it was only Canada which rejected the idea, later interviews suggest both the Canadian and US navies were relieved NORAD was not expanded beyond maritime warning.

9 USNORTHCOM's area of responsibility includes air, land, and sea approaches and encompasses the continental United States, Alaska, Canada, Mexico, and the surrounding waters out to approximately 500 nautical miles. It also includes the Gulf of Mexico, the Straits of Florida, portions of the Caribbean region including The Bahamas, Puerto Rico, and the U.S. Virgin Islands. The commander of USNORTHCOM is responsible for theatre security cooperation with Canada, Mexico, and The Bahamas. See US Northern Command, "About USNORTHCOM," US Northern Command, https://www.northcom.mil/About-USNORTHCOM/ (accessed 21 September 2021).

10 In the Agreement signed in 2006, maritime warning "consists of processing, assessing, and disseminating intelligence and information related to the respective maritime areas and internal waterways of, and the

maritime approaches to, Canada and the United States, and warning of maritime threats to, or attacks against North America utilizing mutual support arrangements with other commands and agencies, to enable identification, validation, and response by national commands and agencies responsible for maritime defense and security. Through these tasks NORAD shall develop a comprehensive shared understanding of maritime activities to better identify potential maritime threats to North American security. Maritime surveillance and control shall continue to be exercised by national commands and, as appropriate, coordinated bilaterally."

11 To coordinate a response, Canada created the interdepartmental Maritime Emergency Response Protocol (MERP) and the United States the Maritime Operational Threat Response (MOTR). In 2014, Canada and the United States signed the Maritime Domain Awareness (MDA) Partnership Charter, and with it the MERP-MOTR Strategic Integrated Protocol for cross-border coordination. For details, see Andrea Charron et al., *Left of Bang: NORAD's Maritime Warning Mission and North American Domain Awareness* (Winnipeg: Centre for Defence and Security Studies, University of Manitoba, 2015), 39–41, https://umanitoba.ca/centres/cdss/media/0_NORAD_Maritime_Warning_Mission_Final_Report_8_Oct_2015.pdf.

12 Naval assets could be "CHOPed" (change of operational control) over to NORAD command on an as-needed basis. For example, on 9/11 a US aircraft carrier "CHOPed" its air assets over to NORAD.

13 For full details of the intelligence-sharing process, see Charron et al., *Left of Bang*.

14 There are three MSOCs in Canada, located on the East and West Coasts and the Great Lakes. The former two are led by National Defence/RCN and the latter by the RCMP. Besides the RCN and the RCMP, the CCG, Transport Canada, the Canadian Border Services Agency (CBSA), and Fisheries and Oceans are present.

15 NMIO is led by a rear admiral and partners with 17 US military and civilian agencies. NMIO's focus is global as opposed to MSOC's more national focus.

16 The commander of NAVNORTH is also the commander of US Fleet Forces Command.

17 For a detailed analysis, see Charron et al., *Left of Bang*, 23–4.

18 The maritime COP used to be received by the NJ-32 (the NORAD operations' intelligence cell), but since 2019, it is sent directly to the watch floor. The change is a function of which maritime experts are assigned

to NORAD and suggests NORAD is still discovering its maritime role.

19 Guy Thomas, "A Maritime Traffic-Tracking System Cornerstone of Maritime Homeland Defense," *Naval War College Review* 56, no. 4 (Autumn 2003): 137–52, 138, https://www.hsdl.org/?view&did=454154.

20 Recall, the N2C2 is fully integrated, except for J-3 (Operations). There is an N/J3 = NORAD Joint Operations Directorate and an NC/J3 = USNORTHCOM Operations Directorate.

21 Canada, however, did not follow suit, except in the provision of RCN personnel. There are no NAVCanada personnel present at NORAD Headquarters. As CANUS cooperation in the maritime and land domains, notwithstanding MW, is strictly bilateral in nature, the image of other Canadian government departmental (OGD) representation as liaisons to USNORTHCOM remains politically problematic.

22 NORAD shares its information with other militaries, government agencies, and security partners that have a need to know by issuing maritime warnings and advisories. Maritime advisories are for issues of national-level interest that do not pose an immediate threat, whereas maritime warnings are for issues that are likely to cause damage or pose a threat. By sharing maritime advisories and warning information, NORAD supports multinational, interagency efforts to respond to threats originating from the maritime domain.

23 Individual agencies and departments were aware of the ship, but they were not able to share the information effectively. Note, all intelligence is information but not all information is intelligence. Intelligence is information that informs (government) policy. See Mark M. Lowenthal, *Intelligence: From Secrets to Policy*, 6th ed. (Thousand Oaks, CA: CQ Press, 2015), 2.

24 Beginning in 2019 on the US side, NAVNORTH must provide the USNORTHCOM commander with a situation report of action taken after an advisory is provided by NORAD. There is no requirement for an update to the NORAD commander on the Canadian side.

25 The need for a common lexicon stemmed from significant terminology differences and the lack of a common threshold for evaluation and decisions, which had depended on the type of event relative to agency mandates. A letter and number system was developed eventually. We are grateful to the *Canadian Naval Review* for letting us use some of our research from Andrea Charron and Jim Fergusson, "NORAD's Maritime Warning Role: Origins and Future," *Canadian Naval Review* 17, no. 2

(2021): 10–14, and to the personnel at NORAD and MSOC East for assistance, especially with the advisory count numbers.

26 Keith Johnson and Dan De Luce, "Busting North Korea's Sanctions-Evading Fleet," *Foreign Policy*, 28 February 2018, https://foreignpolicy.com/2018/02/28/busting-north-koreas-sanctions-evading-fleet-ofac-treasury-shipping/; Michelle Nichols, "Photos Capture North Korea Ships' Sanctions Busting in Chinese Waters: U.N. Report," *Reuters*, 17 April 2020, https://www.reuters.com/article/us-northkorea-sanctions-un-idUSKBN21Z349.

27 There was a limited degree of cooperation in World War I. After an appeal to the United States in 1917 for assistance, it dispatched patrol boats and a flying squadron to Canada. See Michael Hadley and Roger Sarty, *Tin-Pots and Pirate Ships: Canadian Naval Forces and German Sea Raiders 1880–1918* (Montreal and Kington: McGill-Queen's University Press, 1991).

28 The RN-USN-RCN naval relationship is close and distinct among all the allies' cooperation to this day.

29 For details of USN culture, see the relevant chapters in Carl Builder, *The Masks of War: American Military Styles* (Baltimore, MD: Johns Hopkins University Press, 1989).

30 Alfred Thayer Mahan, *The Influence of Sea Power upon History, 1660–1783* (Boston, MA: Little, Brown and Company, 1890).

31 According to Builder, Mahan is the USN's prophet. On the Forward Maritime Strategy, see US Marine Corps, US Navy and US Coast Guard, *Forward, Engaged, Ready: A Cooperative Strategy for 21st Century Seapower* (Washington, DC: US Marine Corps, US Navy and US Coast Guard, 2015), 9–18, https://www.globalsecurity.org/military/library/policy/navy/21st-century-seapower_strategy_201503.pdf.

32 Michael Byers, *Who Owns the Arctic: Understanding Sovereignty Disputes in the Arctic* (Vancouver, BC: Douglas & McIntyre, 2009), 75–7.

33 Canadian Air-Sea Transportable Brigade Group (CAST).

34 Originally stood up in 2005, the SNMGs rotated as NATO's maritime rapid reaction force, and undertake missions, training, and exercises. While the RCN committed naval vessels, the USN did not.

35 NATO, "Trident Juncture," https://www.nato.int/cps/en/natohq/157833.htm (last modified 29 October 2018).

36 The GIUK-Norway gap represents a relative choke point for Russian naval forces and is north of potential Russian SLCM launch points. Although this is classified, the United States also deployed in this area

the deep-water Sound Surveillance System (SOSUS), which is still in operation, designed to track submarines by employing passive sonar acoustics.

37 Russia, as of 2020, possesses 10 nuclear-powered strategic ballistic missile submarines (SSBNs) and China has 4, although that number is increasing quickly. See Amy Woolf, *Russia's Nuclear Weapons: Doctrine, Forces and Modernization* (Washington, DC: Congressional Research Service, 5 August 2019), https://crsreports.congress.gov/product/pdf/R/R45861/2; Ronald O'Rourke, *China Naval Modernization: Implications for U.S. Navy Capabilities – Background and Issues for Congress* (Washington, DC: Congressional Research Service, 21 May 2020), https://crsreports.congress.gov/product/pdf/RL/RL33153/236.

38 Department of National Defence, "NTOG Represents RCN at International Maritime Exercise 2019," Government of Canada, 27 December 2019, https://www.canada.ca/en/department-national-defence/maple-leaf/defence/2019/12/ntog-represents-rcn-international-maritime-exercise-2019.html.

CHAPTER FOUR

1 NASA, "Remarkable Drop in Sea Ice Raises Questions," 25 September 2007, https://www.nasa.gov/vision/earth/environment/arctic_minimum.html; Environment and Climate Change Canada, "Top 10 Weather Stories for 2007: 1. Vanishing Ice at the Top of the World," https://ec.gc.ca/meteo-weather/default.asp?lang=En&n=14D00DAA-1 (last modified 8 August 2017).

2 The Arctic Council, with a mandate to protect the environment and promote sustainable development, consists of eight Arctic member states and six Indigenous groups (the Permanent Participants), non-Arctic observer states, and several nongovernmental and parliamentary observers. The Arctic Council celebrated 25 years in 2021 as Russia assumed the Chair for the second time from 2021 to 2023, to be followed by Norway. The Russian invasion of Ukraine in February 2022 resulted in the hiatus of all Arctic Council activity.

3 The Associated Press, "A Look at Estonia's Cyber Attack in 2007," *NBC News*, 8 July 2009, http://www.nbcnews.com/id/31801246/ns/technology_and_science-security/t/look-estonias-cyber-attack/#.Xu-xvKZ7nIU.

4 Michael Kofman, "Russian Performance in the Russo-Georgian War Revisited," *War on the Rocks*, 4 September 2018, https://warontherocks

.com/2018/09/russian-performance-in-the-russo-georgian-war-revisited/; Independent International Fact-Finding Mission on the Conflict in Georgia, *Report*, vol. 1 (Brussels: Independent International Fact-Finding Mission on the Conflict in Georgia, 2009), https://www.echr.coe.int/Documents/HUDOC_38263_08_Annexes_ENG.pdf.

5 US Department of State, "New START Treaty," https://www.state.gov/new-start/ (last modified 23 September 2021).

6 "Agreement Between the Government of Canada and the Government of the United States of America on the North American Aerospace Defense Command," E105060, 28 April 2006, https://www.treaty-accord.gc.ca/text-texte.aspx?id=105060.

7 Canadian Forces Base North Bay in Ontario is responsible for providing surveillance, identification, control, and warning for the aerospace defence of Canada and North America at the Sector Air Operations Centre.

8 Auditor General of Canada, "Chapter 6: Modernizing the NORAD systems in Canada National Defence," in *Report of the Auditor General of Canada to the House of Commons* (Ottawa: Office of the Auditor General of Canada, May 2007), 24–5, https://www.oag-bvg.gc.ca/internet/English/parl_oag_200705_06_e_17481.html#ch6hd3a.

9 Dimitri Trenin, "The Revival of the Russian Military: How Moscow Reloaded," *Foreign Affairs* 95, no. 3 (May/June 2016): 23–9.

10 North American Aerospace Defense Command, Office of the Command Historian, *A Brief History of NORAD as of 13 May 2016* (Colorado Springs, CO: NORAD, 2016), 11, https://www.norad.mil/Portals/29/Documents/History/A%20Brief%20History%20of%20NORAD_May2016.pdf?ver=2016-07-07-114925-133.

11 "Agreement on Cooperation on Aeronautical and Maritime Search and Rescue in the Arctic," 2011, https://oaarchive.arctic-council.org/handle/11374/531.

12 US Northern Command, *Statement of General Terence J. O'Shaughnessy, United States Air Force Commander United States Northern Command and North American Aerospace Defense Command before the Senate Armed Services Committee 13 February 2020* (Washington, DC: US Northern Command, 2020), 2, https://www.armed-services.senate.gov/imo/media/doc/OShaughnessy_02-13-20.pdf.

13 Office of the Secretary of Defense, *Annual Report to Congress: Military and Security Developments Involving the People's Republic of China 2020* (Washington, DC: Office of the Secretary of Defense, 2020), https://media.defense.gov/2020/Sep/01/2002488689/-1/-1/1/2020-DOD-

CHINA-MILITARY-POWER-REPORT-FINAL.PDF. Note on page xi: "China continues to undermine the integrity of the U.S. science and technology research enterprise through a variety of actions such as hidden diversions of research, resources, and intellectual property."

14 For an excellent review of China's ambitions and actions in the Arctic and Antarctica see Anne-Marie Brady, *China as a Polar Great Power* (Cambridge: Cambridge University Press, 2017). Dr Brady has been subjected to a campaign of intimidation by President Xi's government.

15 Jim Garamone, "Panetta Describes US Shift to Asia Pacific," Department of Defense, 1 June 2012, https://archive.defense.gov/news/newsarticle.aspx?id=116591; and see the shift in the Unified Command Plan at https://www.pacom.mil/About-USINDOPACOM/USPACOM-Area-of-Responsibility/. Most shifts in assets came in the form of reducing "cuts" to the USN to broaden support in the region. See Mark E. Manyin et al., *Pivot to the Pacific: The Obama Administration's "Rebalancing Toward Asia"* (Washington, DC: Congressional Research Services, 28 March 2012), 12, https://sgp.fas.org/crs/natsec/R42448.pdf.

16 US analysis labels this doctrine "anti-access/area-denial" (A2D). Andrew Krepinevich, Barry Watts, and Robert Work, *Meeting the Anti-Access and Area-Denial Challenge* (Washington, DC: Center for Strategic and Budgetary Assessments, 2011), http://csbaonline.org/publications/2003/05/a2ad-anti-access-area-denial/.

17 Permanent Court of Arbitration, "In the matter of the South China Sea arbitration before an arbitral tribunal constituted under Annex VII to the 1982 United Nations Convention on the Law of the Sea between the Republic of the Philippines and the People's Republic of China," PCA Case No. 2013-19 (12 July 2016), https://pca-cpa.org/wp-content/uploads/sites/6/2016/07/PH-CN-20160712-Award.pdf.

18 Debates (Hansard) No. 188 – June 6, 2017 (42–1) - House of Commons of Canada. ... Chrystia Freeland (Minister of Foreign Affairs, Lib.). https://www.ourcommons.ca/DocumentViewer/en/42-1/house/sitting-188/hansard.

19 The NWS was completed in 1985. The series of long- and short-range radars are largely dependent on 1970s technology. See Andrea Charron and Jim Fergusson, *Rediscovering the Cost of Deterrence* (Calgary, AB: Canadian Global Affairs Institute, September 2019), https://www.cgai.ca/rediscovering_the_cost_of_deterrence.

20 Article 30 reads: "1. Military activities shall not take place in the lands or territories of indigenous peoples, unless justified by a relevant public interest or otherwise freely agreed with or requested by the indigenous

peoples concerned. 2. States shall undertake effective consultations with the indigenous peoples concerned, through appropriate procedures and in particular through their representative institutions, prior to using their lands or territories for military activities." 13 September 2007, https://www.un.org/development/desa/indigenouspeoples/wp-content/uploads/sites/19/2018/11/UNDRIP_E_web.pdf.

21 During the Cold War, both the United States and the Soviet Union undertook research on manoeuvrable ballistic missile warheads, then known as Manoeuvrable Re-entry Vehicles (MARVs), but concluded that the technology was not available. Instead, both deployed Multiple Independently Targeted Re-Entry Vehicles (MIRVs), which enabled the deployment of several nuclear warheads on a single missile, each capable of independent targeting relative to the missile's ballistic flight path, but flying a direct path once released from the missile's "bus." Another and worrying trend is renewed attention to directed-energy weapons (high-energy lasers, high-power microwaves, and charged-particle electron beams), studied in the 1960s, but now receiving attention once more.

22 In their support to the NORAD mission, Canadian personnel are seconded to US AWACs aircraft. Furthermore, the United States is upgrading aircraft with new sensors and targeting capabilities to deal with these advanced cruise missile threats. US Department of Defense, *Missile Defence Review* (Washington, DC: US Department of Defense, 2019), https://www.defense.gov/Portals/1/Interactive/2018/11-2019-Missile-Defense-Review/The%202019%20MDR_Executive%20Summary.pdf.

23 Russia has apparently tested, unsuccessfully, a nuclear-powered cruise missile, termed Skyfall, with an indeterminate range and an estimated speed of Mach 8. See David Axe, "Why Russia's Nuclear-Powered 'Skyfall' Missile Is Bad News," *The National Interest*, 22 October 2019, https://nationalinterest.org/blog/buzz/why-russias-nuclear-powered-skyfall-missile-bad-news-90116.

24 The INF Treaty was signed between the Soviet Union and the United States in 1978 for an indefinite period. It banned intermediate-range (500 to 5,500 km) ballistic missiles and GLCMs. After several years of American charges of Russian cheating, the United States gave its six months' notice in February 2019 of its intent to withdraw as permitted under the Treaty, bringing the Treaty to an end on 2 August 2019. See Andrew S. Erickson, "Good Riddance to the INF Treaty," *Foreign Affairs*, 29 August 2019, https://www.foreignaffairs.com/articles/china/2019-08-

29/good-riddance-inf-treaty; US Department of State, "U.S. Withdrawal from the INF Treaty on August 2, 2019," 2 August 2019, https://www.state.gov/u-s-withdrawal-from-the-inf-treaty-on-august-2-2019/.

25 Hypersonic weapons have speeds of Mach 5 or more (above 6,125 kilometres per hour, although the speed of sound varies with altitude and temperature). See International Institute for Strategic Studies, "The Speed of War: Faster Weapons; Faster Organisations," in *Strategic Survey 2018: The Annual Assessment of Geopolitics* (London: International Institute for Strategic Studies, 2018), 23–32, https://www.iiss.org/publications/strategic-survey/strategic-survey-2018-the-annual-assessment-of-geopolitics/ss18-04-strategic-policy-issues-4.

26 Department of National Defence, *Strong, Secure and Engaged: Canada's Defence Policy* (Ottawa: Department of National Defence, 2017), https://www.canada.ca/en/department-national-defence/corporate/reports-publications/canada-defence-policy.html.

27 Department of National Defence, *Defence Investment Plan 2018* (Ottawa: Department of National Defence, 2018), https://www.canada.ca/en/department-national-defence/corporate/reports-publications/defence-investment-plan-2018.html; Department of National Defence, "Update 2019: Defence Investment Plan," Government of Canada, https://www.canada.ca/en/department-national-defence/corporate/reports-publications/defence-investment-plan-2018/2019-dip.html (last modified 4 June 2019).

28 US Department of Defense, *Missile Defense Review* (Washington, DC: US Department of Defense, 2019), xi, https://www.defense.gov/Portals/1/Interactive/2018/11-2019-Missile-Defense-Review/The%202019%20MDR_Executive%20Summary.pdf; President of the United States, "Pillar 1: Protect the American People, the Homeland, and the American Way of Life," in *National Security Strategy of the United States of America* (Washington, DC: Executive Office of the President, December 2017), https://trumpwhitehouse.archives.gov/wp-content/uploads/2017/12/NSS-Final-12-18-2017-0905.pdf; Government of Canada, *Budget 2021: A Recovery Plan for Jobs, Growth and Resilience* (Ottawa: Government of Canada, 2021), 289–90, https://www.budget.gc.ca/2021/pdf/budget-2021-en.pdf.

29 Office of the Prime Minister of Canada, "Minister of National Defence Mandate Letter," Government of Canada, 13 December 2019, https://pm.gc.ca/en/mandate-letters/2019/12/13/minister-national-defence-mandate-letter: "Work with the Minister of Foreign Affairs, the Minister of Northern Affairs and partners through the Arctic and Northern Policy Framework to develop better surveillance (including

by renewing the North Warning System), defence and rapid-response capabilities in the North and in the maritime and air approaches to Canada, to strengthen continental defence, protect Canada's rights and sovereignty and demonstrate international leadership with respect to the navigation of Arctic waters."

30 Kyle Mizokami, "How Quantum Radar Could Completely Change Warfare," *Popular Mechanics*, 24 August 2019, https://www.popularmechanics.com/military/a28818232/quantum-radar/; International Institute for Strategic Studies, "Quantum Computing and Defence," in *Military Balance 2019* (London: International Institute for Strategic Studies, February 2019), 18–20, https://www.iiss.org/publications/the-military-balance/the-military-balance-2019/quantum-computing-and-defence. Quantum radar could provide a much more detailed image of targets while remaining difficult to detect.

31 The fourth-generation F-18 Super Hornet, which remains a potential candidate for CF-18 replacement, also possesses this capability.

32 Called the Joint Land Attack Cruise Missile Defense Elevated Netted Sensor System (JLENS; colloquially known as a spy balloon), this capability was tested by the United States and NORAD, but after a number of incidents and with costs mounting, the program was cancelled in 2017. Jen Judson, "After Blimp Broke Free and Crashed, JLENS Program Hangs by a Thread," *Defense News*, 30 October 2015, https://www.defensenews.com/home/2015/10/30/after-blimp-broke-free-and-crashed-jlens-program-hangs-by-a-thread/; Jen Judson, "After Blimp's Wild Ride, JLENS Program Will Fly Again, NORAD Says," *Defense News*, 11 February 2016, https://www.defensenews.com/breaking-news/2016/02/11/after-blimp-s-wild-ride-jlens-program-will-fly-again-norad-says/; Jen Jedson, "Congress Nails Runaway Blimp's Coffin Shut," *Defense News*, 27 May 2016, https://www.defensenews.com/land/2016/05/27/congress-nails-runaway-blimp-s-coffin-shut/.

33 This may include undersea sensors, similar to the longstanding North Atlantic Sound Surveillance System (SOSUS) system. The permanent Arctic ice cap has long been the base for the stationing of Soviet/Russian nuclear-powered strategic ballistic missile submarine(s) (SSBNs), and the site of the attempt by the USN to track them employing nuclear submarine hunter-killers.

34 The new Canadian Arctic and Offshore Patrol Ship only possesses a first-year ice capability, and whether it is capable of carrying some form of anti–cruise missile capability is an open question. Large, all-year icebreakers are under American and Canadian coast guard command, not

navy. While the USCG can undertake defence activities under Title 10, the Canadian Coast Guard (CCG) is not legally mandated (nor equipped or trained) to do so. While both are in the process of acquiring a new fleet, there is no indication that either will deploy anti–cruise missile capabilities.

35 RADARSAT is a Canadian Space Agency program that provides crucial information to many government departments, including Agriculture and Agri-Foods Canada and DND/CAF. The Polar Epsilon project leveraged RADARSAT-2 to provide DND/CAF with Arctic surveillance in support of Canada's sovereignty, near-real-time ship detection, and maritime surveillance. Combining RADARSAT-2 images with space-based Automatic Identification System (AIS) data enables the identification of ships and the detection of dark ships (those that are supposed to transmit AIS signals but do not), both in Canadian waters and elsewhere. Canadian Space Agency, "RADARSAT Data to Serve Canadians," Government of Canada, https://www.asc-csa.gc.ca/eng/satellites/radarsat/data-serve-canadians.asp (last modified 19 December 2019).

36 US Northern Command, *Statement of General Terence J. O'Shaughnessy*, 9.

37 The Canadian Northern Economic Agency's Northern Communications & Information Systems Working Group had Imaituk Inc. prepare an "Arctic Communications Infrastructure Assessment (ACIA) Report" in 2011 (https://www.aciareport.ca/). The report highlighted the difficulties and limited infrastructure in the Canadian Arctic then. Nearly ten years later, there are still serious gaps, although space-based satellites and cubesats are aiding local communities as well as government departments.

38 The Government of the Northwest Territories has awarded a contract to Associated Engineering (BC) Ltd for CAD$729,541.30 to plan and design services related to the lengthening of the Inuvik Airport's runway in 2019; see https://contracts.fin.gov.nt.ca/psc/fsprdsp/SUPPLIER/ERP/c/GNT_SS.GNT_EVENT_DTL.GBL?AUC_ID=0000003784&AUC_ROUND=1&AUC_VERSION=&BUSINESS_UNIT=GNWT1&PAGE=GNT_EVENT_DTL&. See also Department of National Defence, "NORAD Operation Spring Forward Concludes in Canada's North," Government of Canada, https://www.canada.ca/en/news/archive/2014/04/norad-operation-spring-forward-concludes-canada-north.html (last modified 12 April 2014). Additional sites being researched include Coral Harbour and Hall Beach in Nunavut and Puvirnituq, Kuujjuaq, and Raglan Mine in northern Quebec.

39 The initial costs for the initial three radar lines across Canada in the 1950s was shared roughly on a one-third (Canada) / two-thirds (United States) basis. Cost sharing for the NWS in the 1980s was 40-60. The United States bears all of the costs for NORAD-related infrastructure in the United States.

40 Related, the Canadian commander of CANR and the American deputy commander are dual-hatted as the Joint Forces Air Component Commander (JFACC) and deputy commander.

41 US Department of the Air Force, *Arctic Strategy* (Washington, DC: US Department of the Air Force, 21 July 2020), 2, https://www.af.mil/Portals/1/documents/2020SAF/July/ArcticStrategy.pdf.

42 Scott Gilmore, "The Canadian North Is the Least Defended Territory on Earth," *Maclean's Magazine*, 17 March 2017, https://www.macleans.ca/politics/the-canadian-north-is-the-least-defended-territory-on-earth/; Rob Huebert, "Submarines, Oil Tankers, and Icebreakers: Trying to Understand Canadian Arctic Sovereignty and Security," *International Journal* 66, no. 4 (2011): 809–24; Rob Huebert, *The Newly Emerging Arctic Security Environment* (Calgary, AB: Canadian Defence and Foreign Affairs Institute, March 2010), https://d3n8a8pro7vhmx.cloudfront.net/cdfai/pages/41/attachments/original/1413661956/The_Newly_Emerging_Arctic_Security_Environment.pdf?1413661956; Aurel Braun and Stephen J. Blank, "Why Is Russia Getting Ready for War in the Arctic?" *iPolitics*, 27 February 2017, https://ipolitics.ca/2017/02/27/why-is-russia-getting-ready-for-war-in-the-arctic/; Aural Braun and Stephen J. Blank, *The Cold War Reality behind Russia's Charm Offensive: Why Canada Needs a Realistic Defence Policy* (Ottawa: Macdonald-Laurier Institute, April 2020), https://macdonaldlaurier.ca/files/pdf/20200401_MLI_Arctic_Policy_Braun-Blank_PAPER_FWeb.pdf; Scott G. Borgerson, "Arctic Meltdown: The Economic and Security Implications of Global Warming," *Foreign Affairs* 87, no. 2 (2008): 63–77; Scott G. Borgerson, "Coming Arctic Boom: As the Ice Melts, the Region Heats Up," *Foreign Affairs* 92, no. 4 (2013): 76–89.

43 Center for Strategic and International Studies, "Competing in the Grey Zone: Countering Competition in the Space between War and Peace," https://www.csis.org/features/competing-gray-zone (accessed 21 September 2021).

44 PAME, *Shipping in the Northwest Passage: Comparing 2013–2019: Arctic Shipping Status Report* (Tromsø, Norway: PAME, April 2021), 16–17,

https://www.arctic-council.org/news/report-on-shipping-in-the-northwest-passage-launched/. The study concluded that vessel traffic in the NWP is mainly destinational and Canadian-flagged.

45 The commander of USNORTHCOM is the US military's Arctic capabilities advocate. See also US Northern Command, *Statement of General Terence J. O'Shaughnessy*, 2.

46 The two existing ground stations are located at Aldergrove, British Columbia, and on the East Coast in Masstown, Nova Scotia. See Government of Canada, "Government of Canada Announces Location of Satellite Reception Ground Stations for Polar Epsilon," 30 March 2009, https://www.canada.ca/en/news/archive/2009/03/government-canada-announces-location-satellite-reception-ground-stations-polar-epsilon.html?=undefined&.

47 The United States has an uneven record of environmental cleanup of former American bases and related infrastructure. A B-52 crashed at Thule, Greenland on 21 January 1968, releasing toxic and radioactive chemicals. A joint Danish-American effort to clean the area has not satisfied local residents, especially those who aided in the cleanup process without proper personal protection equipment. In 2003, the Inuit of Greenland applied to the Danish Supreme Court for access to Thule USAF base. Ole Spiermann, "Hingitaq 53, Qajutaq Petersen, and Others v. Prime Minister's Office (Qaanaaq Municipality and Greenland Home Rule Government Intervening in Support of the Appellants)," *The American Journal of International Law* 98, no. 3 (July 2004): 572–8. The court ruled the Inuit could not take back the land from the base, but they were entitled to compensation.

48 The announcement in January 2022 that an Inuit majority-owned corporation, Nasittuq, won the Government of Canada's seven-year NWS maintenance contract is very positive.

CHAPTER FIVE

1 In even simpler terms: command = authority and control = how to exercise authority. Ch. 2 of Richard Goette's *Sovereignty and Command in Canada-US Continental Air Defence, 1940–1957* (Vancouver, BC: UBC Press, 2018) is dedicated to C^2 and the decisions made to establish the North American Air Defence Command.

2 The CJCS is not in the operational chain of command for NORAD or any combatant command. The service chiefs, however, are the main advisors for force employment purposes and so they do link to USNORTHCOM

for ongoing training needs, but not NORAD, as all NORAD personnel are sent to it fully trained.

3 See NORAD and USNORTHCOM, *Strategy: Executive Summary* (Colorado Springs, CO: NORAD and USNORTHCOM, March 2021), https://www.northcom.mil/Portals/28/(U)%20NORAD-USNORTHCOM%20Strategy%20EXSUM%20-%20Signed.pdf.

4 "Agreement Between the Government of Canada and the Government of the United States of America on the North American Aerospace Defense Command," E105060 (28 April 2006), https://www.treaty-accord.gc.ca/text-texte.aspx?id=105060 See 2c.

5 Joint Rescue Coordination Centre (JRCC) Trenton leads and directs all SAR operations in the Trenton search and rescue region (SRR), which covers central Canada including Hudson's Bay, James Bay, and the Canadian portions of the Great Lakes and the Arctic Ocean (approximately 10 million square kilometres).

6 For example, when the US F-15 fleet was grounded after an accident in 2007, Canadian CF-18s were transferred under NORAD authority to ANR.

7 CONR divides its area of responsibility into 2 sectors: the Western Air Defense Sector (WADS) and the Eastern Air Defense Sector (EADS). ANR and CANR have single air defence sectors.

8 For a comprehensive discussion on JFACCs and the CFACC concept, see LCol M.A. French, "NORAD A New Command and Control Model to Improve Agility and Responsiveness (The NORAD CFACC Concept," (MA thesis, Canadian Forces College, 2016), https://www.cfc.forces.gc.ca/259/290/317/286/french.pdf.

9 Of course, NORAD can be considered latently joint, as land and maritime defence assets can be cut over to the command. For example, on 9/11, a US aircraft carrier's assets, located off the coast of New York, were CHOPed (changed of operational control) to NORAD command.

10 French, "NORAD A New Command," 48.

11 Congressional Research Service, *Joint All Domain Command and Control* (Washington, DC: Congressional Research Service, 1 July 2021), https://crsreports.congress.gov/product/pdf/IF/IF11493. DoD is leading a Joint Cross-Functional Team to explore JADC2 as the concept evolves. The team includes representatives from the offices of the DoD Chief Information Officer (CIO), the Undersecretary of Defense for Research and Engineering, and the Undersecretary of Defense for Acquisition and Sustainment. The DoD CIO has stated it plans to use 5G technologies to enable JADC2.

12 Ibid., 1.
13 GIDE or Global Information Dominance Experiments are designed to enable cross–Combatant Command collaboration to generate globally integrated effects using artificial intelligence (AI)–enabled information.
14 Bi-National Planning Group, *Final Report on Canada and the United States (CANUS) Enhanced Military Cooperation* (Colorado Springs, CO: Bi-National Planning Group, 13 March 2006), https://www.hsdl.org/?abstract&did=462647.
15 As these exercises deal with a range of crisis and war scenarios, their details are highly classified.
16 Commander Joint Force Command Norfolk reports to Supreme Allied Command Europe, who is dual-hatted as commander EUCOM. SACEUR reports to US Atlantic Fleet, who in turn reports to USNORTHCOM.
17 Gen (ret) Terrence O'Shaughnessy and Brig Gen Peter M. Fesler, *Hardening the Shield: A Credible Deterrent & Capable Defense for North America* (Washington, DC: Canada Institute, Wilson Center, September 2020), https://www.wilsoncenter.org/publication/hardening-shield-credible-deterrent-capable-defense-north-america. Of course any attack on the United States by a state actor could quickly result in an escalation, including a nuclear exchange.

CHAPTER SIX

1 In the final outcome, the USAF acquired all responsibility and thus control over fixed-wing aircraft, while the Army acquired the same for rotary-wing craft (helicopters). The USN's carrier-based aircraft and fixed/rotary-wing Marine force capabilities were unaffected. See Vandenberg-Collins Agreement, 1 August 1950, reproduced in Richard I. Wolf, *The United States Air Force: Basic Documents on Roles and Missions* (Washington, DC: Office of Air Force History, 1987), 221–2.
2 Recognizing the implications of ballistic missile technology, the USN invested in the development of long-range submarine-launched ballistic missiles (SLBMs) and nuclear-powered submarine (SSBN) launchers, although they would be assigned to the US-dominated Strategic Air Command (SAC) and subsequently US Strategic Command (USSTRATCOM).
3 Canada launched Alouette I, a defence research satellite, in 1962. It was designed to study the impact of the ionosphere on radio communications.
4 In 1967, the Science Secretariat of the Privy Council Office commis-

sioned Special Study No. 1 entitled *Atmosphere and Space Programs in Canada*, which became known as the Chapman Report after the lead author (with P.A. Forsyth, P.A. Lapp, and G.N. Patterson): https://s3.ca-central-1.amazonaws.com/sqreports/Special-Study-No.-1-Upper-Atmosphere-and-Space-Programs-in-Canada.pdf.

5 For a detailed study on Canada's first thirty years of military space, see Andrew Godefroy, *Defence and Discovery: Canada's Military Space Program, 1945–74* (Vancouver, BC: UBC Press, 2011).

6 The Congressionally mandated *2001 Space Commission Report*, chaired by Donald Rumsfeld, argued in favour of adopting "air and space" over "aerospace," with the USAF retaining responsibility for space. See Commission to Assess United States National Security Space Management and Organization, *Report of the Commission to Assess United States National Security Space Management and Organization* (Washington, DC: Commission to Assess United States National Security Space Management and Organization, 2001), https://aerospace.csis.org/wp-content/uploads/2018/09/RumsfeldCommission.pdf. In 2003, the flagship *USAF Aerospace Power Journal* was renamed the *Air and Space Power Journal.*

7 "Exchange of Notes Constituting an Agreement Between the Government of Canada and the Government of the United States of America on the Modernization of the North American Air Defence System," E101003 CTS 1985 No. 8 (18 March 1985). See under "financial responsibilities," sect. 19a, https://www.treaty-accord.gc.ca/text-texte.aspx?id=101003.

8 Reportedly, these satellites are capable of identifying air-breathing assets, including cruise missiles, based on their heat signatures.

9 Known as plumenology, every ballistic missile's plume or heat signature upon launch is unique, and this data is vital not only to distinguish type and range, but also to differentiate a ballistic missile from a civilian rocket launch.

10 For details, see James Fergusson, *Canada and Ballistic Missile Defence 1954–2009: Déjà Vu All Over Again* (Vancouver, BC: UBC Press, 2010), 122–5.

11 The link was not, however, entirely severed. US Air Force Space Command remains co-located with NORAD Headquarters at Peterson Air Force Base in Colorado Springs, which was renamed Peterson Space Force Base in 2021. USSPACECOM was re-established 29 August 2009 with a re-emphasized focus on space as a warfighting domain.

12 The satellites are equipped with a synthetic aperture radar (SAR) instrument which acquires images of the Earth, day or night, in all weather and through cloud cover, smoke, and haze.

13 Prior to the stand-up of DG Space, DSPACED had been eliminated and its components assigned to the Chief of Force Development and distributed on a functional basis therein.

14 The other classes are subsonic (less than the speed of sound or Mach 1) and supersonic (between Mach 1 and 5).

15 Kelley M. Sayler, *Hypersonic Weapons: Background and Issues for Congress* (Washington, DC: Congressional Research Service, 26 April 2011), https://fas.org/sgp/crs/weapons/R45811.pdf. For technical details, see Richard H. Speier, George Nacouzi, Carrie A. Lee, and Richard M. Moore, *Hypersonic Missile Proliferation: Hindering the Spread of a New Class of Weapons* (Santa Monica, CA: Rand Corporation, 2017).

16 Sub-orbital space is the area in which there is insufficient atmosphere for powered flight, but insufficient altitude for an object to remain in orbit. Ramjet or scramjet technology compresses the sparse air molecules to permit flight.

17 The US cancelled and dismantled its ABM Treaty–compliant ABM system, known as Safeguard, in 1976, except for the co-located radar at Cavalier, North Dakota, which was assigned to the BMEW system. The Soviet Union has maintained its Treaty-compliant system around Moscow.

18 Eric Gomez, "Russia Claims Its New Nuclear Weapons Are a Response to U.S. Missile Defense," *The National Interest*, 15 March 2020, https://nationalinterest.org/blog/buzz/russia-claims-its-new-nuclear-weapons-are-response-us-missile-defense-132747.

19 Known as the Hypersonic and Ballistic Missile Tracking Space Sensor (HBTSS), the likely constellation will be located in LEO, and linked to the existing space-based sensor system. Although details are unknown, it is likely related directly to the former space-based infrared low development program.

20 See, relative to the entire cruise missile problem, Congressional Budget Office, *National Cruise Missile Defence: Issues and Alternatives* (Washington, DC: Congressional Budget Office, 2021), https://www.cbo.gov/system/files/2021-02/56950-CMD.pdf.

21 This capability entailed F-15 aircraft armed with air-to-LEO missiles. The first successful test occurred in 1985. Roughly a year later, Congress cut funding for the program. See Paul Glenshaw, "The First Space Ace: F-15 vs. Satellite," *Air and Space Magazine*, April 2018, https://www.airspacemag.com/military-aviation/first-space-ace-180968349/.

22 For the full story of the complicated history and evolution of Canadian policy, see Fergusson, *Canada and Ballistic Missile Defence*.

23 The system consisted of two interceptors. Sprint had a range of 20 and Spartan of 500 miles. Both employed nuclear warheads set to detonate at the point the incoming warhead entered the terminal phase of its flight upon re-entering the atmosphere.

24 As a function of the physics of ballistic missiles, the earlier they are intercepted in their flight path, the greater the area that can be defended. For example, if a missile is intercepted in its lift-off or boost phase, a global defence is possible. If it is intercepted in its flight through outer space or during the mid-course phase, then only continental defence is possible.

25 The deployed Safeguard system, prior to its cancellation and dismantlement in 1976, was deployed at Cavalier, North Dakota to defend the Grand Forks ICBM field as permitted by the 1972 ABM Treaty and 1974 ABM Protocol. The ABM radar was transferred to the BMEW system.

26 Roughly a year before NORAD renewal in 1968, SecDef McNamara proposed to separate NORAD renewal from ABM, and proposed the insertion of an ABM exclusion clause in the agreement if Canada so desired. The exclusion clause remained in place until 1981, and its elimination was a direct function of the ABM Treaty's prohibition on third-party involvement, which rendered it redundant.

27 An at-sea radar is a possibility, similar to that deployed for the GMD system. However, its location would likely place it in Canadian or Danish (Greenland) ice-filled waters.

28 For example, Canadian NORAD personnel seconded to the USPACECOM's 50th Space Wing at Schriever just outside Colorado Springs and the Canadian liaison officer to BMDO were relegated to the unclassified domain.

29 The 1967 *Treaty on Principles Governing the Activities of States in the Exploration and Use of Outer Space, including the Moon and Other Celestial Bodies,* otherwise known as the Outer Space Treaty, outlines basic rules about the use of "outer space," but does not define "outer space." In 2017, the chairman of the UN space law working group supported 100 km as a defining altitude boundary. The *Von Kármán Line*, treating airspace as ending (and space beginning) at the point where it is impossible to fly an aircraft, is problematic given changing technology. An *orbiting line* defines the boundary where airspace ends (and outer space begins) at the lowest perigee of an orbiting satellite, but again technology makes this boundary changeable. See Timothy Nelson, "Where Does Space Begin? The Decades-Long Legal Mission to Find the Border between Air and Space," *SpaceNews*, 26 March 2019, https://spacenews.com

/op-ed-where-does-space-begin-the-decades-long-legal-mission-to-find-the-border-between-air-and-space/.

30 Many satellites have limited manoeuvring capabilities as a function of their solar panels.

31 Carin Zissis, "China's Anti-Satellite Test," Council on Foreign Relations, 22 February 2007, https://www.cfr.org/backgrounder/chinas-anti-satellite-test.

32 Jim Wolf, "U.S. Shot Raises Tensions and Worries over Satellites," *Reuters*, 21 February 2008, https://www.reuters.com/article/us-satellite-intercept-vulnerability/u-s-shot-raises-tensions-and-worries-over-satellites-idUSN2144210520080222.

33 On 15 July 2020, US officials claimed that Russia had undertaken a space-based, non-destructive anti-satellite weapons test by employing an object released by another satellite, the third such test since 2018, when a similar object was released near a US spy satellite. Russia rejected the claim, labelling the object a satellite inspector. US Space Command, "Russia Conducts Space-Based Anti-Satellite Test," 23 July 2020, https://www.spacecom.mil/MEDIA/NEWS-ARTICLES/Article/2285098/russia-conducts-space-based-anti-satellite-weapons-test/.

34 It also prohibits their deployment on other celestial bodies or their stationing in space by other means: UN General Assembly, Resolution 2222 (XXI), *Treaty on the Principles Governing the Activities of States in the Exploration or Use of Outer Space, Including the Moon and Other Celestial Bodies*, A/RES/2222(XXI), 19 December 1967, https://digitallibrary.un.org/record/203169?ln=en#record-files-collapse-header.

35 Following the signing of the Outer Space Treaty, the United States claimed that the Soviet Union was potentially in violation as a function of its development of a fractional orbital bombardment system (FOBS). Specifically, this entailed the launch of an ICBM on a southern trajectory, whereby it would enter a fractional orbit transiting beneath the South Pole on its way to North American targets. The issue disappeared with the Soviet cancellation of its Fractional Orbital Bombardment System (FOBS), a low-earth-orbit nuclear weapons delivery system developed in the 1960s.

CHAPTER SEVEN

1 Office of the Prime Minister of Canada, "Joint Statement from President Donald J. Trump and Prime Minister Justin Trudeau," Government of Canada, 13 February 2017, https://pm.gc.ca/en/news/statements

/2017/02/13/joint-statement-president-donald-j-trump-and-prime-minister-justin.

2 Department of National Defence, *Strong, Secure and Engaged: Canada's Defence Policy* (Ottawa: Department of National Defence, 2017), 90, http://dgpaapp.forces.gc.ca/en/canada-defence-policy/docs/canada-defence-policy-report.pdf.

3 The White House, "Roadmap for a Renewed U.S.-Canada Partnership," 23 February 2021, https://www.whitehouse.gov/briefing-room/statements-releases/2021/02/23/roadmap-for-a-renewed-u-s-canada-partnership/.

4 NORAD and USNORTHCOM, *Strategy: Executive Summary* (Colorado Springs, CO: NORAD and USNORTHCOM, March 2021), 3, https://www.northcom.mil/Portals/28/(U)%20NORAD-USNORTHCOM%20Strategy%20EXSUM%20-%20Signed.pdf.

5 Government of Canada, House of Commons Debates, 19th Parliament, 3rd Session, vol. 3 (10 June 1942), 3236, https://parl.canadiana.ca/view/oop.debates_HOC1903_03/1061?r=0&s=1.

6 Joshua Rovner, "Warfighting in Cyberspace," *War on the Rocks*, 17 March 2021, https://warontherocks.com/2021/03/warfighting-in-cyberspace/.

7 The *Posse Comitatus Act*, 18 U.S. Code, Section 1385. For both countries, in a national emergency, armed force can be applied in a policing role. In addition, the US National Guard, under the jurisdiction of state governors (Title 32 of the United States Code), can be employed in policing roles as well. The exception is the US Coast Guard's constabulary role under its Title Fourteen authority.

8 In 2003, the Northeast electrical power grid collapsed after the power company's alarm (cyber) system failed to detect a collapsed power line, which led to a cascade of power line failures across the grid. See J.R. Minkel, "The 2003 Northeast Blackout – Five Years Later," *Scientific American*, 13 August 2008, https://www.scientificamerican.com/article/2003-blackout-five-years-later/. The last major quake on the West Coast occurred in 1700 with a magnitude of 9.0, and research indicates a roughly 300- to 500-year window for another event. See Miles Bodmer and Doug Tooney, "Where the Pacific Northwest's 'Big One' Is More Likely to Strike," *Scientific American*, 5 August 2018, https://www.scientificamerican.com/article/where-the-pacific-northwest-rsquo-s-ldquo-big-one-rdquo-is-more-likely-to-strike/.

9 For example, the 2005 Security and Prosperity for North America Agreement included a section on emergency response to work on

updating existing bilateral agreements on cross-border assistance, including in the cyber domain. See M. Angeles Villarreal and Jennifer M. Lake, *Security and Prosperity Partnership of North America: An Overview and Selected Issues* (Washington, DC: Congressional Research Service, 27 May 2009), https://fas.org/sgp/crs/row/RS22701.pdf.

10 This was identified in the 2005 International Policy Statement. See Government of Canada, *Canada's International Policy Statement: A Role of Pride and Influence in the World; Overview* (Ottawa: Government of Canada, 2005), http://aix1.uottawa.ca/~rparis/IPS_2005.pdf.

11 Limited (ostensibly) to US military commands, a watch conference looks at anomalous cyber events, and an events conference relates to response decisions. Above these is a national event conference run by the Pentagon that brings together other government agencies. It appears that this is the only access point for Canada as a function of NORAD. See Randall DeGering. "What Is NORAD's Role in a Cyber Attack Warning?" *Homeland Security Affairs* 12, essay 5 (May 2016), https://www.hsaj.org/articles/10648.

12 John R. Hoehn, *Joint All-Domain Command and Control: Background and Issues for Congress* (Washington, DC: Congressional Research Service, 18 March 2021), https://crsreports.congress.gov/product/pdf/R/R46725/2.

13 Congressional Research Service, *Artificial Intelligence and National Security* (Washington, DC: Congressional Research Service, 10 November 2020), https://fas.org/sgp/crs/natsec/R45178.pdf.

14 Government of Canada, "All Domain Situational Awareness Science and Technology Program," https://www.canada.ca/en/defence-research-development/programs/all-domain-situational-awareness-program.html (last modified 12 February 2018).

15 As during the Cold War, a Canadian government would likely accept long-range offensive strike forces transiting through Canadian airspace and provide emergency landing rights to US forces.

16 Currently, Canada has no plans to acquire either area or point defences for North American defences, although it has committed in *Strong, Secure and Engaged* (2017) to acquire point air defences for forces deployed overseas. Its CF-18 fighter replacement will likely include the acquisition of air-to-air missiles capable of dealing with both cruise missiles and hypersonics.

17 In the case of Canada, although no funds were attached to North American defence and NORAD modernization, the governmental mandate to both was established in the prime minister's mandate letter to the minister of National Defence following the 2019 election. In the 2021 bud-

get, the government allocated $163.4 million over five years to support NORAD modernization and $88.8 million over five years to maintain existing NORAD Arctic capabilities. See Office of the Prime Minister of Canada, "Minister of National Defence Mandate Letter," Government of Canada, 19 December 2019, https://pm.gc.ca/en/mandate-letters/2019/12/13/minister-national-defence-mandate-letter; Justin Massie and Camille Raymond, "Federal Budget 2021: Defence and Security," *Open Canada*, 28 April 2021, https://opencanada.org/federal-budget-2021-defence-and-security/.

18 See Jean-Christophe Boucher, "The Politics of Sovereignty: Canada-United States Defence Relations," in *Defending Canadian Sovereignty: New Threat, New Challenges*, edited by Jean-Christophe Boucher, Pierre-Gerlier Forest, and Louis Bélanger (Ottawa: Department of National Defence, 2019), https://publications.gc.ca/collections/collection_2019/mdn-dnd/D2-408-2019-eng.pdf.

19 See Aileen Moreton-Robinson, ed., *Sovereign Subjects: Indigenous Sovereignty Matters* (London: Routledge, 2007).

20 UN *Declaration on the Rights of Indigenous Peoples* (2007), Article 30 especially.

21 In the case of Canada, this is found with the Joint Strategic Planning Staff and Canada Joint Operations Command (CJOC).

22 Theoretically, the scale of defence integration can be measured in degrees between bilateralism, multilateralism, and binationalism. For example, a fully integrated binational North American relationship would possess fully integrated North American defence forces, rather than national forces assigned to the binational command, and North American defence elements that would remain strictly national.

23 See Michel Fortmann and David G. Haglund, "Canada and the Issue of Homeland Security: Does the Kingston Dispensation Still Hold?" *Canadian Military Journal* 3, no. 1 (Spring 2002): 17–22, http://www.journal.forces.gc.ca/vo3/no1/doc/17-22-eng.pdf.

Index

The letter f appearing before a locator indicates a figure.